Setting Up a Weather Station and Understanding the Weather

A Guide for the Amateur Meteorologist

Setting Up a Weather Station and Understanding the Weather

A Guide for the Amateur Meteorologist

Roger Brugge

THE CROWOOD PRESS

First published in 2016 by
The Crowood Press Ltd
Ramsbury, Marlborough
Wiltshire SN8 2HR

www.crowood.com

British Library Cataloguing-in-Publication Data
A catalogue record for this book is available from the British Library.

ISBN 978 1 78500 161 1

Disclaimer
The author and the publisher do not accept any responsibility in any manner
whatsoever for any error or omission, or any loss, damage, injury, adverse outcome,
or liability of any kind incurred as a result of the use of any of the information
contained in this book, or reliance upon it. If in doubt about any aspect of
meteorology readers are advised to seek professional advice.

All images are from the author's collection unless otherwise stated.

Typeset by Jean Cussons Typesetting, Diss, Norfolk
Printed and bound in India by Replika Press Pvt Ltd

CONTENTS

PREFACE AND ACKNOWLEDGEMENTS   6

1. INTRODUCTION   7
2. GETTING STARTED   12
3. WEATHER TYPES   21
4. NON-INSTRUMENTAL OBSERVATIONS OF WIND AND VISIBILITY   34
5. CLOUDS   41
6. STATE OF THE GROUND   60
7. OPTICAL PHENOMENA   67
8. THUNDER, DUST, ASH AND HAIL   78
9. ATMOSPHERIC PRESSURE   84
10. PRECIPITATION   97
11. THERMOMETER SCREENS   112
12. AIR TEMPERATURE AND HUMIDITY   119
13. SOIL AND SURFACE TEMPERATURES   134
14. EVAPORATION   144
15. INSTRUMENTAL OBSERVATIONS OF THE WIND   148
16. SUNSHINE AND SOLAR RADIATION   156
17. LOCAL WEATHER AND CLIMATE   166
18. SHARING YOUR OBSERVATIONS AND FURTHER LEARNING   172

GLOSSARY   180
INSTRUMENT AND SOFTWARE SUPPLIERS   181
REFERENCES AND FURTHER READING   184
INDEX   190

PREFACE AND ACKNOWLEDGEMENTS

I have been a weather observer for over forty years, for much of that time as part of a thriving amateur observing community in the UK – many of whom, like myself (at least originally), were 'self-taught observers' and used equipment that had not changed for a century. In fact, in the UK the origins of weather observing date back over 150 years when equipment was expensive and, to some extent, running a weather station was the preserve of those with both time and money.

The advent of modern electronic weather sensors means that weather observing is now within the reach of almost everybody. No longer does the observer need to visit the instruments every day – electronic sensors can be left running unattended for long periods of time, leaving the observer with more time to analyse and investigate the weather conditions that they report. Observing equipment is nowadays quite varied in design, and relatively cheap.

This book aims to provide some guidelines for the newcomer to weather observing (particularly in the UK), based on official guidance but making allowance for the limitations inevitably imposed on hobbyist sites. Some of the ideas in this book have been expanded from short notes and words of advice provided over the years to the Climatological Observers Link. Numerous references to additional reading material are also provided for those wishing to learn more about specific aspects of weather and weather observing.

My thanks are due to many colleagues and friends who have taught me about meteorology and weather observing, particularly those in the Department of Meteorology at the University of Reading and in the Climatological Observers Link. I am grateful to Les Cowley, who commented on, and provided diagrams for, the chapter on optical phenomena. Special thanks are also due to Stephen Burt for the many useful discussions about weather observing that we have had over recent years; Stephen also proofread early drafts of some chapters and suggested some improvements. I would also like to thank the Department of Meteorology of the University of Reading for access to their weather observations, some of which have been used in this book.

Finally, I would like to thank those who kindly provided photographs or diagrams that appear in this book – Edwina Brugge (my wife, who proofread many of the final chapters), Stephen Burt (CloudBank Images Ltd), Robin Andrea Chanin, Les Cowley, Jonathan Dancaster, Martin Grosshög, Ole Jul Larsen, The Met Office, Donald Perkins, Susan Petry, Angus Tyner, Bill Wade, Graham Webster and Nicholas White.

Roger Brugge, August 2015

I. INTRODUCTION

WHY OBSERVE THE WEATHER?

Why watch and record the weather? Perhaps the best reason is that the weather and its impacts affect us all and that learning more about the weather and how to observe it can be both fun and instructive. Weather observing can be done photographically with a camera, in the form of a day-to-day diary with pencil and paper (or computer), or with instruments. No two clouds/storms/seasons are ever the same, so there is always something new to observe and something new to learn.

Many of the amateur weather observers that I know pursue weather-related activities, either for their work or as a hobby. The effects of weather can last:

- For a few hours (how heavy will the rain be and will I need an umbrella?)
- A few days (winter snowfalls or thundery floods might be examples here)
- Over the longer term (how hot was last summer and how did it compare with a typical summer?)

For those with an outdoor job or hobby, the weather can play a crucial role in day-to-day activities.

With some simple observations, you can begin to answer questions like 'what is the height of that cloud base?' or 'why did the wind change last night as the humidity rose, after an otherwise fine day?' You can begin to understand the peculiarities of the weather in your locality, or maybe predict the minimum temperature for tomorrow morning.

Having an even longer timescale, the subject of climate change is one that cannot have escaped your attention in recent years. Those with a long observational record (maybe twenty years or more), even from several sites, will be able to see the effects of climate change (particularly the rise in summer maximum temperatures) emerging from their own measurements.

Fig. 1. Deep cumulus clouds developing into thundery cumulonimbus clouds at Holdenby House, Northamptonshire. How warm and sultry is it today compared to yesterday? Well, your temperature and humidity measurements will help you find out.
EDWINA BRUGGE

We are all familiar with weather forecasts, the production of which relies at the outset on millions of weather observations that help determine the state of the weather across the globe at all levels of the atmosphere. While the observations for these forecasts are taken, on the whole, by professional meteorologists (often with very expensive equipment, such as satellites), there are many amateurs for whom observing the local weather is a hobby. It can become an all-consuming passion as statistics build up over the months and years, records are broken and different extreme weather types are encountered and recorded. Indeed, the earliest weather observers were often amateurs, a phrase which in meteorology is used to denote a person for whom the weather is not their main source of income or profession.

Many amateurs can help make important contributions to the science of weather and to the provision of weather data by maintaining well-kept records. Indeed, since there is no longer an official weather station in my home town, I have been asked on several occasions for copies of some of my own records from my home weather station by the police (investigating local crimes), solicitors, researchers and individuals pursuing insurance claims resulting from storm damage.

Perhaps you'll be lucky and see a tornado or a funnel cloud from a safe distance; maybe you'll measure some 15–20mm diameter hailstones or witness some other extreme weather conditions.

Weather has been the main hobby of mine for some forty years now. Learning about climates in school geography lessons, it soon became apparent to me that conditions at the local Ringway (Manchester) Airport (daily data from there were published in one of the national papers in those days) were sometimes quite different from those experienced at my home, which was surrounded by a large garden and was located in an inner suburb of the city. Moreover, both sets of measurements often departed from those that might be expected based on climatology – and both differed (for various reasons) from those made in the centre of Manchester at the local (rooftop) weather centre.

SIX'S MAXIMUM-MINIMUM THERMOMETER

This thermometer (named after the eighteenth-century inventor James Six) is no longer used for the accurate recording of daily maximum and minimum temperature extremes, but is easy to purchase at most garden centres and can be found in many greenhouses as a result. The thermometer consists of a single U-shaped tube, the tubes usually being labelled 'min' and 'max'. The bulb at the top of the minimum ('min') reading arm is full of alcohol; the other contains low-pressure alcohol vapour. In between these two is a column of mercury or, nowadays, mercury-free liquid.

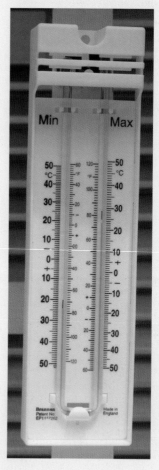

Fig. 2. Six's maximum-minimum thermometer. The minimum and maximum temperatures recorded since the instrument was last reset can be found by noting the value of the temperature scale at the bottom of each of the grey markers.

MASON'S WET AND DRY BULB HYGROMETER

The principle of Mason's wet and dry bulb hygrometer dates back to the mid-nineteenth century, with the instrument consisting of two identical thermometers that are used to measure the temperature and humidity. As the name suggests, one thermometer is kept permanently wet by means of a tightly fitted sleeve that is wrapped around the thermometer bulb and draws water towards the bulb by capillary action from a reservoir of distilled water. The other (dry bulb) thermometer measures the air temperature. The wet bulb thermometer is cooled by evaporation and records a lower temperature than the dry bulb, the difference between the two readings being a measure of the humidity of the air.

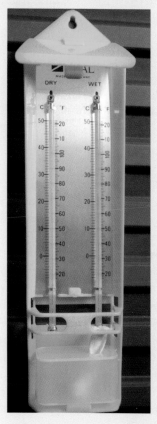

Fig. 3. **Mason's wet and dry bulb hygrometer, showing the dry and wet bulb thermometers and the reservoir of water that feeds the wick surrounding the wet bulb.**

Armed with a homemade raingauge (comprising a jar, plastic funnel and a measuring cylinder), a Six's thermometer and a Mason's wet and dry bulb hygrometer inside a homemade thermometer screen (made from louvred wooden walls mounted on an old tree stump), my early observations were to be the beginnings of a lifelong hobby. Being still a schoolboy at the time I began observing, and with

THE CLIMATOLOGICAL OBSERVERS LINK

The Climatological Observers Link (COL) is an organization of people who are interested in the weather. Its members are mainly amateur meteorologists, but many professionals and observers from schools, universities and research establishments also belong to COL. Many members run weather stations and keep records, ranging from daily rainfall and temperature measurements, with their observations and analyses maintained in log books or spreadsheets, to numerous weather parameters recorded every few minutes using elaborate electronic equipment, often displayed in real time on their own websites.

COL has published a monthly summary of UK weather since May 1970 – shortly after it was formed. This is largely comprised of the contributions of the members themselves, including summaries of their monthly weather observations and notes on the weather, and this is now the most comprehensive source of monthly weather information available in Britain.

COL also runs an online weather forum, as well as holding regular regional events and meetings for those with an interest in weather observing. More information about COL can be found on their website, www.colweather.org.uk.

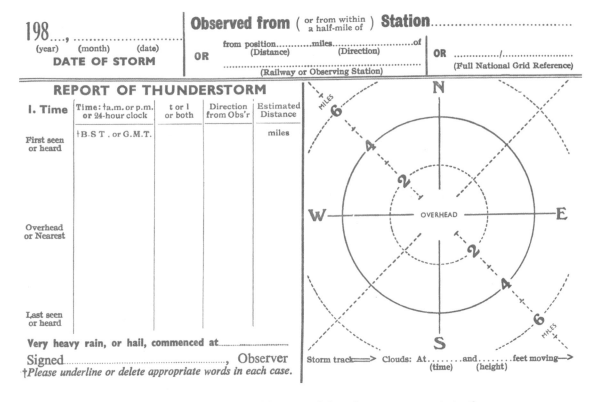

Fig. 4. A report card as used during the 1980s to send thunderstorm reports to the Thunderstorm Census Organisation. By locating the direction of any lightning flash and then counting the time between the flash and subsequent thunder both the direction and distance from the observer of the lightning could be plotted. Assuming that all flashes came from the same storm, the movement of the storm with time could be plotted on the right-hand side of the card. AUTHOR/JONATHAN WEBB

weather being a scientific subject requiring technical (expensive) instrumentation, it was a few years before I owned what might be regarded as a 'proper weather station'.

However, these days weather observing equipment has evolved from the 'traditional' instrumentation that dominated weather observing around the world from about the 1850s (and in some places even earlier by a century or so) until late in the twentieth century. Now, one can buy reasonably priced electronic equipment via the internet or in local electrical stores in many high streets. Such equipment allows the keen amateur to monitor aspects of the weather continuously, rather than by just making one or two observations

each day. There are also observations that can be made without resorting to instruments – observations, which, strangely enough, many modern-day professional systems cannot make.

Of course, once you start to observe the weather you may wish to share those observations with others. I spent many hours as a young observer watching the movement of thunderstorms across the local skies. Observations were made using special report cards, which were then sent to the Thunderstorm Census Organisation (TCO). Often this meant forgoing a couple of hours of sleep on thundery nights in the summer. Nowadays the role played by TCO has been taken over by the Tornado and Storm Research Organisation and there are also other organizations to which amateur observers can submit regular daily or monthly weather summaries and occasional reports of interesting weather events.

One such organization is COL, the UK's Climatological Observers Link, which was formed in the 1970s by a group of amateur meteorologists. Many of the guidelines in this book are based upon the observing practices promoted by COL – thereby allowing observers to compare their observations with those of other sites, both amateur and professional.

BOOK LAYOUT

Hopefully, this book will draw you into the subject of weather observing using some relatively inexpensive equipment and encourage you to consider making 'weather observing' one of your hobbies.

The book is unapologetically aimed at those who are new, or relatively new, to weather observing. There is a lot about the science of meteorology that the amateur can learn from their own observations – and this book will give some insights and pointers here too.

Following this introductory chapter the book deals with setting up a weather station and then with observations that can be made without resorting to any instruments. Instrumental observations are then covered, in order of increasing complexity. Thus air pressure, rainfall and air temperature are treated first, with wind and soil temperatures, sunshine and evaporation following later.

For each observation type, some indication of 'best observing practice', what to record in your weather register, and the reasons for making the observation are explained.

Mention is also made of organizations and web pages, books and magazines that the newcomer to weather observing might find useful. Having made observations, many observers like to share their results and to see how they compare with measurements made at other sites, whether across town or on the other side of the world, or even with records made a hundred years ago; again some pointers are provided here.

Useful references and sources of further reading are shown using the superscript symbols, with a full reference to these being given at the end of the book.

2. GETTING STARTED

SETTING UP A WEATHER STATION

This chapter provides an introduction to setting up a weather station with the aim of keeping long-term records. Changing the position of your weather station can have an effect on the measurements of some elements of the weather – so these sections provide some pointers towards 'best practice' for the amateur observer. Likewise, changing the observation time can change your weather statistics, so for the serious observer some thought should be given to these matters at the outset.

Readers wondering how to make a start in weather observing having been presented with some new instrument (or those interested in making non-instrumental observations) may decide to jump ahead to the appropriate chapter covering those observations – but please return to this chapter soon!

AN AUTOMATIC SYSTEM OR INDIVIDUAL INSTRUMENTS?

Many long-established amateur observing sites, including mine, have been built up over a period of time by means of a series of instrument purchases. Such a series was often the result of cost considerations; weather observing is a science, and scientific equipment can be expensive. Maybe the station began with a simple raingauge and some basic thermometers; then a standard raingauge was added, followed by a better thermometer screen to house standard thermometers; later perhaps an automatic weather station was purchased. Often such improvements were made when an existing instrument was broken or failed to function correctly.

The way in which we measure the weather is currently changing rapidly. Modern electronics, personal computers and laptops along with wireless technology have led to the availability of inexpensive sensors for weather observing that are often of very

Fig. 5. A roadside automatic weather station. Note the nearby trees – not all roadside weather stations are in locations that might be classified as good.

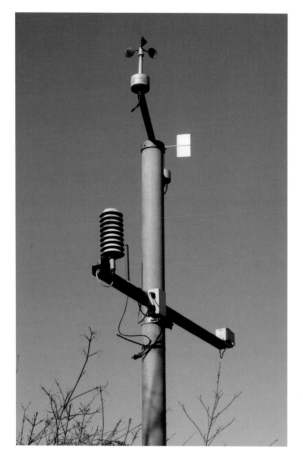

Fig. 6. Close-up of the roadside automatic weather station shown in Fig. 5. Along the arms at the top of the post are located the cup anemometer and wind vane, while the lower arm contains the thermometer screen (left) and the wetness sensor (right).

good quality. An additional spur in this direction has been provided by international legislation that is steadily outlawing the sale of some instruments containing mercury – in particular thermometers.

An Automatic Weather Station (AWS) consists of one or more electronic devices that measure common elements of the weather, such as air temperature and pressure, wind and rainfall. As long as the required power continues to be provided – either in the form of batteries or a mains supply of electricity – an AWS will continue to report the weather for days, months and (hopefully) years into

the future with only minimal effort required on the part of the observer.

In the amateur market, AWS equipment may consist of a display-only instrument (meaning that the measurements cannot be stored for later use). For a serious amateur observer the AWS should have a logging capability – meaning that the observations can be stored on a computer for later analysis (maybe in case anything of interest occurs).

Most observers will have seen an AWS by the side of a main road or at the side of a motorway. The locations of, and some observations from, some of these AWSs can be found on Vaisala's traffic weather website.[1] The data collected by such instruments aid decision making when it comes to deciding when to send gritters out in very cold weather, for example. Road temperatures can also be measured with surface and subsurface sensors, which, along with the residual salt content on the road, can provide an indication of the freezing temperature of moisture on the road. Figure 7 shows a different type of AWS seen on Guernsey.

Fig. 7. An automatic weather station on the island of Guernsey. The white object in the foreground is the raingauge.

In contrast, a manual weather station, comprising the more traditional thermometers, raingauge and perhaps a barometer, needs watching, with observations being made at regular intervals. While such a manual approach might seem time-consuming, it is probably true that any new observer will quickly become more aware of the weather if such equipment is used – there's nothing like standing outside in 'continuous heavy rain' and a force 6 wind when making the daily observations to gain an appreciation of the impact and vagaries of the weather.

However, an AWS will gather a lot more data and allow the observer to analyse conditions 'after the event', thereby gaining an understanding of the minute-by-minute changes in wind speed and direction, rainfall rates and temperature changes across cold fronts, for example. Alternatively, you might use the observations to examine the change in wind and temperature during a thunderstorm. Of course the weather changes throughout the day; all these changes will be captured by an AWS for later study.

TYPES OF AWS

An AWS in its basic form consists of a sensor and a logger – the former to measure the weather element and the latter to store that information. These equate to, in the manual observation case, the instrument (for example thermometer) and observer's notebook. Usually the logger is connected to the observer's personal computer on a regular (or permanent) basis in order to download and store for perpetuity the observations. Without regular downloads, the logger will eventually run out of memory and overwrite the earliest observations that it holds.

The advent of wireless technology means that it is nowadays more usual to have a set of outdoor sensors that are connected to a transmitting device that relays the observations indoors to a display console – thereby allowing the owner to visualize the weather from the comfort of indoors in real time (the observations are relayed to the console every few seconds). With cheaper AWSs the consoles can also be connected to a PC (maybe using

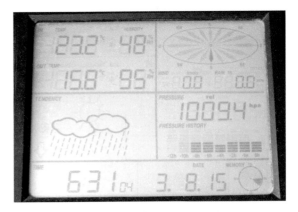

Fig. 8.   An example of a display console for an automatic weather station. Indoor and outdoor temperature and relative humidity (top left), wind and rainfall in the past hour (top right), pressure tendency and weather forecast (centre left) and pressure and pressure history (centre right) are shown, along with the time and date. Note that the weather forecast is only indicative and seems (in the case of this display) to be based upon the rate of change of pressure.

a dedicated cable) from time to time to archive the observations.

Nowadays, a feature of modern weather stations is their ease of connection to a personal computer and the ease with which they may be used to upload observations to a live weather website. For such a capability a mid-range priced weather station is usually required – priced at £250–£300 upwards (as of January 2016). As with any scientific equipment, cheap weather stations may seem a good way into the hobby, but can prove disappointing when some of the sensors turn out to be inaccurate or unreliable – or the outdoor sensors fail after a few weeks.

As a starting point, an AWS should provide you with observations of barometric pressure, air temperature and humidity, wind speed and direction, as well as rainfall. To measure such elements using traditional instruments might cost you around £300 (£150 for an entry-level thermometer screen, £50 for a raingauge, £50 for an aneroid barometer, £50 for a Six's thermometer and a Mason's hygrometer) – assuming that the wind is estimated 'by eye'.

If you purchase an AWS, check to see if all the sensors are wired closely together; if the sensors are too close it may be difficult to use them all effectively. The air temperature should be measured at about head height, the rainfall at just above ground level, while the wind needs to be measured ideally above the rooftop in a back garden weather station. This might be problematic if all the sensors in your cheap AWS are connected to a central controller by cables no more than 1m or so in length.

The solution might be to use one AWS to measure one type of meteorological parameter (for example temperature) and then simply ignore the other measurements. Rainfall could always be measured using a stand-alone manual raingauge. Indeed, it is recommended that such a raingauge is installed. Then, once you have decided that weather observing is a hobby you would like to pursue further, maybe you can upgrade to a better AWS that allows the sensors to be exposed in separate locations.

An alternative is to buy different sensors for different observations – but if these sensors are made by different manufacturers then maybe different data loggers would be needed. In many cases an aptitude for basic computer programming is an advantage, as you may want to combine the different outputs into one computer file for each calendar month. Such an approach does, however, lend itself to the purchasing of weather instruments as a gift – a wireless temperature sensor or a wireless raingauge are the obvious candidates here, although the former may also require the addition of a small thermometer screen to shelter it from sunshine.

A few automatic weather stations have their displays and sensors combined into a single piece of equipment. This means that you can only view the observations in situ – usually this means mounting the equipment close to the house in order to view the weather conditions from indoors. Of course the presence of the house will affect the measurements. Output from such instruments may not be amenable to being logged near-automatically onto a computer.

For those who wish to deepen their knowledge and understanding of weather observing and instrumentation I would also recommend reading Stephen Burt's excellent book on the subject,[2] which is aimed at both the amateur and professional weather observer.

OBSERVATION TIME

There are, broadly speaking, two types of weather station in the UK. Weather stations report a mixture of real-time weather observations (these are synoptic stations) and once-daily summaries.

Synoptic observations are often used as a source of weather data by weather forecast models. They are also made as a means of determining the current state of the atmosphere by those for whom the weather can be of immediate importance and are often sited at locations such as airports and airfields. Before the advent of automatic equipment, synoptic weather stations were sometimes manned

---

BST, GMT OR UTC?

For weather measurements to be comparable from place to place, or over a long period of time at the same site, the time at which the measurements are made and the period covered by the observations need to be common as far as possible. Operational weather observations are made according to the common time standard of Coordinated Universal Time (UTC). UTC and Greenwich Mean Time (GMT) are, to within a second, equivalent and are treated as being identical in this book.

In the UK, GMT is adopted during the winter and British Summer Time (BST; GMT + 1 hour) during the summer, with the changeover occurring on the last Sundays in March and October. Observations made at 0900 GMT in winter should be continued during the summer months as close as possible to 1000 BST, with corresponding time changes being made to any observations made at other times of the day.

around the clock to enable hourly observations to be made.

Weather information is also useful for statistical or climatological purposes; in particular the daily maximum and minimum temperatures, sunshine and rainfall totals fall into this category. In addition, stations making once-daily climatological observations often also record the number of days with certain weather phenomena, soil temperatures and measurements of cloud, wind and visibility at 0900 GMT. Many of them also keep as complete a record as possible of the evolution of the weather during the day.

Many amateur weather observers in the UK strive to maintain their weather stations as close as possible to this 'climatological station model'. While not all are able to make a daily 0900 GMT observation, most are able to make a regular daily observation between 0600 GMT and 0900 GMT. It is important to try to maintain observations at this 'morning observing hour' as many meteorological phenomena do exhibit diurnal variations – and it is easier to compare observations if any diurnal effects can be reduced.

WHERE TO INSTALL EQUIPMENT

The majority of amateur weather stations are located in back gardens and do tend to be slightly sheltered as a result. However, with a little thought, good observations can still be made. A few amateurs may be fortunate to be able to find a site with more of an open aspect, for example in a local school.

While site security is not normally an issue with back garden weather stations, it must be considered when the stations are in an area with public access. Too many stations have had to reduce the types of observations made, due to persistent vandalism, and some have closed permanently after damage or theft. Unfortunately, a compromise often has to be made between the changes needed to secure a site against intruders and the need to maintain an open aspect to enable the weather to reach the instruments. A raingauge located in the shadow of a tall fence is rather pointless, while the site owner might object to the installation of a tall, electrified fence around the instruments!

Garden weather stations may also need some protection from animals and young children. If the raingauge is sited on the lawn, then perhaps a small, low-level (20cm-tall) mesh netting located half a metre from the raingauge will prevent the family's pet labrador from making use of it every morning. Placing the thermometer screen too close to the garden swing in a corner of the garden, or close to a hedge, might be as bad as placing it too close to the house.

At this point it is also worthwhile mentioning that different observations need to be made at different heights above the ground. Thus wind measurements should be made (ideally) above rooftop level at an enclosed amateur site, otherwise the wind flow is distorted by the presence of building and trees, for example. Even if any trees or building are a few tens of metres downwind of the wind sensor (in the direction of the prevailing wind) it is quite likely that the distortion of the airflow around these trees or buildings will take place over several hundred metres, resulting in reduced wind speeds and variable wind directions.

Temperatures are usually measured in a white thermometer screen (which protects the instruments from the effects of rain and direct sunshine), with the instruments at a height of about 1.25m above the ground, while rainfall is measured traditionally at 30cm above the ground. Temperature measurements can be largely determined by the nature of the thermometer screen into which they are placed. Thus, using a grey or black thermometer screen will usually result in higher-than-expected temperatures being recorded as the sun's heat will be absorbed by the body of the screen and create a locally warm enclosure of air – into which you have placed a thermometer.

The Royal Meteorological Society has published a useful document that discusses the siting of instruments.[3]

Site/Instrument Exposure – a Simple Assessment System

Every site is different and consequently objective methods are required to distinguish between sites.

Only then can differences in readings between two sites be judged to be due to the different weather characteristics of the sites rather than being due to differences in the type of instruments being used or to differences in instrumental exposure.

One simple measure of assessing the site exposure was first introduced some 150 years ago by the British Rainfall Organization. Originally devised to assess the exposure of raingauges in the British Isles, it determines the ratio of the distance between an obstacle (for example, a tree or a building) and an instrument to the height of the obstacle. Over the years a ratio of 2 has become accepted as a reasonable minimum ratio – thus any obstacle should ideally be a distance equivalent to twice its height away from the instrument.

In order to facilitate the comparison of observations between sites, the Climatological Observers Link (COL, see Chapter 1) has made use of a series of station grading schemes, the most recent dating

Table 1	The station grading scheme of COL

The first column shows the overall station grade assigned to the weather station.

COL station grading	Station characteristics
A	Standard site; records are likely to be indistinguishable from those obtained at other standard sites
B	Sheltered site; standard instruments are used but a sheltered exposure may result in some differences in readings when compared to standard sites
C1	Very sheltered site; although standard instruments are employed, the very sheltered nature of the site may result in significant differences when compared to records at standard sites
C2	Non-standard instruments or exposure; limitations in the exposure or instrumentation may create significant differences when compared with those from a standard site
U	Site details at least partially unknown; this will include new and ungraded sites

Table 2	The exposure assessment scheme of COL

Here h is the height of any obstacle.

COL exposure grading	Site characteristics
5	Very open exposure; no obstructions within 10h or more of temperature or rainfall instruments
4	Open exposure; most obstructions/heated buildings 5h or more from temperature or rainfall instruments, none within 2h
3	Standard exposure; no significant obstructions or heated buildings within 2h of temperature or rainfall instruments
2	Restricted exposure; most obstructions/heated buildings at least 2h from temperature or rainfall instruments, none within 1h
1	Sheltered exposure; significant obstructions or heated buildings within 1h of temperature or rainfall instruments
0	Very sheltered exposure; site obstructions or sensor exposure severely limit exposure to sunshine, wind and rainfall
R	Rooftop site
U	Exposure unstated or unknown

back to 2009. The scheme is based around some key instrument and site characteristics, as follows:

- The exposure and standard of each type of instrument, principally those for measuring temperature, rainfall and sunshine
- The observation times
- The site exposure
- The urban profile of the site
- Observations made at the site, which may be reported to standard (national) rainfall or climatological networks

The overall station grade is then summarized using a one- or two-letter/number combination as shown in Table 1, while the shelter component of the scheme is shown in Table 2.

Another, non-instrumental contribution to the station grading is that of the urban profile. The COL station grading scheme adopts the scheme of Timothy Oke (*see* Table 1 in Oke's guide to siting weather stations)[4] and uses the categories shown in Table 3.

KEEPING A RECORD

Having made a set of weather observations, you should keep them in a safe place for future reference – either to allow the calculation of monthly summaries at the end of each month, or to allow you to refer back when comparing the weather month by month. This record can be either in the form of a paper copy, or in some sort of electronic file. In either case, we will refer to this as the 'register of weather observations' or 'register'.

Although some publishers have diaries or registers for such a purpose, many amateurs may find that their observations do not match the columns in such books. Keeping your own records in some kind of notebook (better than a set of loose-leaf papers, which have a tendency to become lost over time) is ideal for the amateur – and you can then simply include additional columns as the collection of equipment expands.

For observers who use non-electronic equipment, a good way forward is to devise your own spreadsheet using computer software such as

Table 3 The **COL** urban climate zone indicator	
These are taken from reference[4] – Table 1 in that document (which shows some typical skylines) may also help you to determine the correct rating.	
COL urban climate indicator	**Site characteristics**
1	Intensely developed urban zone with detached close-set high-rise buildings with cladding; for example downtown towers
2	Intensely developed high-density urban zone with 2- to 5-storey attached or very close-set buildings often of brick or stone; for example old city core
3	Highly developed, medium-density urban zone with rows of detached but close-set houses, stores and apartments; for example urban housing
4	Highly developed, low-density urban zone with large low buildings and paved parking; for example shopping mall, warehouses
5	Medium development, low-density suburban zone with 1- or 2-storey houses; for example suburban housing
6	Mixed-use zone with large buildings in open landscape; for example institutions such as hospital, university, airport
7	Semi-rural development with scattered houses in natural or agricultural area; for example farms, estates
U	Urban climate zone unstated or unknown

Table 4   Part of the January 2014 summary sheet from the author's Maidenhead weather station

DD	N	ww	Max	Min	Gmin	10	100	SS	Rain	Sun	S	L	F	Press
1	8	02	10.5	3.7	−1.1	5.1	7.9	0	14.3	0.0	0	0	0	996.5
2	1	01	10.4	5.1	2.0	6.3	7.9	0	4.6	4.9	0	0	0	995.5
3	1	21	10.2	5.2	1.1	6.7	7.9	0	19.8	1.7	0	0	0	994.0
4	8	65	8.2	5.9	−3.5	6.1	8.0	0	6.4	0.0	0	0	0	991.0
5	1	02	12.4	−0.8	−3.7	3.4	7.9	0	6.5	0.0	0	0	0	1004.0
6	2	02	12.1	−0.5	−2.1	7.2	7.9	0	3.8	1.2	0	0	0	994.5
7	8	02	11.4	9.2	6.3	7.1	7.9	0	4.0	3.2	0	0	0	1001.0
8	7	02	11.8	7.0	2.0	5.7	8.0	0	3.1	0.5	0	0	0	1014.0
9	6	21	9.6	7.0	2.6	7.9	8.1	0	0.0	4.3	0	0	0	1003.0
...														
23	8	02	8.8	1.9	−1.5	4.2	7.6	0	1.1	4.1	0	0	0	1011.0
24	8	03	8.2	0.5	0.3	3.6	7.5	0	8.8	0.0	0	0	0	1014.0
25	7	02	11.2	3.0	2.0	6.1	7.4	0	2.5	1.6	0	0	0	1014.5
26	8	02	9.2	3.4	1.0	4.6	7.4	0	8.2	0.8	0	0	0	1005.5
27	8	25	8.9	1.3	−2.0	3.7	7.4	0	5.7	3.8	0	0	0	990.0
28	7	03	10.6	3.2	−1.0	3.9	7.4	0	3.3	3.8	0	0	0	984.5
29	8	02	5.3	5.0	1.6	5.1	7.2	0	20.0	0.0	0	0	0	993.5
30	8	15	5.2	3.1	2.6	4.3	7.1	0	0.1	0.0	0	0	0	1002.5
31	8	02	9.4	2.8	0.2	4.5	7.1	0	15.0	0.0	0	0	1	1003.0
High			12.4	9.2	6.3	7.9	8.1		20.0	6.5				1019.5
Low			5.2	−2.4	−5.3	2.7	7.1							984.5
Average	5.3		9.5	2.6	−0.6	5.2	7.7							1002.3
Total									163.1	68.6	0	0	2	
Normal	6.0		7.8	1.9	−0.8	3.8	6.7		61.0	57.5	2.9	1.5	1.8	1017.1

For clarity, many columns have been omitted (and also data for the 10th to 22nd), as have the accompanying graphs and statistical summary. Nevertheless, the unusually wet beginning and end of the month can be seen, along with the lack of snow during the entire month. Key: DD – date; N, ww – total cloud amount (oktas) and present weather code at 0700 GMT (*see* Chapters 3 and 5); Max, Min, Gmin – maximum and minimum air, and minimum grass temperature (°C); 10, 100 – soil temperature at depths of 10cm and 100cm (°C); SS – snow depth at 0700 GMT (cm); Rain – precipitation (mm); Sun – sunshine duration (hours); S – snow (5) or sleet (1) falls; L – 50 per cent snow cover at 0900 GMT (1); F – fog (1) at 0900 GMT; Press – air pressure at 0900 GMT (mb). The final five rows show the highest and lowest values observed during the month, the average or the total for the month, and (Normal) the long-term climatological average for January based on observations from previous years.

Excel. This way you can easily produce site-specific monthly summaries for circulation to family and friends, and maybe the local history section of your local library. An example of some monthly summary data from my Maidenhead station can be seen in Table 4.

FUTURE-PROOFING YOUR RECORDS

Electronic equipment records the weather around the clock and usually comes with its own software (computer programs) to enable the data to be stored. Be warned, though – computers and software are frequently updated and the hardware and software version that you use now may not be usable twenty years into the future. At one point in time my monthly files were stored in Word3 files on small 3.5in floppy disks – the latter cannot now be plugged into my laptop without the use of additional hardware.

So it might be worthwhile keeping a printed copy

of any file and also saving a printed copy as an Adobe PDF file. In addition, as you upgrade your software in future years, try to create upgraded versions of any data files – by loading in the old copies and then resaving them in the new format. Thus anyone who has old Excel data files with an '.xls' filename extension might wish to resave them with an '.xlsx' extension. Old files can usually be read by new versions of software, although sometimes reading old file types will not work for very old versions. This updating is easier if the number of files is kept to a minimum; each of my own daily observations is stored in two different files – one for each calendar month and one file that contains everything. My 25-year record of daily observations amounts to a file with a size of only 5 megabytes – quite small by the standards of today's computers.

Even paper records can be lost (by flood, fire or burglary, for example) – so having a paper duplicate of any data stored in a paper file might prove useful. But keeping additional copies of any electronic records is even more useful. Most computer users will at some point in time find that their computer fails to work – perhaps due to some spam email received that has made a mess of the computer's file systems or some other virus (or malware) that has not been quarantined and removed. Maybe the computer just wears out and needs to be replaced with minimal possibility of retrieving any old data files. So it is essential to keep a backup copy of any electronic files – preferably on a separate hard disk and ideally in a second location (maybe in a drawer at work).

Here are some tips for ensuring that your data have a long lifetime:

- Make regular backups of your data. If you have an AWS that gathers data every few seconds or minutes, then maybe a backup copy should be made at least once daily. Automatic software can do that without intervention once set up.
- Back up electronic data onto an external disk drive or USB stick (ideally make two copies). Periodically ensure that any old drives or sticks can still be read.

- Be aware that old photocopies may fade with time. Perhaps they could be scanned into PDF files?
- Try to keep any copies (paper or disk copies) in a separate location – at the office or with a relative.
- Share your observations with others, both individuals and groups; for example with COL (*see* Chapter 1).
- Ensure that your will (or at the very least a note or codicil stored with your will) indicates what is to happen to your records in the event of your death. Perhaps the local history section of your library (or local public records office) might be interested in a copy? All too often many years of hard work (and valuable data) simply end up in a rubbish skip.

METADATA

Metadata can be defined briefly as 'data about data'. As your weather station develops and new instruments are acquired, you will slowly tend to forget the details of the early instruments and the dates during which they were used. It is useful, therefore, to keep notes about:

- The instruments (type, manufacturer, any serial number, date of installation and removal)
- The site (where all the instruments are sited; any trees or bushes that were removed; any new buildings that were added to the site)

It is also useful to have some photographs of the site – preferably one each facing north, south, west and east – as a pictorial record of any changes. You could take one set of photographs in winter and one in summer, to show the growth of vegetation – and repeat this every two to three years. More importantly, when your observations are used by others at a later date, they will have an idea whether your raingauge was in the centre of a large lawn, or under the clothes line (yes, this does happen!) or quite close to a fence – and is this fence in the direction of the prevailing wind and hence the direction from where the rain tends to arrive?

3. WEATHER TYPES

PRESENT AND PAST WEATHER

In addition to instrumental observations, many weather observers maintain a diary of weather phenomena that occur at their weather station. Such a diary may include one or more of the following types of entry:

1. Present weather observation made at the observing time(s)
2. A descriptive diary of the weather throughout the day
3. A daily count of certain types of weather phenomena

Before describing each of these entries and how to record them in your weather register, we will first define the weather phenomena that we may wish to record.

These definitions are agreed by international convention and the World Meteorological Organization, so that observers in different countries can be sure they are measuring or describing the same phenomena. Many national meteorological services also publish guides to their own observers – those for observers in the UK can be found in the Met Office's *Observer's Handbook*[5] and *Meteorological Glossary*.[6]

TYPES OF WEATHER

Most weather phenomena are termed meteors. *The International Cloud Atlas (volume I)*[7] gives the following definition: 'A meteor is a phenomenon, other than a cloud, observed in the atmosphere or on the surface of the earth, which consists of a precipitation, a suspension or a deposit of aqueous or non-aqueous liquid or solid particles, or a phenomenon of the nature of an optical or electrical manifestation.'

Meteors are classified into four groups – hydrometeors, lithometeors, electrometeors and photometeors. The latter category is comprised of optical phenomena that are discussed more fully in Chapter 7.

HYDROMETEORS

A hydrometeor is a meteor consisting of an aggregate of liquid or solid water particles suspended in, or falling through, the atmosphere, blown by the wind from the earth's surface, or deposited on objects on the ground or in free air.

The most common hydrometeors are described below.

Rain and Drizzle

Rain consists of precipitation of liquid water particles in the form of drops of more than 0.5mm in diameter. Drizzle consists of fairly uniform precipitation of fine droplets of water of no more than 0.5mm in diameter. Drizzle is fine enough to have no effect upon the surface of puddles, whereas raindrops create rings as they hit puddles. Freezing rain or drizzle consists of drops that freeze on impact with the ground or other objects.

Snow and Sleet

Snow consists of solid precipitation of ice crystals, most of which are branched, falling from a cloud. The form of snow varies considerably according to the temperature at which the crystals form and the conditions in which they develop. Snow occurs in a variety of forms: as minute ice crystals at temperatures well below 0°C, but as larger snowflakes at temperatures around 0°C. Snowflakes are aggregates of ice crystals. In the UK sleet is a mixture of rain and snow, or drizzle and snow. Note that in the USA, sleet is defined as being pellets of ice composed of frozen

Fig. 9.   An evening view of deep lying snow in Maidenhead, with present weather conditions of 'continuous fall of slight snow'. The snow depth was 5cm and the ground was entirely snow-covered. Note that surfaces like the main road and areas underneath the trees (where the snow depth was reduced because of the overhanging branches) are not considered when describing the general surface snow conditions.

or mostly frozen raindrops, or refrozen partially melted snowflakes.

Snow Pellets and Snow Grains
Snow pellets consist of precipitation of white and opaque ice particles, which are spherical or sometimes conical with a diameter in the range of

Fig. 10.   A fall of snow pellets, shown on a hailpad (see Chapter 8). The snow pellets make only minimal marks on the hailpad's foil as they are quite light. DONALD PERKINS

2–5mm. The pellets are brittle and easily crushed; they bounce and often break up when falling on hard ground. Snow pellets generally fall in the form of showers, when temperatures are around 0°C. Snow grains are a precipitation type formed of very small white and opaque grains of ice. These grains are fairly flat or elongated, with a diameter generally less than 1mm. Snow grains do not bounce or shatter upon hitting hard ground; they usually fall in small quantities, mostly from stratus cloud or fog, and not in the form of showers.

Hail, Ice Pellets, Diamond Dust and Ice Prisms

Hail is precipitation formed of small balls or pieces of ice (hailstones) with a diameter of 5mm or more. The stones fall from cumulonimbus clouds during thunderstorms. Ice pellets are precipitation composed of transparent or translucent pellets of ice, which are roughly spherical and have a diameter of less than 5mm. Sometimes large hailstones may be formed of agglomerations of smaller stones.

Diamond dust consists of extremely small ice crystals, and usually forms low in the atmosphere at temperatures below −30°C. The name diamond dust comes from the sparkling effect created when light reflects on the ice crystals in the air. They are

---

SNOW PELLETS, DIAMOND DUST OR SNOW?

Snow – the familiar snowflake, comprised of many ice crystals; feathery in appearance

Sleet – a mixture of rain (or drizzle) and snow falling simultaneously

Snow pellets – white ice particles, usually rounded, that bounce on hard ground

Snow grains – white ice particles, rice grain-like in shape and less than 1mm in diameter

Diamond dust – small ice crystals, often falling from a clear sky, that glitter in sunshine; rare in the UK

Ice prisms – ice crystals in the form of needles, columns or plates; rare in the UK

Ice pellets – usually spherical, clear ice particles with a diameter less than 5mm

Small hail – translucent ice particles, usually spherical, with a diameter usually less than 5mm

Hail – transparent or opaque particles of ice from cumulonimbus clouds; often, but not always, spherical

Note that these are definitions as used in the UK and some may differ elsewhere.

Fig. 11.   **Hailstones that fell in a small area in the upper part of Nidderdale (Yorkshire, England) in July 2015 during a violent thunderstorm, with ruler scales numbered in centimetres (upper) and inches (lower). Local damage was considerable – especially to windows, skylights, plastic roofs and cars. Some sheep were also injured.**

BILL WADE

usually seen in polar regions, but can occur at higher temperatures (for example −10°C) in the UK.

Ice prisms are unbranched ice crystals in the form of needles, columns or plates, often so tiny they seem to be suspended in the air. They rarely fall in the British Isles but are frequent in polar regions.

Drifting Snow

This is an aggregate of snow particles raised by the wind to small heights above the ground. The visibility is not greatly reduced at eye level.

Blowing Snow

This consists of snow particles raised by the wind to moderate or great heights above the ground. Visibility at eye level can sometimes be very poor, and the concentration of particles may sometimes be sufficient to hide the sky and even the sun. Particles of blowing snow will generally be smaller in size than those of falling snow.

Fog

Fog is a suspension of very small droplets in the air reducing the visibility at the surface to below 1,000m. Thick fog is said to exist when the visibility drops below 200m, while dense fog occurs when the visibility falls below 50m. Sometimes the visibility varies in different directions, such that towards some points of the compass it exceeds 1,000m. The fog is then described by the phrase 'fog patches'.

Mist

Mist is a suspension of very small droplets in the air reducing the visibility at the surface. The term is used when the visibility is 1,000m or more, with the relatively humidity in the range 95–100 per cent.

Freezing Fog and Ice Fog

Freezing fog is a suspension of very small super-cooled water droplets in the air, reducing visibility at the surface to below 1,000m, which may freeze on contact with solid objects, leading to rime accretion. Even with just a slight breeze, this accretion of water droplets will often tend to occur on just one side of any obstacle such as a tree trunk or pole, leading to horizontal feathers of ice pointing into the wind. A related phenomenon is that of ice fog, which consists of a suspension of minute ice crystals in the air reducing the visibility at the surface to below 1,000m.

Fig. 12. Shallow fog seen during early morning in autumn in Maidenhead. Note how the tree tops in the middle distance are visible, but not their trunks.

Shallow Fog

This is fog lying on the surface of the sea or ground, the depth being about 2m over land and 10m over sea. Visibility may well be over 1,000m above the fog layer. It is for this reason the visibility measurement must be made at ground level.

Dew and Hoar Frost

Dew is a deposit of water drops on objects at or near the ground, produced by the condensation of water vapour from the surrounding clear air. It occurs because it is often that part of the atmosphere closest to the ground overnight that cools most rapidly, thereby becoming temporarily saturated.

Under clear, frosty nights in winter, soft ice crystals may form on vegetation or any object that has been chilled below freezing point by cooling of the near-surface air. This is hoar frost, a deposit of ice having a crystalline appearance, generally assuming the form of scales, needles, feathers or fans. It is formed in manner similar to that of dew, but at a temperature below 0°C. In this case the vapour in the air is deposited as solid ice without going through the water phase. However, the deposit may frequently be formed of drops of dew that have subsequently been frozen.

Rime

Rime is a deposit of ice composed of grains more or less separated by trapped air, sometimes containing crystalline branches protruding more or less horizontally from a vertical surface. The thickness of the rime should be noted. It is produced by the rapid freezing of very small, supercooled water droplets on solid objects. Near the ground, rime is deposited by wind or air movement on the upwind side of obstacles. In mountainous areas, where the water source may be cloud droplets, rime may form quickly and be quite dense and hard.

Glaze and Ground Ice

Glaze is a mainly uniform, clear deposit of ice formed by the freezing of supercooled drizzle or rain on objects with a surface temperature below,

Fig. 13. Hoar frost seen as spikes on smooth-edged leaves following an early morning spell of freezing fog. EDWINA BRUGGE

or just slightly above, 0°C. It occurs when rain or drizzle falls through a layer of subfreezing temperatures of sufficient depth to reach the ground with a temperature close to freezing point. It may also be formed by rain or drizzle falling out of warmer air and freezing upon impact with surfaces having a temperature well below 0°C.

Fig. 14. This hoar frost on the tree was formed during a clear, cold night, although some mist formed by dawn. This mist, and subsequent clouding over of the sky, later raised the temperature near the ground, especially under the trees, where surface hoar frost is much less evident.

Glaze differs from ground ice, which is formed by the freezing of moisture on a previously wet and warm surface, or by the freezing of melted snow on the ground, or by lying snow being compacted by heavy traffic.

Spouts and Funnel Clouds (Tornado Cloud or Waterspout)

These are phenomena consisting of an often violent whirlwind, revealed by a cloud column or inverted cone (funnel cloud – see Fig. 15) protruding from the base of a cumulonimbus, or of a bush composed of water droplets raised from the surface of the sea (a waterspout), or of dust, sand or litter over land (a tornado). The axis of the funnel cloud may be vertical, inclined or sometimes appear long and sinuous. The cloud column in the UK is usually of the order of tens of metres in diameter, although in the USA diameters may range up to several hundreds of metres. Sometimes several spouts are seen associated with a single cloud.

When the phenomenon touches the ground it is known as a tornado; over the sea touchdown creates a waterspout; while the name funnel cloud is used while the spout remains detached from the surface.

Fig. 15. Funnel cloud observed at 12.15pm on 1 December 2010 at Ashford, Co. Wicklow (Republic of Ireland). The funnel cloud had just moved onshore and five minutes later was obscured from view by falling snow. ANGUS TYNER

HAVE YOU OBSERVED A TORNADO, FUNNEL CLOUD OR WHIRLWIND?

If so, then the Tornado and Storm Research Organisation (TORRO) would like to hear all about it from you. They have a popular Facebook page at www.facebook.com/pages/Torro-the-UKs-Tornado-and-Storm-Research-Organisation/249176491778442?fref=nf that can be used for reports, and they also have a Twitter account, @TorroUK, that is becoming increasingly popular. These have enabled them to receive reports almost instantaneously and then put out alerts to others in the area on social media to have a look out.

The more traditional method for making reports is via the report form on their website at www.torro.org.uk/site/report_form.php; they also have a 'mail a big file' link so that photographs and videos can be sent through as well – see www.torro.org.uk/site/uploads.php or www.mailbigfile.com/torro.

They publish all their monthly whirlwind reports in the *International Journal of Meteorology*, and produce annual reports that feature in the July or August issue of this publication each year.

Spouts are sometimes very destructive, although in the UK they tend to be short-lived. Far from being rare in the UK, however, there are on average about forty tornadoes a year.[8, 9]

LITHOMETEORS

A lithometeor is an ensemble of particles most of which are solid and non-aqueous. The particles are more or less suspended in the air, or lifted by the wind from the ground.

TEN UK TORNADO AND WHIRLWIND FACTS

These are taken from the website of the Tornado and Storm Research Organisation (TORRO).[10]

1. The origin of a tornado is often associated with well-developed thunderstorm cells on cold fronts.
2. Some tornadoes form out to sea as strong waterspouts that sometimes cross the coast, so a waterspout may become a tornado as the rotating funnel moves from sea to land.
3. A powerful and well-documented example of a waterspout that became a tornado is that of Selsey on the south coast of England, overnight on 7–8 January 1998.[11] When the waterspout made landfall, it carved a trail of damage a kilometre wide through the town as it damaged hundreds of buildings in less than ten minutes.
4. Most UK tornado reports come from the Midlands, central southern and southeast England and East Anglia. Tornadoes are rare in Northern Ireland and Scotland.
5. In Britain, on 23 November 1981, as many as 105 tornadoes broke out in five and a half hours as a cold front crossed a comparatively small part of England from northwest to southeast.
6. The country with the highest number of reported tornadoes per unit area is England.
7. In the UK a tornado will typically last for a few minutes, track across the land for 2–5km and have a diameter of 20–100m. Wind speeds are usually about 70–100mph. In contrast, a hurricane is an intense area of low pressure that only forms in the tropics where the sea surface temperature is at least 27°C. A hurricane core has a diameter of around 150km but the cloudy area associated with the system will extend over a much larger area such that it is easily visible on satellite imagery. Hurricanes will rapidly dissipate once they make landfall and they lose their source of surface moisture.
8. The majority of lesser whirlwinds are typified by a more or less vertical, whirling column of rising air that is warmer than its surroundings. More frequently formed on warm, sunny days in clear dry air, these are wind devils – also known as land devils and water devils. Depending upon the nature of entrained matter that makes them visible, they may also be called dust devils, sand devils, snow devils, fire devils and so on.
9. On 21 May 1950, a tornado which touched down at Little London (Buckinghamshire) tracked 107km to Coveney (Cambridgeshire), the longest-known tornado track in the UK. From there it continued as a funnel cloud, travelling another 53km to Shipham (Norfolk), where it was last seen disappearing out across the North Sea.
10. The earliest tornado known in Britain is also the equal severest on record here. This was a violent tornado that hit St Mary le Bow in central London on 23 October 1091.

Haze

Haze is a suspension of extremely small, dry particles in the air, invisible to the naked eye but sufficiently numerous to give the air an opalescent appearance. There is no upper or lower limit to horizontal visibility in the presence of which haze may be reported. Haze gives a yellowish or reddish tinge to distant objects or lights seen through it, while dark objects appear bluish.

Dust Haze and Smoke Haze

Dust haze is a suspension of dust or small sand particles in the air, raised from the ground by a duststorm or sandstorm. Dust haze is only reported when there is a lack of strong wind sufficient to raise dust from the ground. In the UK a suspension of sand particles in the air may have been caused by a gusty wind whipping up dry sand off a nearby coastal beach.

Smoke haze is a suspension in the air of small particles produced by combustion. In the UK this is often the result of the incomplete burning of coal, although it can sometimes be due to local agricultural fires. It is reported when visibility impairment can definitely be attributed to smoke.

Drifting or Blowing Dust or Sand

These conditions require a sufficiently strong wind to create a mix of small particles of dust or sand raised, from the ground, to small (drifting dust/sand) or moderate (blowing dust/sand) heights. In the case of drifting phenomena, the visibility is not noticeably diminished at eye level. If visibility is noticeably reduced at eye level then the term 'blowing' is used instead; the particle concentration may be sufficient to hide the sky and even the sun.

Duststorms or sandstorms are a collection of particles of dust or sand lifted to great heights by a strong and turbulent wind. They generally occur in regions where the ground is covered by loose dust or sand and so are unlikely to happen in the UK, although on occasions may travel some distance from the source. The 'fen blow' of East Anglia is a similar phenomenon that lifts dust or soil particles into the air at low levels.

In a slight or moderate duststorm or sandstorm the visibility is below 1,000m but not below 200m, and the sky is usually not obscured. In severe events the visibility drops below 200m and the sky and clouds are usually hidden.

ELECTROMETEORS

An electrometeor is a visible or audible manifestation of atmospheric electricity, of which thunderstorms are the most common type.

Thunderstorms

Thunderstorms consist of one or more electrical discharges (lightning) and a sharp or rumbling sound (thunder). Thunderstorms are usually (but not always) accompanied by precipitation.

A thunderstorm is reported as being at the station from the time that thunder is first heard (whether or not lightning or precipitation is occurring). In the UK the practice is that 'thunderstorm at the time of observation' is reported if thunder is heard in the ten minutes preceding the time of observation. If no thunder is heard for a period of ten minutes or more, the thunderstorm is deemed to have ended.

Lightning is a luminous phenomenon accompanying a sudden electrical discharge that usually takes places from within a cloud. Four types of lightning are recognized:

- **Ground discharges** (sometimes known as thunderbolts or cloud-ground discharges) – this type of lightning occurs between cloud and ground, and appears as a streak or ribbon of light.
- **Cloud discharges** (sometimes known as sheet lightning) – this type occurs within a thundercloud and appears as a diffuse flash of light.
- **Air discharges** (sometimes known as streak lightning) – this type is of the form of sinuous discharges, passing from a thundercloud to the air, and not reaching the ground.
- **Ball lightning** – this is reported as being in the form of a luminous globe, thought to be 10–20cm in diameter. It moves slowly in the air and usually disappears with a violent explosion.

Thunder is a sharp or rumbling sound that accompanies lightning and is caused by the sudden heating and expansion of air by lightning. The distance of the observer from the lightning source may be esti-

---

SOME DEFINITIONS USED WHEN OBSERVING THE WEATHER

Precipitation – this is the general term given to water (either in drops or as ice particles) formed in the atmosphere and falling to the ground. Thus, strictly speaking, a raingauge measures precipitation, as this includes falls of sleet, snow and hail, dew and hoar frost.

Within sight of the station or at a distance – the phenomenon is observed not to be occurring at the station. This often applies to thunderstorms (which may be observed not to approach the weather station), rain (which can sometimes be seen falling from distant clouds) and mist or fog.

Recent/during the past hour – sometimes the 'current weather' observation can refer to phenomena that have occurred at the station within the past hour, but have now ceased. They may however be evident at some distance away from the station.

Continuous precipitation – precipitation falling without cessation for one hour or more.

Intermittent precipitation – precipitation that has not fallen continuously for an hour or longer.

Showers – these are said to occur when the precipitation falls from convective (that is cumulus or cumulonimbus) clouds. They often start and end suddenly and may have large changes in intensity over a short period of time.

---

mated by noting the interval between seeing the flash and hearing the thunder, counting 1km for every three seconds of elapsed time.

In the UK the precipitation from thunderstorms is usually in the form of hail or rain, although in winter it can be in the form of sleet or snow – the so-called thundersnow phenomenon. With conditions near the ground being colder in winter, the air close to the ground can be cold enough for snow rather than rain to be present here. When thundersnow occurs during the hours of darkness, the lightning seems brighter because it is reflected against the snowflakes. Falling snow can muffle the thunder.

PHOTOMETEOR

A photometeor is a luminous phenomenon produced by the reflection, refraction, diffraction or interference of light from the sun or the moon. More details of such phenomena can be found in Chapter 7.

OTHER PHENOMENA

There are several other phenomena that should also be recorded as weather observations when they occur.

Squall

A squall is a strong wind that rises suddenly – increasing by at least 18mph (16 knots) or three scales on the Beaufort wind scale – lasts for at least one minute and then dies away. It is of longer duration than a gust. Squalls are frequently associated with the passage of cold fronts or thunderstorms; when they occur along a line (the line of the front) they are called line squalls. Line squalls are typically accompanied by a sharp temperature fall, a clockwise change in wind direction, a rise of relative humidity and a roll-shaped cloud.

Gale

A gale is said to occur when the average wind speed reaches at least 39mph (34 knots) for a period of at least ten minutes. It does not apply simply because the wind has gusted to such speeds.

HOW HEAVY IS 'HEAVY RAIN'?

Precipitation intensity is usually defined in terms of the rate of fall of the precipitation. When reporting rainfall intensity as part of the 'present weather' description, the observer should report the intensity last observed. Ideally the intensity should be judged using some form of rainfall rate-measuring instrument – but can often be judged by eye quite accurately by most observers. Table 5 gives the definitions of the precipitation intensities.

Fig. 16.   Heavy rainfall bouncing off puddles in a car park. Over 7mm of rain fell in just under an hour in this heavy downpour in Maidenhead during the early evening of 8 July 2014.

Table 5	A summary of precipitation intensities in the UK		

In the case of mixed precipitation (for example rain and hail) the intensity of each type of precipitation is not given separately, but the heaviest precipitation is used to denote the intensity of the mixture.

Weather type	Intensity	Description
Drizzle	Slight	Dampens ground surfaces with little runoff
	Moderate	Causes windows and road surfaces to stream with moisture
	Heavy	Impairs visibility and accumulates in the raingauge at a rate of up to 1mm per hour
Rain	Slight	Scattered large or more numerous smaller drops; rainfall rate not more than 0.5mm per hour
	Moderate	Rainfall rate between 0.5 and 4mm per hour, fast enough for puddles to form rapidly
	Heavy	Rainfall rate more than 4mm per hour; a downpour that makes a pouring noise on roofs and can form a spray of fine droplets by splashing on road surfaces and other objects
Showers	Slight	Precipitation rate less than 2mm per hour although enough rain may fall to create puddles
	Moderate	Precipitation rate between 2 and 10mm per hour
	Heavy	Precipitation rate between 10 and 50mm per hour
	Violent	Precipitation rate more than 50mm per hour
Snow or snow showers	Slight	Few flakes and of small size; the rate of accumulation does not exceed 0.5cm per hour
	Moderate	Snowfall consists of large flakes falling sufficiently thickly to impair visibility substantially. Snow depth increases at up to 4cm per hour
	Heavy	Visibility is considerably reduced by falling snow and the snow depth increases by more than 4cm per hour
Hail	Slight	Small hailstones, not enough to whiten the ground
	Moderate	A fall of hail sufficient to whiten the ground and to produce an appreciable amount of precipitation when melted
	Heavy	Heavy hail showers are rare in the UK and include at least some stones exceeding 6mm in diameter. Crops are damaged and leaves knocked off trees

Table 6	The Beaufort letters and their meanings
Symbol	Meaning
	State of the sky and clouds
b	Total cloud amount 0/8 to 2/8 (0–2 oktas)
bc	Total cloud amount 3/8 to 5/8 (3–5 oktas)
c	Total cloud amount 6/8 to 8/8 (6–8 oktas)
o	Overcast with a uniform layer of cloud covering the sky
	Precipitation and related phenomena
r	Rain or freezing rain
d	Drizzle or freezing drizzle
s	Snow
h	Hail, snow pellets, ice pellets, diamond dust
l	Lightning
t	Thunder
sh	Snow grains
w	Dew
x	Hoar frost
	Visibility-related phenomena
f	Fog or ice fog
fe	Wet fog
fs	Shallow fog
m	Mist
ks	Drifting or blowing snow
kz	Duststorm or sandstorm
z	Haze
	Other symbols
i	Intermittent
j	At a distance/within sight
p	Shower
y	Dry air, relative humidity less than 60 per cent
u	Ugly, threatening sky
e	Wet air, without precipitation
v	Unusually good visibility
g	Gale, mean speed 34–47 knots over a period of at least 10 minutes
G	Storm, mean speed 48 knots or more over a period of at least 10 minutes
kq	Line squall
q	Squall

The Beaufort letters can be combined, thus 'dr' denotes rain and drizzle, 'rs' means sleet (rain and snow) and 'tlr' indicates a thunderstorm (thunder, lightning and rain).

PRESENT WEATHER CODES

Meteorologists often use a two-digit numerical code (in the range 00 to 99) to describe the weather conditions at the observation time. This saves using a potentially long-winded description of the current weather and enables the current weather to be easily understood by any meteorologist, whatever their native tongue. In addition, the observer can use supplementary notes in the weather register to amplify any description of the weather.

These and other codes useful to weather observers can be found in the World Meteorological Organization's *Manual on Codes*.[12]

BEAUFORT LETTERS

A continuous description of the significant weather at the station may be kept by means of Beaufort letters. These give (most) weather types an alphabetic symbol, which, along with other symbols denoting time, continuity and intensity, for example, allow a shorthand diary to be maintained. The system of letters was first used by Francis (later Admiral Sir Francis) Beaufort early in the 1800s but has been considerably revised since then. The symbols are shown in Table 6.

INTENSITY OF PRECIPITATION

The intensity of phenomena is indicated as follows when using Beaufort letters:

- **Slight** – by the addition of the subscript 'o' to the lowercase Beaufort letter
- **Moderate** – by the use of the lowercase Beaufort letter
- **Heavy, severe or intense** – by the use of the uppercase Beaufort letter
- **Violent** – by the addition of the subscript '2' to the uppercase Beaufort letter

Here is an example:

- $t_o l_o R$ – heavy rain with slight thunder and lightning

CONTINUITY OF PRECIPITATION

When using Beaufort letters, continuity of precipitation is indicated by repeating the symbol(s) while the letter 'i' denotes intermittent phenomena, for example:

- intermittent slight snow – is_o
- continuous heavy rain – RR
- continuous slight drizzle and rain – $d_o r_o d_o r_o$

When indicating shower intensity only the precipitation letter is changed, not the symbol 'p', so, for example 'pR' denotes a shower of heavy rain. Thunderstorm intensity (intensity of thunder and lightning) is considered separately from that of the precipitation.

WITHIN SIGHT

The letter 'j' is used in combination with the letter(s) denoting the phenomena to record phenomena occurring within sight of, but not at, the station. For precipitation, the symbol 'jp' is used rather than (say) 'jr', since the type and intensity of the precipitation is not recorded as this may be difficult to determine.

FOG

Fog continuity is governed by rules similar to that for precipitation. When fog patches drift over the station from time to time, intermittent fog (if) is recorded. If fog patches can be seen by the observer, but the visibility at the station remains 1,000m or greater, then fog within sight (jf) is recorded.

USE OF A HYPHEN

The hyphen (-) may be used to indicate a change in weather, in order to avoid ambiguity. Thus, 'r-s' indicates rain turning to snow, while 'rs' denotes sleet.

OTHER NOTATION

When describing the weather over a period of time (for example in the form of a 24-hour diary of the weather), it may be useful to add other phrases to explain the trends and timings of weather phenomena. All times should be GMT time reported using the 24-hour clock. Examples of this are:

- **bec** – becoming ('f bec m' would indicate fog changing to mist)
- **ocnl** – occasional
- **tempo** – temporarily
- **'am', 'pm', 'evng'** – morning, afternoon, evening. The quote marks are used to avoid 'pm' being interpreted as a shower of mist, for example.
- **1100–1200** – 1100 GMT to 1200 GMT (for example 'rr 1100–1200 bec RR 1200–1400')
- **The comma can be used for clarification** – for example 'css 0930–1200, cS 1210' – in this case making it clear that the heavy snowfall occurred at 1210 GMT. Likewise 'f, s' means fog followed by snow, rather than shallow fog.

ENTRIES IN THE OBSERVATION REGISTER

It is useful to keep a separate column in the weather register for each of the following phenomena observed during the period 0000 GMT to 2400 GMT:

A. **Snow or sleet** – enter '5' when there are falls of snow, snow grains or snow pellets; '1' when sleet but not snow falls; '0' when none of these falls.

B. **Hail/ice pellets** – enter '0' if there are no falls of ice pellets or hail; '4' if ice pellets but not hail are observed; '5' if hail 5–9mm in diameter falls; '6' if hail 10–19mm in diameter falls; or '7' if hail 20mm or more in diameter falls.

C. **Thunder** – enter '0' if no thunder is heard or '1' if thunder is heard.

D. **Gale** – enter '0' for no gale, or '1' if a gale occurs.

In all cases, if more than one type of the phenomenon occurs, then use the highest appropriate code. Thus if both snow and sleet fall, then code 5 is used to denote the type of 'snow day'.

In addition, a note should be made of the following observations at 0900 GMT (or the closest morning observation hour to this time):

E. **Fog** – enter '0' if the visibility is at least 1,000m in all directions, '1' if the visibility is below 1,000m in any direction. *See also* Chapter 4.

F. **Lying snow** – enter '0' if the extent of the ground coverage if less than 50 per cent, '1' if the extent is 50 per cent or more. *See also* Chapter 6.

The following columns relating to a description of the weather may also appear in the register of observations:

G. The present weather at observation time, using the two-digit numerical code.[12]

H. A diary of weather experienced during the day.

I. Notes used to clarify or describe further any phenomena observed.

The number of days with snow/sleet falling each month is the number of entries in (A) that are greater than 0. The number of days with ice pellets falling each month is the number of entries in (B) with a value of 4. The number of days with hail falling each month is the number of entries in (B) with a value of 5 or more.

4. NON-INSTRUMENTAL OBSERVATIONS OF WIND AND VISIBILITY

This chapter describes how to make observations of the wind and visibility without the aid of instruments. While professional wind measurements are made using accurate wind vanes and anemometers, wind is a notoriously difficult quantity to measure correctly and a newcomer to weather observing can make a start to recording the wind by using objects around the weather station.

WIND

Wind is a very variable element of the weather; it is the movement of air resulting from the differential heating of the earth by the sun. This variation in heating leads to variations in air pressure (for example the familiar 'high' and 'low' pressure areas shown on pressure charts). These differences in air pressure lead to wind as air under high pressure tries to move towards an area of lower pressure. The larger the pressure difference, the greater the wind speed.

Wind speeds vary considerably close to the surface of the earth. The roughness of the earth's surface, due to everything from blades of grass to buildings and trees, acts to slow the wind down – the closer the air is to the ground, the greater the effect. For this reason winds are usually measured at a standard height – usually 10m above the ground, assuming there are no obstacles nearby.

According to the Met Office[13] the strongest gust ever recorded in the UK was one of 150 knots (173mph) at Cairngorm Summit on 20 March 1986. Strong gusts can also occur at sea level along the coasts; gusts over 100 knots in such locations are not unheard of. The strongest winds tend to occur in autumn and winter in the UK – the seasons when severe storms arriving over the UK from the direction of the Atlantic Ocean tend to be most prevalent.

Average annual surface wind speeds over low level areas of England tend to average out at 6–10 knots, and they generally increase with increasing altitude to over 20 knots in parts of the Scottish Highlands.

KNOTS OR MILES PER HOUR?

Wind speeds presented in this book will, for the most part, be given in units of knots. The knot is a speed equal to one nautical mile per hour. The use of this unit reflects the historical connection of Britain's Royal Navy with the measurement of wind speed in the seventeenth and eighteenth centuries – and the desire for the wind speed and ship speed to use the same unit of measurement.

Nowadays, wind speeds in the UK are generally reported in knots although many countries, including the Republic of Ireland, use units of metres per second. Table 7 shows how to convert from one unit to another.

Table 7 Conversion factors from one unit of wind speed to another

The conversion factors are accurate to three decimal places.

	m/s	km/h	mph	knot
1 m/s =	1	3.6	2.237	1.944
1 km/h =	0.278	1	0.621	0.540
1 mph =	0.447	1.609	1	0.869
1 knot =	0.514	1.852	1.151	1

Wind direction is, meteorologically, defined as the direction from which the wind blows or arrives. Furthermore, it should be specified using 'true' and not 'magnetic' compass directions. Thus a southerly wind blows over the observer from a southerly direction. In the UK the surface wind blows most frequently from a southwesterly quadrant – see Fig. 17.

The prevailing wind direction has an important effect on the surface air temperatures experienced in the British Isles. Water, having a larger heat capacity than surface soils, requires a larger change in heat content than the land surface to warm up or cool down. In addition, water will spread out any temperature changes more rapidly over depth by virtue of the fact that water can move upwards and downwards. This means that the surface of Atlantic Ocean will be cooler in summer and warmer in winter than adjacent (European) land masses. Thus a prevailing wind from the southwest will tend to make the British Isles milder in winter and cooler in summer than one blowing from the direction of nearby Europe.

Wind speeds vary diurnally. The sun heats up the ground and this heat in turn is transferred into the air in contact with the ground – an effect that is greater when the sun is high in the sky than at night, for example. This heat transfer does not occur at the same rate everywhere, leading to relatively warm and cool patches in close proximity, which in turn leads to air motions that attempt to even out these differences. Before dawn, winds are often at their lightest – one of the reasons why fogs tend to disperse once the sun rises. Another reason for fogs around dawn is that the air may no longer remain saturated as the sun begins to warm it. As a result it is important to make a note of the time of any wind observations.

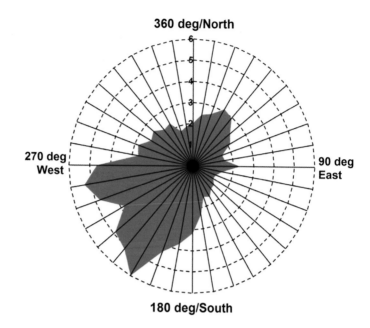

Fig. 17. A wind rose (or wind direction frequency chart) compiled using hourly surface wind direction observations made at London's Heathrow Airport during 2000–2013. Observations are plotted every 10 degrees and show that winds from the southwest quadrant are much more prevalent than those from other directions. The wind occurrence is plotted as a percentage of the total occurrence.

While accurate wind measurements use some form of wind vane and anemometer, it is possible to get a reasonable estimate of the wind conditions by eye.

WIND SPEED

Whether you are a meteorologist or not, the phrase 'gale force' will be a familiar term. The word 'force' refers to a measure on the Beaufort wind scale, a method of estimating the wind speed over sea that is usually credited to Francis (later Admiral Sir Francis) Beaufort. He, it was claimed, invented his scale around the beginning of the nineteenth century; it was first mentioned in his private log in 1806. In fact, accounts from 1704 by Daniel Defoe, in his description of a severe storm that occurred over the British Isles on 26–27 November 1703, used a very similar scale.[14] Later, in 1780, there are records of a scale that could be used by observers

Table 8   The Beaufort wind scale, as used by observers over land

Note that the speeds shown are mean speeds, usually an average over ten minutes (by convention). Gusts can be considerably greater, particularly where the surface roughness is greater – such as in urban areas. The quoted wind speed is that measured at 10m above ground, not at the surface (which, at head height, may be only 50–70 per cent of these values).

Beaufort scale	Mean speed	Wind speed range	Description	Effects observed on land
Force	knots	knots		
0	0	Less than 1	Calm	Calm; smoke rises vertically
1	2	1–3	Light air	Smoke drift indicates wind direction; wind vanes still
2	5	4–6	Light breeze	Wind felt on face, leaves rustle; wind vanes begin to move
3	9	7–10	Gentle breeze	Leaves and small twigs constantly moving; light flags extended
4	13	11–16	Moderate breeze	Dust, leaves, and loose paper lifted; small tree branches move
5	19	17–21	Fresh breeze	Small trees in leaf begin to sway
6	24	22–27	Strong breeze	Larger tree branches moving; whistling in overhead wires
7	30	28–33	Near gale	Whole trees moving; resistance felt walking against wind
8	37	34–40	Gale	Twigs breaking off trees; wind generally impedes progress
9	44	41–47	Severe gale	Slight structural damage occurs; slates blow off roofs
10	52	48–55	Storm	Seldom experienced on land; trees broken or uprooted, considerable structural damage
11	60	56–63	Violent storm	Very rarely experienced; accompanied by widespread damage
12		64 or more	Hurricane	Devastation

to estimate wind speeds over land.[14] This subsequently underwent further changes and extension – see Table 8.

To use the wind scale, instead of an anemometer to measure wind speed, the observer should identify which type of near-surface condition (as shown in the last column of Table 8) applies, and then read off the corresponding wind speed or force. Thus, if over ten minutes it is noted that the wind is starting to be felt on the face or that wind vanes are beginning to move then the wind is one of force 2 with a speed of about 5 knots.

Remember to take into account any obstruction or shelter and that these conditions ideally apply 10m above the ground. If the observer is standing in a small garden surrounded by 2m-tall fences or buildings, for example, then the effect of the wind might be considerably less than that shown in Table 8.

WIND DIRECTION

The wind direction should also be measured (or in this case estimated) as that applying at (ideally) 10m above the ground. How can that be achieved?

If you are fortunate, your weather station might be within sight of a local church equipped with a wind vane or a building flying a flag (see Fig. 18, for example). Failing that, try to observe the movement of any large trees or tree branches. If you are in an open area away from obstacles such as trees or buildings, try to feel the direction of the wind on your face – or, maybe, throw some grass or small leaves into the air and see how they fall.

Fig. 18.   The wind vane and flag flying over the roof of Great Fosters Hotel in Egham, Surrey. The wind direction – from where the wind blows – is southwesterly.

CAN CLOUD MOTION INDICATE SURFACE WIND DIRECTION?

The apparent movement of cloud across the sky can be used to give an indication of the near-surface wind direction. However, unless an identifiable feature of the cloud can be seen and followed over time, it is possible that the cloud may be forming or growing on one edge, and dissipating on the opposite one; the cloud may appear to be moving in a direction that does not match the flow of the wind.

Another problem is that the wind direction may vary with height. Figure 19 shows the variation of the wind direction with height close to the ground, according to a radiosonde balloon ascent made at the University of Reading. Note how at the ground the wind is blowing almost from the south (close to 200 degrees according to a compass), while at the cloud base (at around 1,100m above the ground) it has veered round to 250 degrees (almost a westerly wind): observing the movement of cloud base would give an erroneous wind direction in this case.

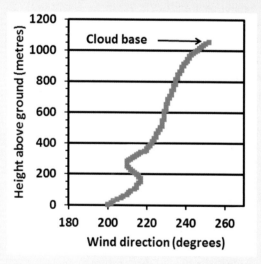

Fig. 19.   Winds recorded close to the ground at the University of Reading on 15 September 2013 during the launch of a weather balloon (radiosonde). Note how the direction changes between the surface and cloud base.

Another method used to measure the wind is the wind sock. This instrument is found mainly at airports and in some open areas, such as on mountain roads, where an easy to see indication of wind direction and strength may be important. The wind blows into the open end of the wind sock closest to the supporting pole.

If used with care, the movement of low clouds can sometimes be used as confirmation of the wind direction determined by one of the methods described above. The lower the cloud the better, as even some low clouds may have a cloud base as high as 1,000m or more.

Due to the errors inherent in determining wind direction without an instrument, it is advisable to report the wind direction according to one of the eight main compass points – see Table 9. If the wind speed is determined to be calm then no wind direction need be recorded as, by convention, no specific direction is reported in such a case.

REGISTER ENTRIES OF WIND

In summary, these entries for wind observations 'made by eye' may be included in the register of observations:

A. The wind direction, entered as a two-digit code or as a compass point.
B. The wind speed, entered in terms of the speed and not the wind force. Make sure the units being used are clear.

VISIBILITY

Visibility is an element of the weather that depends mainly upon the amount of solid and liquid matter present in the atmosphere. Atmospheric visibility is reduced as a result of the scattering of light, rather than by its absorption. This means that light from a distant object is prevented from reaching the eye (that is the object is prevented from being seen) by small particles of solid or liquid matter in the air that deflect the light away from the observer.

Visibility is characteristic, in a general way, of each air mass. In the UK the visibility is generally better in those air masses with a northerly origin, and worse in those that arrive from the south or southeast. Air arriving from the north has passed over little industrialized land by the time it reaches the UK and thus the particulate aerosol matter content is low. Conversely, air arriving from the south or southeast will contain more particulate matter if it has crossed over industrial areas of Europe.

The passage of air over the Atlantic Ocean and North Sea before reaching the UK can also affect the visibility; such air will acquire water vapour by evaporation from the sea before reaching the UK. Onshore winds in the winter along the east coast of the UK can often be foggy because they are cool (arriving from the east) and moist, for example. In warmer conditions fog can be less of a problem as warm air can hold more water vapour before becoming saturated. Even in summer, however, winds from the southwest can lead to foggy conditions in southern parts of the British Isles.

Local variations in visibility are associated with precipitation, atmospheric pollution and other factors. Visibility has a slight diurnal cycle; for

Table 9 Codes used to record wind direction in the register of weather observations	
This code is used worldwide by meteorologists with the wind direction (in degrees) then being equal to ten times the code number. A northerly wind is always recorded as '36' with '00' being used to denote calm.	
Wind direction code – entered in register	**Wind direction**
00	Calm, wind speed less than 1 knot
05	Northeast, NE
09	East, E
14	Southeast, SE
18	South, S
23	Southwest, SW
27	West, W
32	Northwest, NW
36	North, N

example most people will be aware that fog tends to be present more frequently around dawn than later in the day. This is due to the air cooling overnight and it being more likely to be saturated around dawn. Consequently, to ensure consistency of records from month to month it is recommended that observations are made at a standard time each day, ideally at (or as close as possible to) 0900 GMT in the UK. It is difficult to compare visibility measurements at two sites with differing observation hours.

THE MEASUREMENT OF VISIBILITY

Visibility is defined as the greatest distance at which a black object of suitable dimensions can be seen and recognized against the horizon, sky, or, in the case of night observations, could be seen and recognized if the illumination were raised to the normal daylight level. The observation should be made at ground level as there will be occasions when any reduction in visibility may only occur in the lowest 1 or 2 metres of the atmosphere (for example in the presence of shallow fog), while those who have lived in high-rise flats will probably be familiar with the effects of low cloud that obscures the tower top while having minimal effect at ground level.

In practical terms, visibility may be measured by using a set of landmark objects at known distances from the observer. It is expressed in terms of distance (in metres or kilometres), or in terms of visibility categories at climatological stations. The distance of these objects should be determined either by direct measurement (for the nearest objects) or by reference to a large-scale Ordnance Survey map for more distant objects.

It is useful to have objects visible in different directions from the weather station, as the visibility may not be the same in all directions. This may be due to the current weather conditions; for example, the onset of frontal rain from the west may mean the visibility is reduced in that direction while still being quite good towards the east. It may be that fog is more prone to occur in one direction, perhaps due to low-lying wet fields or lakes in that area. If the visibility is noticeably different in different directions, then the lowest visibility should be noted and a note made of the variations.

At weather stations close to the sea, the visibility should be observed in the direction of land; but make a note in your register if you can tell it differs out to sea – especially if it seems foggier over the water.

Ideally, at an amateur weather station in the UK the observer should aim to specify the visibility measurement using the climatological codes of the Met Office (Table 10). Climatological stations employ a single digit code to describe visibility. This is related to the description of visibility as being in one of the categories 'poor', 'moderate', 'good' and so on. These codes can be used conveniently in a computer database as well as the more conventional log book.

Depending upon the location of the weather station, it may (or may not) be possible to determine the visibility distance measurement when the visibility is very good. This may be because no objects further away from the station than a few kilometres may be seen – especially in an urban environment.

This situation applies at my weather station – and in this case I would suggest limiting the upper code value to that distance that can be reasonably accurately determined. So if 'good visibility' can be determined, but not necessarily 'very good visibility', then code '8' and '9' are recorded as a '7' instead.

Determining Visibility at Night

Few amateur observers will observe visibility at night, although at a few stations additional observations may be made after dark. Unless some type of meter is to be used when making observations during darkness, then objects such as lights at known distances and silhouettes of mountains and hills may be used to estimate visibility.

If it is known that the observations are to be made shortly after sunset, then it is worthwhile making a note of visibility at sunset, bearing in mind that the onset of precipitation, for example, may change the visibility somewhat.

Table 10   The UK climatological visibility definitions, and the suggested entries, for use in the register of weather observations to denote the visibility and the incidence of fog (visibility below 1,000m)

These are the Met Office observing codes for climatological stations

Standard distance range	Single digit code entry used in the weather register	General visibility description	Fog present? – weather register entry
Less than 20m	X	Dense fog	1
20–39m	E	Dense fog	1
40–90m	0	Thick fog	1
100–190m	1	Thick fog	1
200–390m	2	Fog	1
400–900m	3	Moderate fog	1
1,000–1,900m	4	Very poor visibility	0
2–4km	5	Poor visibility	0
5–9km	6	Moderate visibility	0
10–19km	7	Good visibility	0
20–39km	8	Very good visibility	0
Over 39km	9	Excellent visibility	0

Days with Fog

For climatological purposes in the UK, a day of fog is defined as a day with visibility of less than 1,000m at 0900 GMT. Note that in some cases reduced visibility may result from conditions other than fog, for example falling snow or blowing sand. However, it is the visibility that matters in this definition, not the cause of the reduction in visibility.

At amateur stations, observations at 0900 GMT may not be possible, and the morning observation time should be used in the definition instead.

The same observation time should be used on all days of the week – if observations are made at a later time at the weekends, this may result in fewer fog days being noted on Saturdays and Sundays, as might the number of days on which 'sky obscured by fog' are reported!

REGISTER ENTRIES OF VISIBILITY

In summary, the following columns relating to the state of ground may appear in the register of observations:

A. The visibility (use the code in Table 10)
B. The presence of fog at the observation time ('0' or '1')
C. The remarks column may contain a note if the fog is patchy or the visibility clearly varies in different directions

As part of the monthly summary it is useful to determine the monthly frequency distribution of the daily visibility (A) in each of the categories shown in Table 10 and the total number of days with fog at the observation time.

5. CLOUDS

Clouds are one of the most beautiful of atmospheric phenomena, coming in a variety of shapes and sizes. No two clouds are ever the same, a fact that makes studying them both fascinating and (at times) difficult – especially if you are trying to classify them!

Clouds are visible aggregates of very small water droplets or ice crystals, or of both. The cloud will also contain liquid or solid particles of other substances – for example those due to salt, smoke, dust or other atmospheric pollutants. These particles, termed aerosols, are important as they provide material on to which water vapour can condense, enabling the condensation process to occur easily.

Clouds form when water vapour in the air condenses into visible water droplets or ice crystals. There is an upper limit to the amount of water vapour that air can hold. This limit is dependent upon the air temperature – warm air can hold more vapour than cold air. Once this limit is reached then saturation occurs. Saturation of the air can happen if:

- Air is lifted (in this case it will cool without any change in water vapour content until saturation occurs)
- Water vapour is added to the air by evaporation
- Warm and moist air is mixed with colder air

The first of these is a common way of producing cloud, and clouds are often associated with rising motion in the lowest part of the atmosphere. This lifting of air can be caused by:

- **Surface heating** – the ground is heated by the sun; then the ground heats the air in contact with it, causing it to rise. The rising columns of air (or thermals) lead to cumulus-type clouds.
- **Frontal surfaces** – these occur when one air mass rises over another at a front – such clouds are often layer- or sheet-type clouds. Some mixing of the two air masses along the front can also lead to cloud formation. Fronts around the UK are often caused by, for example, warm air from the south meeting, and rising above, cooler air from the north.
- **Topography** – a range of hills or mountains can force air to rise as they act as a barrier to the airflow. These clouds are often layer clouds.
- **Convergence** – this happens when air arriving from different directions meets and is forced to rise.
- **Turbulence** – gusty winds, often associated with a change of wind speed with height, can cause turbulence, which gives rise to ascending air motion.

The water in low-level clouds may be present entirely in the form of liquid water, while clouds at higher levels may be formed entirely of ice, as temperatures may fall below −50°C at the height of aircraft contrails, for example.

Clouds also contain water vapour and precipitation – the latter being liquid, solid or a mixture of both, depending upon the air temperature.

Clouds provide us with most of our precipitation (for example, hail, rain and drizzle, and sleet and snow) and a knowledge of the cloud type and how the clouds are evolving in time can provide the amateur observer with the first clues towards a local weather forecast.

Two useful observations of cloud can be easily made by a weather observer, namely the total cloud amount and the cloud type. At professional observing sites, in particular those concerned with aviation, measurements are also made of the cloud base and cloud top heights of individual cloud layers, and of the coverage of the sky by each layer. These measurements generally require equipment of varying

Table 11 The state of the sky and the reported cloud amount to be entered in the register of weather observations	
Cloud amount – entered in register	**Description of the sky**
0	None present – the sky is free of any cloud
1	1 okta; 1 eighth of the sky covered, or less
2–6	2 to 6 oktas; 2 to 6 eighths of the sky covered
7	7 oktas; 7 eighths of the sky covered or more; some sky visible
8	Sky completely covered, no sky visible
9	Sky obscured or the cloud amounts cannot be estimated*

*Sky obscured should be ignored in any arithmetic calculations – for example when calculating monthly averages of cloud cover.

degrees of sophistication. The total cloud amount and cloud type can be determined by eye.

TOTAL CLOUD AMOUNT

Total cloud amount, or cover, is simply the fraction of the sky covered by all the clouds that are visible. The meteorological unit used when describing the cloud amount is the okta (or eighth) of the sky.

In order to estimate cloud amount the sky should be viewed from a position that commands the greatest possible view of the entire sky – pay particular attention to those areas that may be partially obscured close to the horizon by buildings or trees.

A total cloud amount of 0 oktas is recorded only when the sky is completely free of cloud. Even if only a small amount of cloud (including aircraft contrails or power station cloud plume) is visible then 1 okta is reported.

Cloud cover is reported as 8 oktas when no sky is visible – just a small patch of blue sky means that the cloud amount will be reported as 7 oktas. Note that a complete cloud cover of thin, high cloud can give sunny weather – despite the cloud cover being reported as 8 oktas.

When clouds are scattered across the sky it is often useful to imagine the sky to be split into four quarters and then to assess the amount of cloud in each quarter. Table 11 shows the weather

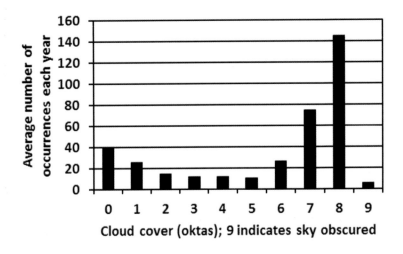

Fig. 20. The average annual cloud cover distribution in Maidenhead, Berkshire, based upon observations made at 0700 GMT each day during 1989–2013. The J-shaped curve is quite typical of cloud cover in temperate latitudes, with about two-thirds of the mornings having a cloud cover of 7 or 8 oktas.

register entries and how they relate to the state of the sky.

Occasionally it will be impossible to determine the cloud amount – usually due to fog or when observing in conditions of total darkness. In such cases an entry of '9' should be made in the register. Even on a moonless night it may be possible to estimate cloud amount by referring to the number and distribution of stars that are visible. Over the course of a year it is remarkable just how many cloudy mornings there are – even in southern England (see Fig. 20).

There is a small variation in cloud cover during the year, as can be seen in Fig. 21. The blue line in this figure shows a tendency towards lower average cloud amounts during the summer months and rather cloudier conditions in winter in Maidenhead at the 0700 GMT observation time. In addition, the cloudiest months have tended to occur in the winter half of the year and the least cloudy months in the summer (the red and green curves, respectively). The day length is longer in summer, leading to more sunshine at this time of the year, but even so, a larger percentage of the daylight hours will have the sun shining – because there tends to be slightly less cloud in summer and hence more opportunity for the sun to shine.

CLOUD TYPES

Clouds vary in shape, size, structure and texture. They also vary in their colour and luminance. Luminance is the measurable quantity that most closely corresponds to the perceived brightness, by the eye, of any cloud. The luminance of a cloud is determined by the amount of light reflected, transmitted and scattered by the particulate matter making up the cloud. This light comes from the sun, sky, the moon or from the surface of the earth – the latter especially when the cloud is viewed over fields of ice or snow.

Clouds formed of ice are usually more transparent than those containing water droplets. The former are thinner due to the relative sparseness of ice crystals compared to the water droplets – in the troposphere (the lowest layer of the atmosphere, in which 'weather' occurs) the higher and colder parts contain less moisture than the lower and warmer parts. Cloud colour depends mostly on the colour of the light that is incident upon the cloud. A layer of haze between the observing eye and the cloud can make distant clouds look red, orange or yellow, for example. Cloud colours can also be influenced by optical phenomena (see Chapter 7) and they also vary according to the height of the cloud and its position relative to the sun and observer – often

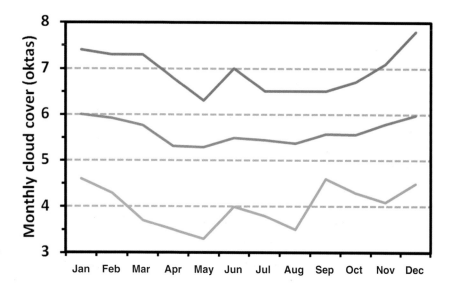

Fig. 21. The average monthly cloud cover distribution at 0700 GMT in Maidenhead, Berkshire, based upon observations made each day during 1989–2014. For each calendar month, the three curves show (from top to bottom) the greatest monthly cloud cover, the average cloud amount, and the lowest monthly cloud cover.

resulting in dark patches of cloud in an otherwise white/grey field of cloud.

For those keen to learn more about clouds there is a wealth of online resources that provide good descriptions. In addition, the Royal Meteorological Society publishes a useful cloud identification chart[15] while the Met Office has an online guide titled *Cloud Types for Observers*.[16] Richard Hamblyn's *The Cloud Book*[17] and Gavin Pretor-Pinney's *The Cloudspotter's Guide*[18] are two other excellent books on the subject. Observers with a keen interest in clouds may be interested in investigating the Cloud Appreciation Society,[19] an organization with a wealth of photographic material about clouds, who often arrange entertaining talks on the subject – from both scientific and artistic viewpoints.

Clouds come in a variety of 'genera', 'species' and 'varieties'. Here, we shall describe the ten main cloud types (see Table 12) or genera. Most clouds are also divided into sub-groups or species, dependent upon the peculiarities or shapes of the clouds. Further subdivisions are then possible due to special features in the appearance of clouds,

and in their degree of transparency. Many, if not most, of these subdivisions are difficult for the newcomer to weather observing to identify or remember; they will not, in general, be discussed further here.

The ten genera of cloud may be divided into three groups according to the height of their cloud base. These come under the categories of high-level cloud (comprising cirrus, cirrocumulus and cirrostratus), medium-level cloud (altocumulus, altostratus and nimbostratus) and low-level cloud (stratocumulus, stratus, cumulus and cumulonimbus).

CLOUD NAMES

The names of clouds are usually combinations of these prefixes or suffixes:

- Stratus/strato – flat/layered and smooth
- Cumulus/cumulo – heaped up, looking like a cauliflower at low and medium levels
- Cirrus/cirro – high-level/wispy
- Alto – medium level
- Nimbus/nimbo – rain-bearing cloud

Table 12   The cloud type (and two-letter commonly used meteorological abbreviation) and the reported cloud type code number that may be entered in the register of weather observations

Often more than one entry will be required to specify the clouds present at the observation time.

Level	Cloud type code entered in register	Cloud type (and two-letter abbreviation)	Typical cloud base (feet)* in the UK
High	0	Cirrus (Ci)	20,000ft or above
	1	Cirrocumulus (Cc)	
	2	Cirrostratus (Cs)	
Medium	3	Altocumulus (Ac)	6,500–20,000ft
	4	Altostratus (As)	
	5	Nimbostratus (Ns)	Surface to 10,000ft
Low	6	Stratocumulus (Sc)	Generally below 6,500ft
	7	Stratus (St)	
	8	Cumulus (Cu)	
	9	Cumulonimbus (Cb)	

*Although metric units are used almost everywhere else in meteorology, cloud heights are generally still quoted in feet, as this is preferred by the aviation industry.

We now describe these ten cloud types, beginning with the high, ice clouds and descending to those clouds found with their base closer to the ground.

CIRRUS

Cirrus (Figs 22–25) is the most common form of high-level clouds. They consist of detached clouds with white, delicate-looking filaments and are typically found at heights greater than 20,000ft. They are formed of ice crystals that originate from the freezing of supercooled water droplets. Cirrus clouds generally occur in fair weather and are aligned by upper-level winds at the height of the cloud, which are usually much stronger than those at the surface. They can range in structure from the 'finger-like' appearance of cirrus fallstreaks to the uniform texture of more extensive cirrus clouds associated with an approaching warm front.

Fig. 22. Cirrus in the form of hooks.
STEPHEN BURT/CLOUDBANK
IMAGES LTD

Fig. 23. Cirrus in the form of fine filaments seeming to spread out of a denser area of cloud.

Fig. 24. Fairly dense cirrus clouds – but still showing some signs of fine delicate structure.

Fig. 25. Dense cirrus (top) at sunset with some stratocumulus showing above the trees.

The fallstreaks form when snowflakes and ice crystals fall from cirrus clouds. The change in wind speed and direction with height, and the fall speed of these ice crystals, then determines the shapes and sizes that the fallstreaks attain. Note that these clouds are sufficiently high that such crystals will not reach the ground – in the absence of any clouds below the cirrus they will eventually evaporate if they fall far enough. Ice crystals fall much more slowly than raindrops, and so the fallstreaks tend to be stretched out horizontally as well as vertically. Cirrus fallstreaks may be almost straight, shaped like a comma or a hook, or seemingly all tangled together. Cirrus clouds can be dense enough to hide the sun or moon.

CONTRAILS (CONDENSATION TRAILS)

Contrails can be seen in the wake of aircraft when the surrounding air is sufficiently humid and cold; the moisture emitted by the engines can then cause localized saturation of the air to form ice clouds. However, if the surrounding air is not that moist, then the ice forming the contrails may be short-lived as turbulence causes the clouds to be mixed with the surrounding air and evaporate. If the air at the aircraft height is sufficiently moist the contrails may persist, being spread out by the upper level winds at the cloud height. Indeed, old trails may spread sufficiently to render them quite similar in appearance to other ice cloud formations seen in the sky.

Fig. 26. Condensation trails (contrails) formed in the wake of aircraft. These can be short-lived (upper) or persist for a few hours (lower).

CIRROCUMULUS

Cirrocumulus clouds are comprised of many small white clouds grouped together at high levels. When seen from the ground, these small clouds appear to be about the width of a finger held at arm's length. Composed almost entirely of ice crystals, the little cloudlets are regularly spaced, often in the form of small grains or ripples in the sky. They are relatively rare and often form from cirrus or cirrostratus.

Fig. 27. Fine cirrocumulus with a cloud base of around 18,000ft. The fine, cellular pattern (much smaller apparent size than that of altocumulus) typical of cirrocumulus is most evident about one-third down the image, while some rippling of the cirrocumulus can be seen towards the centre of the image.

Fig. 28. **A veil of cirrostratus covering the sky, through which the sun can just be seen. Also visible are some darker patches of altostratus that are lower in the sky. These clouds heralded the approach of a warm front.**

CIRROSTRATUS

Cirrostratus is usually seen in the form of a transparent veil of white fibrous ice crystal cloud. It often has a smooth appearance and is sometimes associated with halo phenomena when it appears between the sun and the observer. It can cover the entire sky, possibly heralding the approach of a warm front ahead of a depression, or may sometimes develop from spreading cirrus cloud. The sun may appear to broaden in width and have a whitish or milky appearance.

ALTOCUMULUS

Altocumulus is a cloud found at medium levels, typically 10,000ft above the ground. It can be white or grey, and consist of patches, sheet or layer cloud. It can also take the appearance of cloud turrets, in which case thundery conditions may develop later in the day over quite a wide area.

Over hills and mountains, a lens-shaped altocumulus cloud may develop – lenticular altocumulus. Such clouds are the result of wave-like motions in the atmosphere caused by the presence of the hills, which triggers an upward motion of air arriving over the hills. A series of lens-shaped clouds in a horizontal line may sometimes occur, visible for over 100km downstream of the hill. True lenticular clouds appear to be almost stationary, despite the movement of air through them.

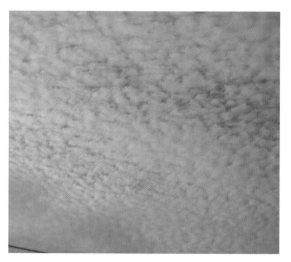

Fig. 29. **An extensive layer of altocumulus cloud in the form of patches.**

Fig. 30. **This sheet of altocumulus soon dissipated and the sun can be seen shining on the underside of the clouds.** EDWINA BRUGGE

Fig. 31. These scattered tufts of altocumulus (at about 9,000ft in altitude) resemble small ragged cumulus clouds. Sometimes these clouds may develop further into altocumulus castellanus, which may then grow both upwards and downwards into thundery cumulonimbus clouds. Both of these types of altocumulus are associated with the development of thundery conditions over a wide area.

Fig. 32. Tufted altocumulus castellanus.
STEPHEN BURT/CLOUDBANK IMAGES LTD

Fig. 33. The sun is visible here through a veil of altostratus that was covering the sky. Also visible are the remains of some poorly developed, rather ragged-looking, pannus-type cumulus. Within five minutes of this photograph being taken the altostratus had thickened sufficiently in front of the sun to hide it entirely.

ALTOSTRATUS AND NIMBOSTRATUS

Altostratus often appears as a greyish or bluish sheet of mid-level cloud, altitude around 10,000ft. The sun or moon can sometimes be seen through this altostratus, particularly if it is thin, but the cloud may then thicken sufficiently to hide even the sun.

Fig. 35. Thick altostratus. This had persisted for most of the day, which was sunless as a result. Records from nearby weather stations showed that the cloud base was about 10,000ft so the cloud was too high for stratus. Any features visible in the cloud would be seen to move only slowly across the sky if the cloud is altostratus; with lower stratus features would move quickly, and low stratus is more likely to be associated with fog or light precipitation.

Even further thickening (and lowering of the cloud base to below 7,000ft) may occur, with the result that some rain or snow falls – in which case the cloud is classified as nimbostratus. However, the amateur may find it difficult to distinguish between precipitating nimbostratus and precipitating ragged (bad weather) cumulus without any knowledge of the actual cloud base height. If the cloud base is high enough, the precipitation produced by this nimbostratus may evaporate before reaching the ground.

Since cirrostratus and altostratus sometimes form from each other it can be difficult to tell them apart when they are viewed from the ground. In general, altostratus does not cause halo phenomena and is thicker than cirrostratus. Being closer to the ground, altostratus appears to move more rapidly across the sky.

STRATOCUMULUS

Stratocumulus has a cloud base usually around 1,000–6,500ft above the ground and is, globally, the most common type of cloud. It can consist of layers or patches and may appear as a series of rounded rolls that are aligned parallel to each other. The stratocumulus layer can appear rather dark if the cloud layer is thick enough or if there are other cloud layers above it.

Stratocumulus can form from the spreading out of cumulus clouds, especially in conditions of high pressure. In such anticyclonic conditions there is often descending air aloft, which causes an inversion (a shallow layer over which the temperature actually increases with height), inhibiting further upwards development of the cumulus. The cloud takes on a flattened appearance and then begins to spread out. The conversion into rolls can be helped when sunset occurs and the tops of the cloud then radiate heat upwards.

Fig. 36. Stratocumulus formed by flattened cumulus. Such a change can happen in the evening when any small cumulus cease their development as the heating power of the sun declines, or when an inversion over the top of the cumulus suppresses further vertical growth.

Fig. 37. Stratocumulus aligned in the form of rolls. These formed under conditions of high pressure.

WHY DO SMALL CUMULUS CLOUDS SOMETIMES DEVELOP INTO LARGE ONES?

Anyone who watches the skies will see that on some days small cumulus clouds remain quite small and scattered, while on other days they will grow to majestic heights and maybe even lead to showery precipitation. The reason for the differences in cloud growth on different occasions is often due to the vertical temperature profile of the lowest part of the atmosphere.

The solid black line with black squares in Fig. 38 shows the temperature between the ground and about 10km up on a particular day. The dew point (see Chapter 12) of the surface air is 15°C – shown by the empty square. Suppose the sunshine warms up the ground a little, thereby enabling the air at the ground to rise. This air will rise and cool (following the dot-dash line) to about 850m before it becomes saturated and cloud forms; so the cloud base will be at 850m. As this air continues to ascend along the dot-dash line, it will find that it is warmer than the surrounding air (the dot-dash line is to the right of the solid black line) and so it will continue to rise – with the water vapour that it holds gradually being converted into cloud water and maybe raindrops. Thus small clouds would initially form and continue to grow upwards as the air ascends.

This ascent continues up to around 10km above the ground, at which height the rising air begins to be colder than the surrounding air – ascent will soon cease and the cloud tops would then appear to exist at about this height. The result would be a sky containing tall, majestic cumulus clouds.

In a different scenario, suppose that the air aloft had been allowed to sink by about 1km – this could easily happen in twenty-four hours under conditions of high pressure. This would create an air temperature profile shown by the red line with triangles. Now any air rising from the surface would (at around 850m) be colder than the surrounding air – the dot-dash line is to the left of the red line – and so the air would tend to sink back down towards the ground. Clouds would be very shallow or non-existent.

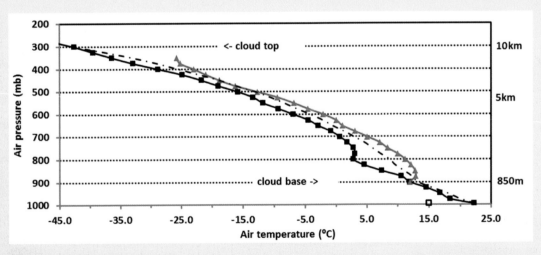

Fig. 38.   **Illustrating why deep cumulus clouds may, or may not, develop. Air temperature increases towards the right and pressure decreases upwards with increasing height.** *See text for a fuller explanation.*

Fig. 39. This rather featureless, low-level stratus cloud, having a cloud base of about 1,000ft above the ground, produced light drizzle about five minutes after the photograph was taken.

STRATUS

Stratus is a grey, sheet-like cloud seen in layers or patches. It usually has a uniform cloud base height but can be ragged in appearance, especially when associated with precipitation. It is a low cloud, often descending close to the ground. Each patch or layer shows no presence of different elements (rolls or cells) and as such stratus can be distinguished from stratocumulus. Low stratus can reduce the visibility, even without giving precipitation.

Fig. 40. Small (heaped) cumulus clouds with some wispy cirrus aloft. They are often called fair weather cumulus as they can develop in response to early morning heating of the ground on a sunny day, without showing any signs of further vertical development. Later, as the setting sun sinks towards the horizon, the clouds may evaporate into a clear sky.

Fig. 41. Cumulus clouds of small (in the foreground) and moderate (above the tree-line) vertical development.

Fig. 42 Cumulus fractus. STEPHEN BURT/CLOUDBANK IMAGES LTD

CUMULUS

Two forms of cumulus clouds will be familiar to any cloud-watcher. Over land, after a cloudless start to a morning, small cumulus clouds may develop as the sun heats up the land surface and this heat, in turn, produces thermals in the lower part of the atmosphere.

Sometimes such clouds, termed fair weather cumulus, will undergo little vertical development during the morning and, once the sun starts to sink lower in the sky, will evaporate as the heat source from the ground is switched off.

Fig. 43. These tall cumulonimbus clouds produced a thunderstorm within ten minutes of this photograph being taken. EDWINA BRUGGE

Fig. 44.   Cumulonimbus with cirrus anvil. STEPHEN BURT/CLOUDBANK IMAGES LTD

DETERMINING THE CLOUD BASE HEIGHT

Convection clouds, for example cumulus and cumulonimbus, often form as a result of sunshine heating the ground. In turn, the warmed ground heats the air just above it, causing it to rise.

As the air rises it expands and cools, but its moisture content remains unchanged. This cooling eventually leads to the air reaching saturation, at which height clouds will begin to form. When saturation occurs, the air temperature, wet bulb temperature and dew point will be identical.

If we know the near surface temperature and either the wet bulb temperature or dew point (see Chapter 12) then we can estimate the cloud base height, because (at least approximately) these decrease at pre-defined rates:

The temperature falls by 9.8 degrees C every kilometre, the wet bulb temperature falls by 5.5 degrees C per kilometre, and the dew point by about 1.8 degrees C per kilometre. The term 'lapse rate' is given by meteorologists to these decreases with height.

Suppose the air temperature is 22.0 degrees C and the dew point 6.0 degrees C; the difference between the two is 16.0 degrees C. The difference between the lapse rates of temperature and dew point is 9.8 − 1.8, or 8.0 degrees C per kilometre.

Thus the air will need to rise 2km before the 16.0 degrees C difference is eroded at a rate of 8.0 degrees C per kilometre. At this height the temperature equals the dew point − meaning that the cloud base at saturation point is 2km.

The cloud base heights of other types of cloud are more difficult to determine, unless there are nearby markers (for example hills of a known height in the distance or aeroplanes that are known to fly at certain heights in the locality) − or maybe tall buildings whose tops may become obscured by low stratus. At airfields, where an accurate knowledge of cloud heights are essential, vertically pointing lidars measure cloud height from reflected laser pulses. Lidar is an acronym for 'light detection and ranging' and operates in a similar manner to radar.

On occasions, if the heating is sufficiently strong or if the upper levels of the atmosphere are conducive to the development of taller clouds, then deep cumulus cloud will develop − looking very much like tall cauliflowers in the sky. Neither of these two clouds tends to produce rainfall.

Rain-producing cumulus clouds do occur − they are termed 'cumulus fractus' and look grey and rather ragged, sometimes appearing in a cloudy sky beneath a grey layer of altostratus or nimbostratus cloud. 'Fractus' simply means 'broken'; the clouds appear to be torn.

Another form of 'cumulus fractus' is shown in Fig. 42. In this case there is often a lot of blue sky to be seen and although the clouds appear ragged and scattered, there is no hint of rain; they appear with less vertical extent than the fair weather cumulus shown in Fig. 40.

CUMULONIMBUS

Deep cumulus clouds may continue to grow vertically, eventually extending from close to the ground to heights of 25,000ft or more. While the lower portions of the cloud may appear similar to cumulus clouds, an anvil-shaped upper part formed of ice cloud may be visible. However, such tops are often invisible to the observer due to the large coverage of clouds across the sky.

Cumulonimbus clouds (Figs 43–44) produce showers and thunderstorms, sometimes accompanied by squalls or hail. It is the large updraughts

Fig. 45. Cumulonimbus cloud with cirrus spissatus (the fibrous cloud at the upper levels of the picture).

within such clouds that are able to support the development of large hail.

Figure 45 is a well-developed cumulonimbus cloud, part of a cluster of similar clouds that stretched around most of the horizon at the time. The tops of such clouds sometimes have hairy or frayed-looking edges and may also be seen in the form of an anvil-shaped cirrus cloud above the cumulonimbus cloud.

Virga

Virga consist of precipitation that does not reach the ground. They are usually seen under cumulus or cumulonimbus (see Fig. 46) and may herald or follow showery conditions in which the precipitation does reach the ground.

CLOUDS AND DEPRESSIONS

Depressions are areas of low pressure, seen on weather charts, that can bring spells of cloud, rain and wind across the British Isles at any time of the year. In a depression the air is rising, forming an area of low pressure at the surface. The rising air cools, condenses and thereby forms cloud. In the northern hemisphere winds near the ground blow in an anticlockwise direction around a depression.

A depression forms when warm and cold air masses meet. Different air masses are associated with distinctive weather types and the boundary between such air masses is indicated by the presence of fronts.

Fig. 46. Virga seen falling from cumulonimbus clouds – it remained dry beneath these clouds at the time this photograph was taken.

On a surface weather chart (*see* Chapter 9), a warm front marks the boundary between cold air and warm air, and shows where warm air is replacing cold air at the surface. A cold front means cold air is advancing and pushing underneath warmer air; cold air is replacing warm air at the surface.

The changing pattern of clouds and weather across a depression can be an indicator of the weather to come (Table 13) although no two depressions are exactly alike. Depressions move at different speeds and may be developing or decaying as they pass overhead. The central pressure (the lowest pressure reading at the centre of the depression) will vary and this will affect the wind speeds; the lower the pressure, the stronger the winds will tend to be. In addition the closer to the centre of the depression the observer is, the more rapidly these differing conditions will be experienced.

ENTRIES IN THE OBSERVATION REGISTER

It is recommended that two columns be used in the register of weather observations. The first can contain the total cloud amount using one of the digits from 0 to 9. At the end of the month the observer can determine the average cloud cover at the observation by simply averaging all the entries in this column – but omit any entries of '9' in the calculation. If observations are done at different times of the day then determine the average at each time if possible.

The second column can contain one or more entries of the digits from 0 to 9 (or the two-letter cloud abbreviations shown in Table 12) describing those clouds present in the sky at the observation time.

Table 13   Cloud and weather conditions associated with a textbook depression

No two depressions are exactly the same. Note that in the northern hemisphere these conditions will be experienced if the observer is on the southern side of the centre of the depression. A wind that backs is one that changes direction in an anticlockwise direction, while one that veers changes in the opposite direction.

		Pressure	Temperature	Cloud	Wind	Precipitation
Direction of increasing time ↓	Ahead of the warm front	Starts to fall steadily	Cool, may start to slowly rise	Cloud base lowers and cloud thickens: cirrus then cirrostratus then altostratus	Speed increases and the wind backs	Rain within 500km or so of the front
	At the warm front	Falling	Rising	Low cloud base: altostratus and nimbostratus	Veers and sometimes becomes blustry	Rain, sometimes heavy
	Warm sector	Steadies	Quite mild	Cloud may thin out or break – but may also remain overcast close to the depression centre	Speed remains steady, backing slightly	Rain turning to drizzle; it may stop if the cloud clears a little
	At the cold front	Begins to rise	A fall, sometimes quite a sudden drop	Thickening deep cloud: cumulus and cumulonimbus	Speed suddenly increases – maybe to gale force; veers sharply	Heavy rain, sometimes with hail and thunder
	To the rear of the cold front	Rising	Cool	Scattered cloud fields: cumulus and cumulonimbus	Squally winds in showers	Showers or rain; maybe wintry depending upon the temperature

6. STATE OF THE GROUND

The state of the ground at the weather station can be used as a proxy for the average weather conditions over a period of time. For example, it is often interesting to look back to identify spells with large number of days when the soil was dry or 'cracked', or when there was snow cover.

The state of the ground can be measured using one or more of four things, namely:

1. A ruler, used to measure the depth of snow – or maybe floodwater!
2. A bare soil plot
3. A grassed area within the weather station
4. An open ground around the weather station that is representative of the local area

The bare soil plot should be, ideally, a square-shaped area of bare soil measuring about 2m along each side (see Fig. 47 for an example), level with the surrounding ground and kept free of weeds. It should be typical of the soil conditions of the weather station and, apart from occasional weeding, should be disturbed as little as possible from day to day. The reason for having such a large bare soil plot is to prevent the surrounding (grass-covered) ground from affecting the centre of the bare plot – by the horizontal movement of moisture as the bare soil begins to dry out, for example.

Both the bare soil plot and the grassed area should be located away from buildings, trees and hedges – or indeed, away from anything that might affect their response to atmospheric conditions.

The open area representative of the ground around the weather station should be fairly flat ground, visible from the station and at a very similar altitude. Any part of the area with surface peculiarities (for example roads, streams, ground under trees, rocky outcrops) should be excluded when the state of the ground is being assessed.

Observations then consist of an assessment of the state of the ground and a measurement of the snow depth. It is suggested that such an observation be made at the same time each day – as near as possible to 0900 GMT.

Fig. 47. **An example of a bare soil plot used to determine the state of the ground at the University of Reading, showing that the plot is also used to contain the station's soil thermometers for measuring both sub-surface temperatures (foreground) and the surface minimum temperature (background). Each thermometer is about 30cm in length.**

STATE OF THE GROUND DESCRIPTION

The World Meteorological Organization uses two sets of numerical codes to describe the state of the ground.[20] one applicable when there is snow or measurable ice cover and one for use in conditions without such cover. Being numerical codes, it is recommended that the observer uses them in the weather register as they will aid the creation of subsequent analyses.

State of ground code, entered in register	Description of ground

Table 14   The numerical code used to describe the state of the ground in the absence of lying snow or measurable ice cover

Note that the definitions of the codes 0–2 and 4 apply to the bare soil plot, while numbers 3 and 5–9 to the open representative area. In all instances, the highest code value applicable is reported. In the UK codes, 0–2 and 9 are the most common unless snow is lying. Taken from the *Manual on Codes*.[20]

State of ground code, entered in register	Description of ground
0	Surface of ground dry (without cracks and no appreciable amount of dust or loose sand)
1	Surface of ground moist
2	Surface of ground wet (standing water in small or large pools on surface)
3	Flooded
4	Surface of ground frozen
5	Glaze on ground
6	Loose, dry dust or sand not covering the ground completely
7	Thin cover of loose, dry dust or sand covering the ground completely
8	Moderate or thick cover of loose dry dust or sand covering the ground completely
9	Extremely dry with cracks
×	Measurement not made; possibly because the ground is snow-covered

STATE OF GROUND WHEN SNOW IS NOT LYING

When there is no lying snow or measurable ice cover, the codes shown in Table 14 apply. To distinguish between codes '0' and '1', I often take a pinch of surface soil between my thumb and forefinger, and if it tends to stick to my skin then I use code '1'.

STATE OF GROUND WHEN ICE OR SNOW IS LYING

When there is lying snow or measurable ice cover the observation codes shown in Table 15 apply.

TOP: **Fig. 48.   Wet lying snow surrounding the raingauge at the University of Reading. The ground conditions this morning in February 2013 were noted as being 'compact/wet snow (with or without ice) covering at least half the ground' with a snow depth of 1cm. The wetness of the snow can be judged from the footprints made by the weather observer.**

BELOW: **Fig. 49.   An example of melting wet snow lying in Maidenhead, January 2014. From a distance the impression is that more than half the ground is covered in snow, but closer inspection (coupled with many grassy areas within sight that were free of snow) indicates that this is not so. A state of ground (with snow/ice cover) code value of 1 was noted in the weather register. The snow depth was only 2–3mm at its deepest.**

Table 15 The numerical code used to describe the state of the ground in the presence of lying snow or measurable ice cover

Code 0 might include an extensive cover of hailstones following a heavy hail shower or thunderstorm; if the cover of ice/snow is predominantly due to ice/hail, then even a 50 per cent cover does not count as a day with lying snow. The lying snow column indicates an occasion when the snow cover is at least 50 per cent. Taken from the *Manual on Codes.*[20]

State of ground code, entered in register	Description of ground	Day with lying snow indicator
0	Ground predominantly covered by ice	0
1	Compact/wet snow (with or without ice) covering less than half the ground	0
2	Compact/wet snow (with or without ice) covering at least half the ground	1
3	Even layer of compact or wet snow covering the ground completely	1
4	Uneven layer of compact or wet snow covering the ground completely	1
5	Loose, dry snow covering less than half the ground	0
6	Loose, dry snow covering at least half the ground (not completely)	1
7	Even layer of loose, dry snow covering the ground completely	1
8	Uneven layer or loose, dry snow covering the ground completely	1
9	Snow covering the ground completely; deep drifts	1
x	Measurement not made – possibly because the ground is not snow-covered	x

Table 16 The average variation of the state of the ground over the year in Maidenhead during 1998–2013 at 0700 GMT

The numbers indicate the number of mornings each month with particular ground conditions.

Month	Dry	Moist	Wet	Frozen	Extremely dry with cracks	Ice or snow lying
January	0.1	22.9	1.3	4.1	0	2.6
February	0	21.8	0.6	3.8	0	2.1
March	3.9	24.7	0.5	1.3	0	0.6
April	6.3	19.1	0.6	0	3.9	0.1
May	7.8	19.6	0.1	0	3.5	0
June	9.7	16.2	0.3	0	3.8	0
July	7.9	17.9	0.4	0	4.8	0
August	8.4	20.5	0.1	0	2.0	0
September	8.2	19.0	0.2	0	2.6	0
October	2.6	27.1	0.8	0	0.5	0
November	0	27.7	1.3	0.9	0	0.1
December	0	23.7	1.3	4.1	0	1.9

DEW AND HOAR FROST

The presence of dew or hoar frost may be described using the Beaufort weather letters (*see* Chapter 3) of 'w' and 'x' respectively in the current weather column of the register – the letters also being used to indicate whether the dew or frost is heavy ('W' or 'X') or light ('w$_o$' or 'x$_o$').

ANNUAL VARIATION OF GROUND STATE CONDITIONS

Table 16 shows the variation of the state of the ground over the period 1998–2013 in Maidenhead. Unsurprisingly, there is little dry ground in winter while extremely dry (or cracked) ground conditions occur from late spring to early autumn. The winter season sees the highest frequency of wet conditions, along with the majority of days with ice or snow on the ground. In wetter parts of the UK the incidence of a dry ground state will be reduced and that of a wet state is likely to be greater.

STATE OF THE GRASS

Observers who are unable to create a suitable patch of bare soil may wish to follow the suggestion of Meaden[21] and record the state of grass instead, by assessing the deposition of water on the grass. The observation should be made as close as possible to 0900 GMT (Table 17). Indeed, both grass and ground state measurements can be kept as a means of identifying the incidence of dew and hoar frost, for example.

LYING SNOW

It is interesting to keep a record of any snow observed to lie on the ground, along with the snow depth. A column in the weather register should be set aside to enter either a '0' or '1' to denote the absence/presence of lying snow; again, this observation should be the one made at the morning observation time to enable a comparison to be made with other sites.

For climatological purposes in the UK a day with lying snow is defined as one when lying snow at the morning observation time (ideally 0900 GMT) covers at least half of the ground. When assessing the snow cover, the observer should note the

Table 17 Meaden's numerical code to describe the state of the grass	
If more than one code applies, the observer should record the highest appropriate value.	
State of grass code entered in register	**Description of grass**
0	Dry; no deposits
1	Wet from dew only
2	Wet from fog (some dew may be present too)
3	Wet from falling rain or drizzle
4	Wet from the melting of the frozen deposits listed as codes 5–9, or from sleet
5	Ice resulting from the freezing of 1–3 or the refreezing of 4, and also including silver frost (frozen, supercooled dew)
6	Ice or glaze resulting from the direct fall of freezing rain or drizzle upon cold surfaces, or ice from hail or ice pellets
7	Hoar frost – the direct deposition of crystals from the air
8	Rime – the direct deposition of crystals from supercooled freezing fog; falling ice prisms or falling ice crystals
9	Snow
x	Measurement not made

conditions over ground that is representative of the station. The 'half of the ground' qualifier is used as it is difficult to assess when the snow cover clears completely – sometimes a very small amount of patchy snow may persist in shaded areas long after the bulk of any lying snow has disappeared. The presence of 'lying snow' conditions is shown in the third column in Table 15.

If the weather station is within sight of high ground, for example nearby mountains or hills, then it may also be possible to observe the snow cover at different altitudes. This cover may vary if the station is in a valley and one side of the valley faces south and the other north – as the presence of sunshine each day will have differing effects on the two valley sides. However, such observations should not replace the standard one applicable to conditions at the weather station.

SNOW DEPTH MEASUREMENT

When snow lies on the ground, a measurement of the total depth can be made with a ruler in an area that is free from drifting and any scouring of the snow by the wind. Take a note of about ten measurements, discard the highest and lowest, and then take the average. The depth should be noted to the nearest whole centimetre.

ENTRIES IN THE OBSERVATION REGISTER

In summary, the following columns relating to the state of surface may appear in the register of observations:

A. State of ground when snow is not lying: entry in the range 0–9 or 'x'

WHAT IS THE DIFFERENCE BETWEEN 10MM OF RAIN AND 10CM OF SNOW?

The answer, in terms of the water content, is 'practically nothing'. If you melt 10 cm of lying snow then you will get a depth of about 10mm of water, depending upon how wet, or light and fluffy, the snow is.

But in terms of its impact, the answer is 'a quite a lot', so it is important to be able to forecast well in advance which will fall in winter. Unfortunately, because of the wintertime temperatures experienced in the UK (often hovering around +4 °C to –4°C), forecasting of snow can be quite difficult here. In colder climates, where mid-winter temperatures are always, say, –5°C or below, then any precipitation will be very unlikely to fall as rain.

Several factors influence whether any forecast precipitation will fall as rain or snow. Altitude is one obvious factor – snow is more likely to fall over higher ground as the air here is cooler, while the warming effect of cities and towns can raise the temperature a degree or so, turning snow into sleet or rain.

Another factor is the air mass type – sometimes in the UK moist and mild air from a direction between south and west meets colder, drier air that arrived from the north or east. Snow may then fall where these two different air masses meet – but the boundary line between snow falling in the colder air and rain in the warmer air can be difficult to forecast. Look for the positions of any fronts in the weather forecast – this might be where the forecasting of snow will be difficult if the temperature is around freezing point.

Observers may be familiar with the cooling sometimes felt after thunderstorms – this can be caused by rain evaporating into surrounding, drier air as it falls. The same can also happen when rain falls near a rain–snow boundary, leading to a possibility of the rain then turning to sleet or snow.

So, when rain is forecast and snow arrives instead, causing the usual transport problems – don't rush to blame the forecaster!

Fig. 50. The snow depth in Maidenhead this morning, 19 January 2013, was 12cm. Some of the snow was still lying in patches a week later. EDWINA BRUGGE

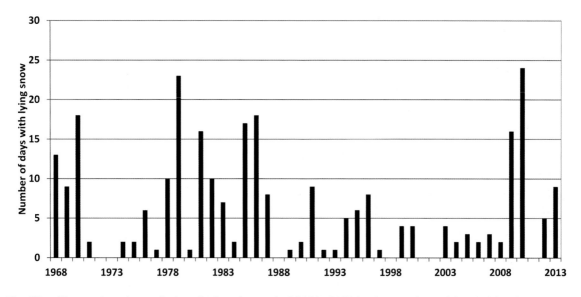

Fig. 51. Illustrating the variation during the period 1968–2013 in the number of days with lying snow at 0900 GMT at the University of Reading's climatological station. Such a variation from year to year is quite typical of that found at many low-level sites in England, with some years having no lying snow.

B. State of ground when snow or ice is lying: entry in the range 0–9 or 'x'
C. Snow lying indicator – at least 50 per cent cover – entry of 0 or 1
D. State of the grass: entry in the range 0–9 or 'x'
E. Snow depth in whole centimetres
F. A note of any dew or hoar frost can be added to a separate current weather column in the register if record (D) is not kept

Note that an entry for both (A) and (B) should be made if the ground state is recorded; one of them will be recorded as 'x'.

Assuming one entry each day is made at the morning observation time, at the end of the month the total of the entries in column C can be determined, as can the total of those in column E. The latter gives an interesting indication of the accumulation and persistence of the snow cover while the former can be compared against any available statistics relating to 'days with lying snow' (for example with data given by Burt and Brugge).[22] Both of these can vary widely from year to year as shown in Figs 51 and 52 – and they also give differing impressions of the winter's snow.

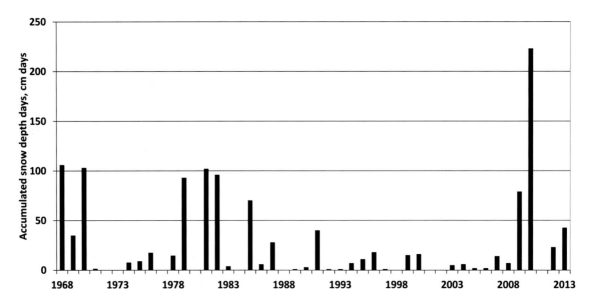

Fig. 52. **The variation of snow depth-day totals observed at the University of Reading during 1968–2013. The depth-day totals are obtained by adding the snow depth of each of the daily observations made at 0900 GMT. The large totals in 2009 and 2010 were due mainly to spells of persistent snow cover during the period 18–26 December 2009 and 6–15 December 2010. A depth of 27cm occurred on 6 January 2010, this being the deepest observed in Reading since January 1963.**

7. OPTICAL PHENOMENA

Light in our atmosphere can produce many optical phenomena. Combined with raindrops, light produces the familiar rainbow while ice crystals (in the higher, colder parts of the atmosphere) create halos that can take the form of simple circles or surprisingly complex geometric patterns. Smaller water droplets found in mist, fog or clouds can help create other effects; for example coronae, fogbows and glories – and then there are mirages, rays and the blue of the sky itself.

This chapter introduces some of these intriguing phenomena. Some can be seen quite frequently; others are rare and, as such, are worth photographing if you do see them. Good sketches and measurements are also worth making at the time, should you wish to seek an explanation as to their formation.

Such is the variety of optical phenomena which may be seen that this chapter can touch only upon a few of them. For those interested, a website that merits further investigation is Les Cowley's Atmospheric Optics.[23] This has many examples of the optical phenomena described in this chapter, along with explanations of many other phenomena. Les Cowley is always happy to receive additional images for the Optics Picture of the Day pages on the website, or to receive questions about optical phenomena.

Many optical phenomena appear close to the direction of the sun or moon but others can be seen in the opposite part of the sky. When conditions near the earth's surface are very cold, they can also form around man-made light sources. The requirement for ice crystals to be present to create many of these phenomena means that the colder, polar regions are often the best locations for seeing a wide variety of optical effects. However, halos in cirrus or cirrostratus clouds (for example) occur frequently in all seasons worldwide – including in the tropics.

PHOTOMETEORS

A photometeor is a luminous phenomenon produced by the reflection, refraction, diffraction or interference of light from the sun or the moon, according to *The International Cloud Atlas*.[24] Such phenomena, of which the rainbow is the one that springs most readily to mind, can be seen in:

- More or less clear air (for example mirage, shimmer, twilight colours and scintillation of stars)
- Inside or on the outside of clouds (for example halos and related phenomena, coronae, glories and iridescence)
- On or inside certain hydrometeors or lithometeors (rainbows, fogbows and crepuscular rays)

RAINBOWS

To see a rainbow (Fig. 53) we need sunshine and falling rain occurring simultaneously. A rainbow is

---

THE COLOURS OF THE RAINBOW

It was the English scientist Isaac Newton who, following his experiments with prisms, divided the spectrum into seven named colours – red, orange, yellow, green, blue, indigo and violet. His use of seven colours came from a belief, following that of the ancient Greeks, that there was a connection between the colours, the musical notes, the known objects in the solar system and the seven days of the week. The human eye is relatively insensitive to indigo and many cannot distinguish indigo from blue and violet.

Fig. 53.   A rainbow seen beneath cumulonimbus cloud immediately following the passage of a rain shower. Rain was still falling from the cloud towards the direction of the rainbow. EDWINA BRUGGE

caused by both reflection and refraction of light in raindrops, resulting in a spectrum of light appearing in the sky. Rainbows caused by sunlight always appear in the section of sky directly opposite the sun.

In a primary rainbow (the rainbow seen when only one arc is visible), the arc is red on the outermost part and violet on the inner side. This rainbow is caused by light being refracted (or bent) when entering a droplet of water, then being reflected inside on the back of the droplet and refracted a second time when leaving the droplet. The primary bow is 42 degrees in radius with its centre opposite the sun.

In a double rainbow, a second arc is seen outside the primary arc, and has the order of the colours reversed. This second rainbow is caused by light reflecting twice inside water droplets. The colouring of a rainbow depends upon the size of the water droplets, with large drops (about 1mm or more in diameter) giving brilliantly coloured bows that show all the colours.

As the sun rises in the sky the top of the bow gets lower. When the sun is 42 degrees or more above the horizon, the whole of the bow is below the horizon and not usually visible. Consequently, early morning and late afternoon are the best times to see rainbows. Inside the rainbow the sky will appear bright because raindrops also direct some sunlight towards here.

22 OR 42 DEGREES?

In this chapter, the use of a measurement in degrees indicates the viewing angle. To visualize the size of something that is 20 degrees in size, stretch out the fingers of your hand at arm's length. The tips of the thumb and little finger then span an angle of roughly 20 degrees.

The bearing between the four main points of the compass is 90 degrees – so about four-and-a-half hand-widths will stretch from (say) north through to east. Similarly, the angle between the horizon and a point directly above the observer is 90 degrees.

Since a rainbow has a radius of 42 degrees, this implies a diameter of 84 degrees; so if you mentally extend the rainbow below the horizon and into a complete circle, then the diameter of this circle would be about four times the distance between the tips of your thumb and little finger, when your arm is outstretched; at its widest, it would stretch almost a quarter of the way around the horizon.

Rainbows can be seen in moonlight – but the lunar rainbow (or 'moonbow') will appear white as the human eye cannot easily distinguish colours in faint light.

HALO PHENOMENA

A halo is produced by refraction or reflection of light through airborne ice crystals, the most common being the 22-degree radius halo around the moon or sun. Other examples of halo phenomena are sun pillars and 22-degree parhelia (also known as mock suns or sundogs).

Often it is the shape and orientation of the ice crystals in the air that are responsible for the type of halo observed. Light is reflected and refracted by the ice crystals and may be split up into the visible colours. In this way the ice crystals behave rather like prisms and mirrors, refracting and reflecting sunlight between their faces, thereby sending shafts of light in particular directions.

THE 22-DEGREE HALO

If faint, then the ring of the 22-degree halo is likely to be seen as white, while a separation of the colours is more obvious in a strong/bright halo. According to the Met Office,[25] in England the 22-degree halo is quite common and can be seen, typically, on one day in three. As such they do not always foretell bad weather, contrary to the saying 'if there is a halo round the sun or moon, then we can all expect rain quite soon'.

Les Cowley[23] notes 'the (22-degree) halo is large… (and) the halo is always the same diameter regardless of its position in the sky. Sometimes only parts of the complete circle are visible.'

Halos can sometimes be quite faint, particularly in a bright sky. Sometimes a halo may be visible if you are wearing sunglasses but almost invisible to the uncovered eye.

Fig. 54. Monochrome image of a 22-degree lunar halo seen through high cirrostratus cloud on a February evening. The white speck in the '8 o'clock' position is Jupiter. The halo can be seen as a faint ring that is slightly further away from the moon than Jupiter in the image.

Fig. 55.   A halo caused by diamond dust taking the appearance of a cross through the sun at the centre of the circular halo. To the left and right sides of the halo are the two mock suns, while an upper tangent arc touches the 22-degree halo directly above the sun. The horizontal halo through the sun is part of the parhelic circle – a colourless circle caused by reflection of sunlight off hexagonal ice crystals. MARTIN GROSSHÖG

MOCK SUN (OR 22-DEGREE PARHELION)

Sometimes called a sundog, these are seen at the same elevation in the sky as, and to the left and right of, the sun – although sometimes only one mock sun is visible. Mock suns are caused by the refraction of sunlight by plate-shaped ice crystals whose large hexagonal faces are horizontal – one such type being the so-called diamond dust crystals, as is the case in Fig. 55. Mock suns can appear coloured (with red closest to the sun) or white.

UPPER AND LOWER TANGENT ARCS

Tangent arcs (as seen in Fig. 55) form when cirrus clouds have well developed column-like ice crystals drifting with their long axes aligned almost horizontally. They are seen above the sun, and below it when the sun is high enough in the sky – in both cases the arcs touch the 22-degree halo, hence their name.

If any colours can be discerned then red will be closest to the sun and bluish colours further away from the sun – this is because red light is refracted less strongly than other colours in white light.

According to Cowley,[23] tangent arc rays pass through the same crystal faces as those of the 22-degree halo and mock suns. The difference in the appearance of the three halo types is due to the orientation of their crystals.

Fig. 56. The white spot is the anthelion, seen in a northwest direction shortly after 0900 GMT in April 2015 in North Yorkshire. This is quite a bright sighting of this phenomenon.
BILL WADE

ANTHELION

The anthelion (Fig. 56) is found at a point (directly opposite the sun) where the parhelic circle is crossed by the Wegener arc (see Fig. 58) and other halos. It is these arcs that may serve to 'brighten' the phenomenon. You will need to be standing with your back to the sun to see it.

MAKING YOUR OWN HALO SIMULATIONS

Les Cowley's website[23] contains a wide selection of optical phenomena, both in the form of photographs and computer simulations. The simulations were created using software called Halosim, a simulation program written by Les Cowley and Michael Schroeder. It is freely available for download from the website. Figures 57 and 58 were created using the software and show some of the types of halos that you might observe. The software creates simulations by accurately tracing up to several million light rays through mathematical models of ice crystals.

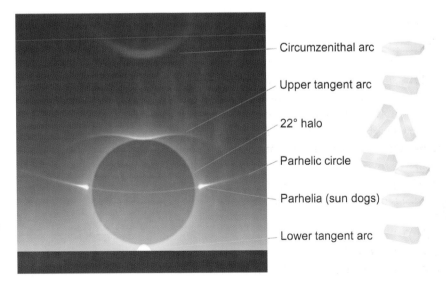

Fig. 57. Some common halos simulated using the Halosim software, illustrating the types and orientation of ice crystal that lead to the creation of these halos. LES COWLEY

— Circumzenithal arc

— Upper tangent arc

— 22° halo

— Parhelic circle

— Parhelia (sun dogs)

— Lower tangent arc

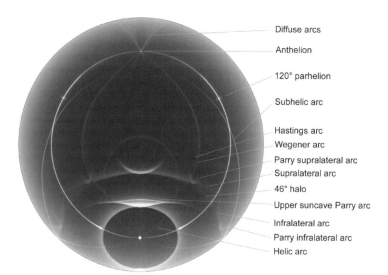

Diffuse arcs
Anthelion
120° parhelion
Subhelic arc
Hastings arc
Wegener arc
Parry supralateral arc
Supralateral arc
46° halo
Upper suncave Parry arc
Infralateral arc
Parry infralateral arc
Helic arc

Fig. 58. Some less commonly observed halos simulated using the Halosim software. The zenith is at the centre of the figure, the horizon is along the edge. LES COWLEY

DIFFRACTION EFFECTS

In atmospheric optics, diffraction is the change in direction of light waves as they pass around an obstacle in their path. The amount of bending depends upon the wavelength of the light, so different colours undergo different amounts of bending and coloured phenomena can then be produced.

CORONA

A corona is a sequence of (usually) no more than three coloured rings of small diameter around the

Fig. 59. Corona and iridescence seen in autumnal altocumulus cloud over Thame, Oxfordshire. NICK WHITE

sun or moon. In each ring the colours range from violet or blue on the inside to red on the outside – the reverse of the colouring of haloes. Coronae are caused by the diffraction of light by water droplets – the clearer the colours, the more uniform are the water droplets forming the rings.

Coronal rings are smaller than those in the 22-degree halo and are most often seen around the moon – being termed the 'lunar corona'.

BISHOP'S RING

This is a dull, reddish-brown ring seen around the sun on a clear day. It was first seen after the eruption of the Krakatoa volcano in 1883 and is caused by the diffraction of light by fine dust or ash high in the atmosphere. The interior of a Bishop's ring is usually much brighter than the surroundings.

THE GLORY

A glory is an optical phenomenon that resembles the halo around the head of a saint – it is seen around the head of the observer on the ground. It consists of one or more concentric, successively dimmer rings, each going from red on the outside to blue on the inside.

Glories are always directly opposite the sun (at the so-called antisolar point) and are best seen from

Fig. 60. Iridescence seen in the eastern sky in California shortly after dawn.
ROBIN ANDREA CHANIN

hills when there is low cloud or mist beneath you and the sun breaks through to shine on it. Then look away from the sun, and downwards. They can also be seen from aircraft and are formed as light is scattered backwards by individual water droplets.

Shadows converge on the antisolar point and so glories are nearly always accompanied by your shadow or that of the aircraft you are in.

IRIDESCENCE

Iridescence, or irisation (both terms derived from Iris, the Greek personification of the rainbow), are the names given to the appearance of colours on clouds due to the diffraction of sunlight by very small cloud particles. These colours can appear banded and almost parallel to a cloud edge or randomly in patches (Fig. 60). Pink or green colours often predominate. When parts of the clouds are thin and have similar size droplets, diffraction can make them shine with colours like a corona. In fact, the colours are essentially coronal fragments.

As the cloud evolves, so the colours can come and go. Iridescence is usually seen on the edges of cirrus and cirrocumulus ice clouds, and sometimes on altocumulus or stratocumulus clouds. Iridescence is seen mostly when part of a cloud is forming, as all the droplets then have a similar history and, consequently, may have a similar size.

A much rarer form of iridescence is that of nacreous, or mother-of-pearl, clouds. They can glow very brightly and are far higher than ordinary tropospheric clouds – at a height of 15–30km above the ground. These clouds are caused by wave-like motion of air, due to the presence of mountain ranges; they can be seen just before dawn or just after sunset.

THE BLUE SKY

Visible sunlight is a mixture of all colours from red to violet (the colours of a rainbow) in the visible part of the electromagnetic radiation spectrum. Each colour has a different wavelength, with reddish colours having a longer wavelength than bluish ones.

When sunlight hits the atmosphere, some is scattered (or deflected) in different directions by air molecules and any dust or aerosol that may be present. The intensity with which radiation is

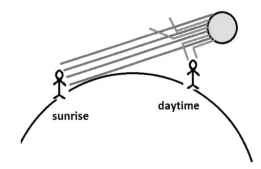

Fig. 61. **Schematic diagram illustrating the scattering of blue light by the atmosphere and the reason that the sky appears blue most of the time, but reddish at sunrise and sunset.**

scattered by small particles, such as air molecules (the so-called 'Rayleigh scattering'), depends upon the wavelength of the radiation being scattered. Short-wavelength blue light is scattered much more strongly than long-wavelength red.

In the absence of large particles (for example dust and haze), wavelengths corresponding to blue light are scattered in all directions, while 'red light' undergoes rather less scattering. So the skies seem

blue and even distant hills may seem to be tinted 'blue'.

Nearer to the horizon, the light we see passes closer to the ground, through low levels in the atmosphere where there is a lot more water vapour and dust. These larger particles in the atmosphere will scatter light of all wavelengths equally. This means that all sunlight colours are scattered, resulting in a paler blue. The same is true when the air is hazy – which is why skies in a northerly (relatively clean) wind in the UK seem bright blue and those in a southerly wind (often bringing dirtier, more polluted, air) often seem whiter.

As the sun begins to rise or set, its light has to pass through a greater thickness of atmosphere to reach your eye. More of the blue light is scattered out of the sun's light path leaving the reds and yellows – hence the red sunsets and sunrises we experience.

If violet light is a shorter wavelength than blue light, why is the sky blue and not violet? Sunlight actually contains little violet light and our eyes are more sensitive to blue than violet – so we tend to see the sky as being blue.

Fig. 62. **A red sunset as seen over northeast Canada on a long-haul flight. The reflection in the foreground is off the airplane wing.**

RED SKY AT NIGHT ...

Everyone is familiar with the saying, 'Red sky at night, shepherd's delight; red sky at morning, shepherd's warning'. A red sky appears when dust and small particles are trapped in the atmosphere by descending air under conditions of high pressure. This scatters blue light, leaving red light to give any clouds a reddish appearance.

In the UK the prevailing winds blow from a westerly direction. A red sky at sunset indicates high pressure is towards the west, meaning that the next day is likely to be dry and settled as these conditions move towards the observer. A reddish tinge to the clouds in the morning implies that high pressure conditions are to be found to the east; the good weather has probably passed, meaning deterioration in the weather is possible. However, the saying is not correct on all occasions.

ONCE IN A BLUE MOON

In addition to the scattering of short wavelength blue light by air molecules and the general scattering

---

THE BENDING OF LIGHT

Light is part of the electromagnetic radiation spectrum. To describe the differences between different types of light like visible and ultraviolet (or, indeed, between the different colours of visible light), scientists talk about the length of the light's waves, or wavelength. The different colours of light, for example, differ in the length of their waves. As a result, the different components of light can be bent differently, revealing the colours and a wealth of optical phenomena to us – as this bending effectively splits up the light before we see it.

Reflection

Reflection of light occurs when it hits a mirror-like surface. In the case of 'total reflection', all the light incident on the surface 'bounces back'.

In meteorology the term albedo is used to describe the reflecting power of a surface and is important, for example, in determining the heat balance of the earth-atmosphere system, either locally or over the globe a whole. The albedo can be dependent upon the wavelength of the radiation (or light) being reflected.

Refraction

When light passes through the boundary between two uniform but different substances (each of a different density, such as air and a water drop), it is bent at a slight angle, a process known as refraction. Different wavelengths are bent to different degrees, and thus refraction plays a part in the appearance of coloured phenomena like rainbows and haloes in the atmosphere.

In the atmosphere this density change may also occur in a non-uniform medium – an example is that caused by large temperature changes in a small depth of air, resulting in relatively large density changes over a small distance. Such variations near the earth's surface also cause refraction and produce mirages.

Diffraction

When light waves pass through a very small gap between obstacles (for example dust particles or air molecules), they carry on between the obstacles, but also spread out from the gap into the area beyond the obstacles. This bending is the process of diffraction. Again, the different wavelengths are bent differently, thereby creating phenomena such as atmospheric coronae and iridescent cloud.

of all wavelengths by larger dust and haze particles, there is an intermediate size of particles (of around one millionth of a metre, or one micron, in diameter) that if present with sufficiently uniform size causes red light to be scattered out of the sun's beam. This action causes the sun or moon to appear blue, hence the familiar saying. Examples of sources of dust capable of this activity include some exceptional duststorms, volcanic eruptions and forest fires.

In 1883 it was reported that people saw blue moons almost every night after the Indonesian volcano Krakatoa exploded. Blue moons were also seen after the volcanic eruptions of Mount St Helens (1980), El Chichón (1983) and Mount Pinatubo (1991).

Another, non-meteorological, phenomenon that has been given the name 'blue moon' is the occasional (once every 2.7 years approximately) occurrence of two full moons in a calendar month. Full moons are separated by twenty-nine days, while most months are thirty or thirty-one days long, so it is possible to fit two full moons in a single month. Neither full moon appears blue in colour.

Both phenomena occur quite rarely, hence the meaning of this popular saying.

OTHER PHENOMENA

MIRAGES

A mirage (displaced image) is an optical phenomenon caused by the bending of light due to refraction close to the surface of the earth. They occur when there are large temperature changes in the vertical, close to the ground, that lead to variations in the air density. Depending upon the variation of temperature with height, the image will be seen either above or below the actual object.

If the ground surface is flat and strongly heated (for example tarmac or desert sand) then the visual illusion may be one of a wet surface and a so-called inferior mirage is created. Here the image appears below the object and seems to be reflected in the wet surface. The wet surface is actually an image of

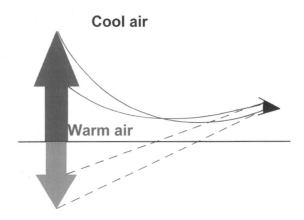

Fig. 63. Schematic diagram of an inferior mirage. The mirage is said to be inferior as the image appears below the object causing it. Light from the green object follows the solid line paths to the eye, being refracted (bent) as it passes through increasingly warmer air. The human brain thinks the light has arrived at the eye in straight lines and that it has followed the dashed lines from the brown image.

the sky. If the surface of the ground is much cooler than the air a little way above it, the light will be bent such that the image appears above the object causing it.

In both cases the mirage is seen because the eye expects the light to have arrived in a straight line from the object towards the eye.

SHIMMER

Weather conditions are never uniform over a large area and small variations close to the ground, particularly in temperature, may cause apparent movement of distant objects – or shimmering. The scintillation (or twinkling) of stars is a similar effect and is more noticeable for stars that are low in the sky, rather than overhead – as these stars are viewed through a greater thickness of near-ground atmosphere. Both effects are due to refraction effects similar to those that give rise to mirages. The atmosphere can also bend light travelling through it due to movement caused by turbulence – this will cause small, localized distortions in the temperature of the atmosphere.

Fig. 64. Crepuscular rays at Cape Cod, after a heavy cloud layer opened up and allowed these brilliant early morning rays through. SUSAN PETRY

CREPUSCULAR RAYS

Crepuscular rays comprise three similar classes of optical phenomena. They commonly appear as sunbeams emerging through gaps in low cloud and appearing to diverge from the position of the sun hidden behind the clouds. In fact this divergence is purely due to perspective, as the sunlight arrives as parallel beams of light. The light is made visible by particles of water or dust in the atmosphere (see Fig. 64).

Sometimes the rays may appear as upward beams, appearing from the cloud tops when the sun is hidden by cumulus or cumulonimbus clouds. The separating darker streaks are due to shadowing caused by parts of the cloud.

The third type consists of reddish-coloured beams that spread out upwards at twilight from the sun when it is below the horizon. The light is scattered to the viewer by dust in the atmosphere and the separation of the light into apparent beams is due to hills below the horizon that cast shadows upwards.

AURORA

The aurora is a light display in the night sky, predominantly seen in the high latitude (Arctic and Antarctic) regions close to the two magnetic poles, but sometimes seen much further away from the poles. In the British Isles it is occasionally seen in southern England, but most often in Scotland or northern England. In northern latitudes these displays are usually called aurora borealis or northern lights; in southern latitudes the terms aurora australis and southern lights are used.

Aurorae are caused by collisions between electrically charged particles, released from the sun, that enter the earth's atmosphere and collide with gases such as oxygen and nitrogen. The most common aurora colour is green, while red, blue or purple colours can also be seen. The aurora can take many forms, these often being described as streamers, arcs, rippling curtains or rays.

Space Weather Forecasting

A recent development in meteorology has been that of 'Space weather forecasting' – that is the forecasting of environmental conditions in near-earth space. Magnetic fields, radiation, particles and other matter ejected from the sun can interact with the earth's upper atmosphere and magnetic field to produce a variety of effects, including the aurora.

Some of these effects can have major impacts on our society, which is heavily dependent upon electrical technology – including interruptions to radio communications and GPS, disruption of power grids and damage to spacecraft.

There are two useful websites, www.swpc. noaa.gov[26] and www.metoffice.gov.uk/publicsector/emergencies/space-weather.[27] that provide further information, and also space weather forecasts that include pointers towards expected auroral activity.

WHAT INFORMATION SHOULD I RECORD?

Clearly, a good photograph or two might be worthwhile, especially if the phenomenon is one you would like to investigate further. Take a note of the date, time and direction towards which the phenomenon was seen, along with the altitude (use hand spans, converted to degrees, above the horizon). In addition, a good sketch illustrating the size of the phenomenon (in degrees) might be useful.

8. THUNDER, DUST, ASH AND HAIL

Rumbles of thunder, along with falls of hail, dust or ash, are quite rare events in the UK; consequently, their occurrences are worth noting. Thunderstorms are relatively easy to observe, while falls of dust or ash can be quite difficult to discern. Hail may melt before you see it while dust or ash may be mistaken for dirt. However, the observing of each of these phenomena can be aided with the help of some simple measuring devices.

THUNDER AND LIGHTNING

LIGHTNING DETECTORS

Lightning arises from thunderstorms – the first signs of which are usually tall cumulonimbus clouds – and is the visual flash that results from an electrical discharge in the air. Thunder is a sharp or rumbling sound that accompanies lightning and is caused by the sudden heating and expansion of the air by the lightning.

Usually, both thunder and lightning will be heard and seen by an observer when a thunderstorm is nearby, but sometimes only thunder (or, indeed, only lightning) will be observed.

Lightning travels at the speed of light and will reach the observer almost instantaneously – a lightning flash that occurs 10km from the observer will take much less than a millisecond to reach the observer. Thunder travels at the speed of sound, and so takes about thirty seconds to reach the observer from a distance of 10km. Thus, as a rule of thumb, the distance of the observer from the lightning source may be estimated by noting the interval between seeing the flash and hearing the thunder, counting 1km for every three seconds of time interval.

However, any thunderstorm has a finite size, typically several kilometres in width, and there can be discharges from different parts of the storm –

Fig. 65 A SkyScan lightning detector. The instrument can be powered by batteries or off the mains supply. Each time the instrument detects a lightning stroke, it emits an audible warning tone and lights the range indicator column for the appropriate distance.

meaning that the perceived distance to the storm will vary slightly with each flash. Monitoring the flash–thunder intervals over a period of time will, however, enable an observer to track the general movement of the thunderstorm.

Figure 65 shows a portable lightning detector that can be purchased by amateur observers from SkyScan.[28] According to the user manual, 'The SkyScan P5-3 lightning detects the presence of lightning/thunderstorm activity occurring within 40 miles of your location. It uses patented technology to determine the distance to the detected stroke. The distances are indicated in four ranges: 0–3 miles (0–5km), 3–8 miles (5–13km), 8–20 miles (13–32km) and 20–40 miles (32–64km).'

Such an instrument is a useful tool for the observer keen on monitoring local thunderstorms; thunderstorms can move quite quickly and if they remain at a distance from the observer it is easy to miss any lightning flashes and for the sound of thunder to be drowned out by the noises of modern life. However, it is unclear how the distance determination is achieved by the instrument, and visual observation of any storms, once the instrument has alerted the observer to their presence, may be equally reliable.

THUNDERSTORM CLIMATOLOGY IN THE UNITED KINGDOM

The incidence of thunderstorms varies widely across the British Isles, being generally highest in East Anglia and southeast England. In these regions thunder occurs on fifteen to twenty days each year on average; the incidence decreases to the north and west with Cornwall, Wales and northwest England having typically only six or seven days with thunder each year. In much of central Scotland the incidence drops to about three days each year, although on the islands of north and west Scotland four or five days of thunder may be expected each year. Similarly, across the Republic of Ireland there are four to seven days with thunder on average each year.

Places in the north and west of the British Isles have a relative high frequency of thunder during the winter months associated with showers that form over the Atlantic Ocean and blow inland. These showers are then damped down as they move over the relatively cool land and many occurrences of thunder may consist of just one or two rumbles.

Thunderstorms (especially severe ones) in southeast England are more typically spring and summer thunderstorms that are triggered by the presence

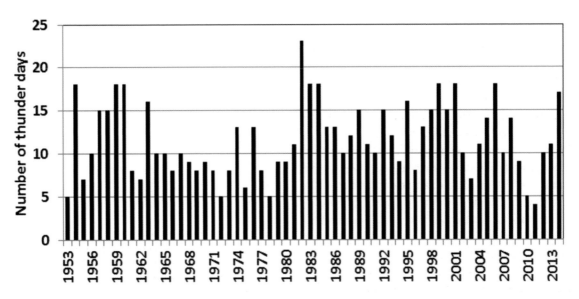

Fig. 66.   **The annual incidence of thunder days in Maidenhead (Berkshire) during 1953–2014.**

of warm or hot air that has arrived from the near continent. These storms can be long-lived and followed across large areas using satellite imagery (see www.sat24.com[29] for example), as warm surface air leads to more vigorous ascent and deeper convection clouds.

The incidence of thunder varies a lot from year to year. For example, in Maidenhead (Berkshire) thunder was heard on an average of thirteen days each year between 1981 and 2010. However, as can be seen in Fig. 66, the annual incidence has varied between four days and twenty-three days over a period of sixty-two years. Similar variations occur in all locations across the British Isles.

LIGHTNING

As well as being of interest from a climatological viewpoint, being able to detect the location of thunderstorms can be important insofar as public safety is concerned. In addition to the obvious dangers posed by lightning, thunderstorms can also be associated with other types of severe weather such as intense rainfall, hail and occasionally tornadoes.

When lightning strikes it sends out pulses of radio waves. Most people will have experienced interference on their radios in a thunderstorm for this very reason. These radio waves can be used to detect lighting strikes. In the UK, the Met Office uses the ATDnet system,[30] which detects these radio wave pulses at a frequency known as VLF (Very Low Frequency) – a much lower frequency than normal radio waves. ATDnet stands for Arrival Time Difference network.

These pulses are known as sferics and are capable of travelling a long way through the atmosphere as they are reflected between the surface of the earth and the ionosphere. The ionosphere is a layer of the earth's atmosphere, above about 60km from the Earth's surface, where ionization by solar and cosmic radiation occurs.

While an individual sensor in the network can detect a sferic, in order to determine the exact location of a thunderstorm (the source of the sferic) a network of sensors is used. When a sferic occurs, the sensors in the network will pick it up at slightly different times and, through a technique known as multilateration, these readings can be used to determine the exact location of the thunderstorm. Multilateration is a form of triangulation, but using time differences rather than angles.

Nowadays there are several sites on the internet that carry real-time plots of sferics, providing a warning of possible thunderstorms that may be heading your way (see, for example, www.blitzortung.org).[31]

ST ELMO'S FIRE

This phenomenon is formed by electrical point discharges that occur when the environmental electric field is high, typically at the tips of sharp conductors

Fig. 67. A lightning strike seen over Brockenhurst at night, from one of a series of storms that affected southern and eastern England on 3–4 July 2015. EDWINA BRUGGE

that concentrate the electric field. The masts of old sailing ships contained just such points and the phenomenon was frequently seen around these masts, often towards the end of thunderstorms. The name was given to the phenomenon by Mediterranean sailors who regarded it as a visitation of their patron saint, Elmo (Erasmus), portraying the imminent end of the thunderstorm and hence being a portent of good weather.

SPRITES

High above cumulonimbus clouds during thunderstorms, very brief bursts of red and blue light, known as 'sprites' and 'blue jets' can sometimes be seen. They are often only visible to those in flight above a storm, and happen so quickly that they are easily missed. Some images of these phenomena can be found at the website of the University of Alaska Geophysical Institute.[32]

Current understanding is that sprites are related to lightning, in which a neutrally charged cloud discharges some of the electricity to ground. Negative charge is normally carried from the cloud to the ground, but occasionally the removal of positive charge leaves the top of the cloud negatively charged. It is then that the sprite occurs – an electrical discharge upwards from the thunderstorm into the ionosphere.

HAILPAD

Hail is a phenomenon that weather observers should aim to record – but how do you record something that can fall for a just a few minutes (and then melt) without maintaining a continual watch on the skies or the ground?

The answer is a hailpad, which may consist of aluminium foil wrapped around a layer of polystyrene. As a cheaper alternative, observer Donald Perkins[33] suggests carefully removing the centre of the lid of a plastic container (maybe 12–15cm in diameter), leaving the rim in one piece. Then place a few stones in the bottom of the container (to prevent it blowing away) and stretch a sheet of aluminium foil over the top, before reattaching the lid to keep the foil in place. The foil should be as smooth and tight as possible. Donald places his hailpad inside a larger plastic plant pot so that it sits 5cm below the rim of the pot and away from the edges. This helps to stop birds from fouling or pecking the aluminium foil layer (*see* Fig. 68).

Fig. 68. A hailpad as constructed by Donald Perkins. The small impressions made in this observation are the result of small ice pellets. DONALD PERKINS

The pad needs to be examined at least daily – preferably late in the day as a day with hail is counted when hail falls between 0000 GMT and 2400 GMT (see Chapter 3). To calibrate the hailpad you will need to examine the device after the first few falls of hail. Donald finds that snow pellets, even large ones, make only a light impression due to their small mass. He finds that ice pellets make a definite mark related to their size while hailstones can penetrate the aluminium foil layer.

An alternative method of hailpad creation, courtesy of the Community Collaborative Rain, Hail and Snow Network, can be found on their website.[34] They use 30cm square pieces of polystyrene covered in foil.

DUSTPAD

Even less common in the UK than thunder and hail are falls of Saharan dust. Sand from the western and central areas of the Sahara Desert can, given suitable conditions, be drawn up into the atmosphere and transported great distances – towards the Caribbean for example, and occasionally to the British Isles. Stephen Burt, a meteorologist at the University of Reading who has studied dust falls over the UK, has identified two main routes for this to happen.[35] One of these is the 'Spanish plume track', or meridional route, in which the dust-laden air is fed northwards to the British Isles from North Africa via Spain. The other route takes a westward path from the Sahara

---

WHAT IS THE SPANISH PLUME?

The Spanish plume (a term often heard on British television during hot or polluted days in spring and summer) happens when warm air from the Iberian Plateau (where temperatures in some areas sometimes exceed 40°C close to the ground) is pushed northwards to reach Britain. The warm air is fed towards the British Isles ahead of an atmospheric cold front that moves towards the east over the Bay of Biscay and western parts of the British Isles. At the surface the air pressure is low over the Atlantic and high over Europe; it is this that leads to a flow of air from the south into the British Isles.

Strong heating of air near the surface over the Iberian Plateau causes it to be warmed at low levels, resulting in ascent and convergence of the air near the ground – thereby pulling in more air at the surface towards the plateau. This leads to a formation of a heat-induced area of low pressure over the Iberian peninsula – marked by the presence of the letter 'L' on pressure maps. The approaching cold front then plays an important role in the further development of the Spanish plume.

Air behind the front is colder and so as it approaches the warm air over western Europe the existing temperature gradients in the west–east direction become enhanced. The warm air from the south then rises rapidly over the cooler air from the west, causing very active convective clouds, such as deep cumulus and cumulonimbus, to develop. The resulting thunderstorms can be quite violent, especially over England.

Severe weather from such events can include:

- Heavy showers and thunderstorms with hail; prolonged thundery conditions can occur with thunderstorms being identifiable for several hours on satellite imagery
- Sudden falls in temperature during these showers and thunderstorms, accompanied by strong gusts of wind
- Possibly even tornadoes, or falls of Saharan dust if this has been fed across the Iberian peninsula before the hot air leaves there

towards the Canary Islands, before the dust is swept into a northeastward-moving trajectory towards the British Isles. Saharan dust was, until relatively recently, often described as 'blood rain' or 'coloured rain', having a colour from brownish red to more of a yellowy colour – the colour being dependent upon the exact source region of the dust in North Africa.

Saharan dust is most easily seen on car wind-screens and conservatory roofs. However, a simple detector can be made using a smooth piece of wood, say 20cm by 20cm in size, painted with white gloss paint so that the collecting surface is horizontal. Daily visits to the detector will be needed – often it will collect deposits of pollen, soot or other particulate matter from the atmosphere, which will need to be wiped off.

Another form of do-it-yourself dustpad can be constructed using an upturned frisbee toy – so that it appears rather like a bowl when viewed from above. The frisbee can either be held in place horizontally and its contents inspected (and then emptied) after each fall – or a small hole can be made in the base of the Frisbee with the contents being drained into a collecting bottle fixed underneath it.

Recent observations, in particular by members of the Climatological Observers Link (see Chapter 1), have suggested that in some years there may be as many as ten Saharan dust events over the British Isles, with dust falling on as many as twenty individual days as a result.

POLLEN AND FALLS OF LOCAL SAND OR SOIL

Occasionally, what looks like a fall of Saharan dust on your car may actually be a deposit of pollen or locally produced sand or soil. In agricultural communities during spring, when the ground is being ploughed, or close to sandy beaches after a spell of dry weather, it is possible that soil or sand may be whipped up into the air by surface winds and deposited a short distance downwind.

In the UK, pollen can be found in the air from January to September, and during this time light and dusty-looking pollen grains can be deposited. Pollen is likely to be seen on a parked car if it has been standing near pollen-producing trees or bushes for a few hours.

VOLCANIC DUST

Very occasionally, your dustpad may be able to pick up volcanic ash, as was the case in April and May 2010 when the eruptions of Eyjafjallajökull in Iceland caused tremendous disruption to air travel across western and northern Europe. In particular, following the first phase of the eruption, during 14–20 April, ash covered large areas of northern Europe; about twenty countries closed their airspace to commercial jet traffic, affecting about 10 million travellers.

Ash fall was observed in places across the British Isles from this eruption, and also following the Grímsvötn volcanic eruption of May 2011. Potential ash samples were collected from across the UK[36] and sent to the British Geological Survey for analysis.

In the event of another eruption the British Geological Survey webpage[37] shows how you can help in the collection of volcanic ash for analysis, while there is also an app[38] that enables people to take photographs, enter quantitative observations and take samples.

ENTRIES IN THE OBSERVATION REGISTER

It is useful to keep a separate column in the weather register for each of the following phenomena (see also Chapter 3) observed during the period 0000 GMT to 2400 GMT:

A. Hail/ice pellets: enter '0' if there are no falls of ice pellets or hail; '4' if ice pellets but not hail are observed; '5' if hail 5–9mm in diameter falls; '6' if hail 10–19mm in diameter falls; or '7' if hail 20mm or more in diameter falls.
B. Thunder: enter '0' if no thunder heard, '1' if thunder is heard.

In addition, daily notes can be made of occasions when falls of dust or ash are observed – along with photographs of the deposits if at all possible.

9. ATMOSPHERIC PRESSURE

It used to be true that the most common meteorological observing instrument likely to be found in many homes was the aneroid barometer (*see* Fig. 69) used to measure the air pressure. Often located in the hallway, the daily ritual probably included a brief 'tap on the glass' front of the instrument (thereby releasing any sluggishness due to friction of the inner workings) before obtaining the current pressure reading, and then a resetting of the pointer to today's value – this resetting allowed the observer to determine whether pressure had risen or fallen compared to the previous reading. In

fact the daily tapping may also provide an indication as to whether the barometer is rising or falling at the observation time.

Modern barometers can be very accurate; air pressure can be measured indoors and, if the measurements are combined with those from other locations, can give meteorologists a very good idea as to current weather conditions in general.

The atmospheric pressure at any point on the earth's surface is the force per unit area exerted by the column of air lying above that point. Thus the air pressure decreases with increasing height above the ground. It is often the pressure tendency (that is whether the pressure is steady, rising or falling) that gives (when measurements from just one instrument are available) a reasonable indication of the approaching weather for the next few hours ahead.

Fig. 69. An aneroid barometer. The dark needle shows the current air pressure while the gold one shows the reading when the instrument was last 'reset'. The dial around the edge ranges from about 940mb to about 1,060mb, or about 28.7in to about 31.3in (of mercury). The aneroid barometer contains a closed sealed capsule with flexible sides – this is the silver circular object behind the glass and just visible under the word 'Change'. Any change in pressure alters the thickness of the capsule and these changes are magnified by a series of levers, causing the black pointer to move around the dial.

Falling air pressure may indicate the approach of an area of low pressure, which often brings cloud and precipitation. Rising air pressure may mean that an area of high pressure is approaching, bringing fair weather. However, the barometer does not, in general, foretell future weather precisely and the words stormy, rain, change, fair and dry that appear of most aneroid barometers are rather misleading. Indeed, many modern entry-level automatic weather station (AWS) consoles come equipped with a 'weather forecast' display that can be equally misleading at times.

A BRIEF HISTORY

It was Evangelista Torricelli[39] who invented the barometer in 1644. He filled a glass tube (of about 1 metre in length) with mercury, inverted it and placed it in a bowl of mercury. The column of mercury in the tube fell to give a column about 760mm above the surface of the mercury in the bowl, and left a vacuum at the top of the tube. Torricelli realized that the weight of the mercury pushing down in the tube on to the mercury in the bowl was exactly the same as the weight of the air pushing down on the mercury exposed in the remainder of the bowl.

Now, 760mm is equivalent to about 30in, and it was these measurements of the height of the mercury column that were used initially to describe the air pressure measurement – as shown on the outer rim in Fig. 69. In 1914 the millibar unit (abbre-

---

MEAN SEA LEVEL PRESSURE ON EARTH

While most household barometers in the British Isles will only rarely venture outside the range 950–1045mb, much larger variations have been observed worldwide, according to the World Meteorological Organization[42] – and even within the British Isles itself (*see* Table 18).

Table 18   Sea level pressure extremes in the UK, Republic of Ireland and worldwide

The data are extracted from various sources.[42, 43, 44] Insufficient data exist concerning the pressure extremes inside tornadoes, although values inside severe tornadoes are quite likely to be lower than those stated here.

Characteristic	Reading	Date and location
Highest sea level air pressure at a station below 750m altitude	1083.8mb	31 December 1968, Agata, Russia
Highest sea level air pressure at a station above 750m altitude	1089.1mb	30 December 2004, Tosontsengel, Mongolia
Lowest sea level air pressure (excluding tornadoes)	870mb	12 December 1979, Eye of Typhoon Tip (16°44'N, 137°46'E)
Highest UK sea level pressure	1053.6mb	31 January 1902, Aberdeen
Lowest UK sea level pressure	925.4mb	26 January 1884, Ochtertyre, Perthshire
Highest Republic of Ireland sea level pressure	1051.9mb	28 January 1905, Valentia, Kerry
Lowest Republic of Ireland sea level pressure	931.2mb	28 November 1838, Limerick

Further information on low and high pressure extremes in the British Isles can be found in two of Stephen Burt's articles in *Weather*.[45, 46]

SOME PRESSURE TERMINOLOGY

From time to time certain phrases are mentioned in weather forecasts that refer to features on pressure charts.

Isobars

These are contours on a pressure chart joining places having the same air pressure at a given height – often at mean sea level.

High

Pressure is said to vary from high (or large) values to low (or small values) on a pressure chart. Often, the word 'high' is used to denote the centre of an area of high pressure. Then, 'high' is used in a relative sense, meaning that the pressure at surrounding locations in all directions away from the centre is lower. Even though pressure at sea level will typically vary between about 990mb and 1030mb in many months at any location in the British Isles, the centre of an area of high pressure might be marked on a chart if the actual pressure reads, say, just 1010mb – provided that this is the highest pressure in a localized region at that time.

In an area of high pressure the air tends to be descending, which inhibits the formation of cloud. The light winds and clear skies can then lead to overnight fog or frost. But high pressure weather can also be cloudy – light winds may be insufficient to create enough turbulence to disperse any existing cloud.

Low

'Low' is used in the opposite sense to the word 'high' and can denote an area of low pressure. In the UK pressure may fall to 970mb (or lower) in such weather systems in the winter.

Depression

A depression is an area of low pressure – literally meaning a depression or lowering of the pressure at a certain height (often at sea level).

Cyclone

Meteorologists also use the word 'cyclone'. The direction of the surface circulation in a cyclone (anticlockwise in the northern hemisphere and clockwise in the southern hemisphere) is opposite to that in an anticyclone. Since a cyclonic circulation and relative low atmospheric pressure usually coexist, it is common practice for the terms 'cyclone' and 'low' to be used interchangeably.

Anticyclone

An anticyclone is the opposite of a cyclone in terms of relative direction of the movement of the winds. Because anticyclonic-type motion and relatively high atmospheric pressure usually coexist, the terms 'anticyclone' and 'high' tend to be used interchangeably. The surface wind in an anticyclone is in a clockwise direction in the northern hemisphere but is anticlockwise in the southern hemisphere.

Ridge

Often called 'a ridge of high pressure', this is the name given to an elongated area of relatively high atmospheric pressure leading off from an anticyclone centre.

Trough

A trough (or 'pressure trough' in this case) is an elongated area of relatively low atmospheric pressure. A trough may also be marked on a pressure map as a thin black line running across the isobars. Such trough lines sometimes mark a line of localized area of wet weather (usually providing a burst of rain and maybe a temporary increase in wind speed or a change in temperature).

Col

A col is the point of intersection of a pressure trough and a ridge in the pressure pattern of a weather map. It is the point of relatively lowest pressure between two highs and also the point of relatively highest pressure between two lows. It can be compared to a saddle point on a topographical map, between two hills and two valleys.

Hurricane, Typhoon, Tropical Cyclone, Cyclone

These are areas of low pressure covering several thousands of square kilometres in the tropics or sub-tropics. A tropical cyclone is the general term for a cyclone that originates over the tropical oceans. Initially classified as a tropical depression, this will become known as a tropical storm once the mean wind speed reaches 39mph; further intensification to a mean speed of 74mph results in a classification of hurricane, typhoon or cyclone – depending upon the location on earth.

At maturity, the tropical cyclone is one of the most intense storms of the world; winds exceeding 150mph are sometimes measured in such weather systems. After formation, tropical cyclones usually move to the west and generally slightly towards the pole. They may then migrate into the mid-latitude westerlies and move back towards the east as a low pressure system.

viated to 'mb' in this chapter) was adopted (shown on the inner ring of number in Fig. 69) and in the international SI system of units[40, 41] this is equivalent to the hectopascal (hPa). The latter is derived from the pascal, which is the SI unit of pressure (or force per unit area). To convert, 30in of mercury is equivalent to 1015.9mb, while 10mb equates to 0.259in of mercury.

Numerous measurements of air pressure are used on surface weather charts to help find surface depressions, high pressure systems, frontal boundaries and other features.

However, since pressure decreases with increasing height, it is important that any surface pressure measurements are 'reduced' down to mean sea level (MSL) to give MSL pressure. It is these MSL pressure readings that you will find plotted on most surface weather charts. Climb a mountain from sea level to a height of 1km and you will find that the air pressure will fall by about 110 millibars. Consequently atmospheric pressure varies more rapidly with height than with horizontal distance.

INSTRUMENTS

SITING AND CHECKING YOUR BAROMETER

Although barometers can be sited indoors, they are sensitive to changes in temperature. As a result, any instrument should be kept in a place free from the effects of direct sunlight, central heating – or indeed, any sudden cooling. Unfortunately, with simple aneroid barometers any correction to MSL pressure is a one-off calibration and will not be able to account for large or sudden temperature changes.

Dial-type aneroid barometers do have a tendency to drift with time, meaning that daily readings may become consistently higher (or lower) than the true value at each reading. This drift can be corrected by comparing your own reading with those from official stations when the air pressure is high – and consequently varies little over large distances.[47]

ANEROID BAROMETERS

Instruments such as the one shown in Fig. 69 need to be set to show the MSL pressure and will then give the pressure (after 'tapping') to the nearest millibar. However, nowadays, better precision is usually obtained even with entry-level AWS pressure sensors.

BAROGRAPHS – SMALL PATTERN AND OPEN-SCALE TYPES

A barograph is the recording form of the aneroid barometer. Fluctuations in air pressure cause the distance between the edges of the two faces of the capsule pile (see Fig. 70) to vary slightly; this change is amplified using levers and is then transmitted to a chart via a pen arm. Typically, changes in pressure over one week are recorded on a sheet of paper wrapped around a drum that is rotated either by clockwork or batteries. Since a continuous record of the pressure is kept, barographs can be used to identify even quite small pressure changes that may occur during thunderstorms or the passage of fronts (see Fig. 71).

Care must be taken to ensure that the timescale of each record is known accurately – a time mark should be put on the chart (ideally each day and certainly close to the start and end of the weekly record when the chart is changed) by opening the lid and depressing the pen about 1–2mm to create a vertical mark on the chart. Make a note of the time when this is done, and then annotate the chart with the time when it is removed.

Small-pattern barographs are the ones usually purchased by amateur observers. The larger, open-scale

Fig. 70.   **A seven-day small-pattern barograph. The partially evacuated capsules can be seen as a column of silvery discs. The chart is secured to a clockwork-drive drum that revolves once every seven days, producing a continuous record of the air pressure. The range of pressure on the chart is 950–1,050mb, the chart being 7.5cm tall.**

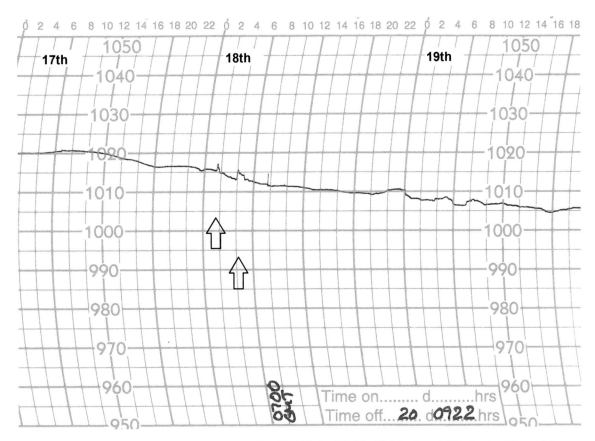

Fig. 71. This barograph trace (barogram) for 17–19 July 2014 in Maidenhead, illustrates the sudden sharp fluctuations (marked by the arrows) associated with thunderstorms early on the 18th. Such jumps in pressure often mark the boundary between the air flowing out from a thunderstorm (cooled by the evaporation of rain close to the ground) and the surrounding air.

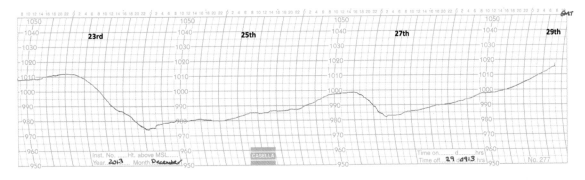

Fig. 72. The Maidenhead barogram for the week of 22–29 December 2013. Note the sharp fall of pressure on the 23rd (about 38mb in 24 hours) associated with a depression that led to stormy conditions on the 23rd and 24th across the British Isles. The lowest pressure reading, as a result of the depression, over land in the British Isles was 936mb at Stornoway on the 24th – the lowest UK pressure recorded since 1886.

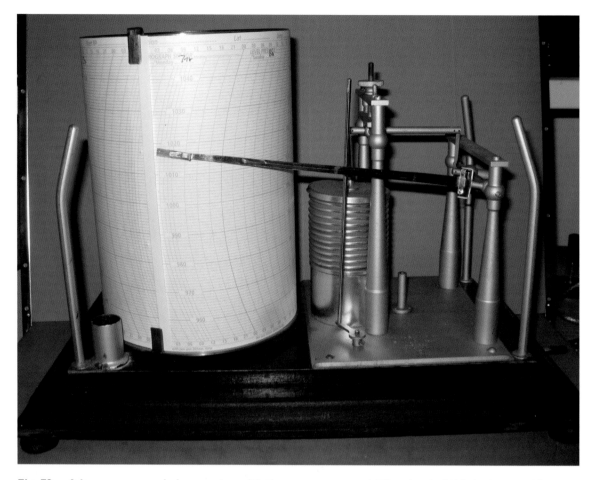

Fig. 73. A large, open-scale barometer with the cover removed. The chart of this instrument is about 17cm tall.

model used to be the type more commonly seen at official observing sites. The smaller version can be used to measure the air pressure to about the nearest 0.5mb; the open-scale barometer (being taller) can be used, with practice, to determine the pressure (and also pressure changes) to the nearest 0.1mb.

Barographs are quite expensive, but they last a lifetime and make an interesting centre point even in a household without any weather observer. Like dial-type aneroid barometers, barographs need frequent checking (maybe once a month) to prevent any drift from occurring in their measurements – when pressure is high, check the MSL pressure at your nearest official station,[47] and adjust the barograph accordingly.

MERCURY BAROMETER

The mercury barometer is rarely used these days in the UK, as the Met Office has been removing them for many years. There are two types, the Fortin and the Kew-pattern. The latter was the standard barometer used in the UK for meteorological observations for many years.

Figure 74 shows the Kew-pattern barometer used at the University of Reading for daily observations of pressure. A vernier scale (Fig. 75) is adjusted and a 'station level pressure' reading is then obtained to the nearest 0.1mb. This is then adjusted to mean sea level, based on the temperature of the barometer and the outside air temperature.

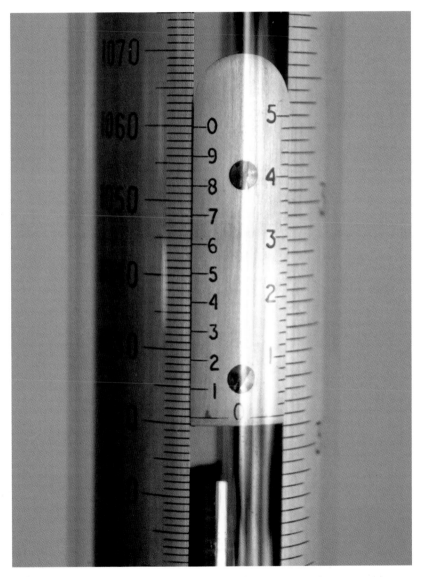

Fig. 74. The Kew-pattern mercury barometer of the Department of Meteorology at the University of Reading. The instrument is about 85cm tall.

Fig. 75. The vernier scale of a mercury barometer. The central part of the scale (with the two screws) is lowered until its lower edge lies just above the level of the mercury column, and the reading is then taken. In this case, before the lowering, the scale reads 1020.8mb.

PRECISION ANEROID BAROMETER

In a precision aneroid barometer (*see*, for example, Fig. 76) an electrical signal is created as the aneroid capsules flex in response to pressure changes. The modern version of the precision aneroid barometer is a small instrument (a few centimetres in size), having a similar precision to that of a mercury barometer. In such instruments it is the station-level pressure that is read, and subsequently converted to MSL pressure. The electrical output from a modern precision barometer can be used as part of an AWS system.

AUTOMATIC WEATHER STATION PRESSURE SENSORS

Nowadays, most entry-level AWS consoles include a pressure sensor that should allow the observer to report the air pressure to the nearest millibar. It is, therefore, important to keep the console out of the sun and away from draughts and temperatures changes. Many of these instruments allow the user to incorporate a one-off correction to MSL pressure.

SURFACE PRESSURE (OR ANALYSIS) CHARTS

Surface pressure charts are widely available on the internet and can also sometimes be seen on television weather forecasts; an example is shown in Fig. 77. What do they mean and why are they so useful?

They are created by joining places with the same MSL pressure, in much the same way as an outdoor map for walkers will contain contours showing the altitude of the ground above sea level. The numbered lines on a surface pressure chart (sometimes called an analysis chart as it shows an analysis of the state of the atmosphere) are called isobars (lines of equal pressure); the charts also show the location of areas of high (H) and low (L) pressure, together with the pressure at these locations. Fronts are also displayed, using darker symbols.

Most charts nowadays are drawn using computer software. At one time they were drawn by hand; the different elements of the weather (for example pressure, cloud, weather conditions and temperature) were all plotted, and this enabled

Fig. 76. A precision aneroid barometer, showing a pressure reading of 1006.8mb. This instrument is an older-type Met Office MK2 instrument.
GRAHAM WEBSTER

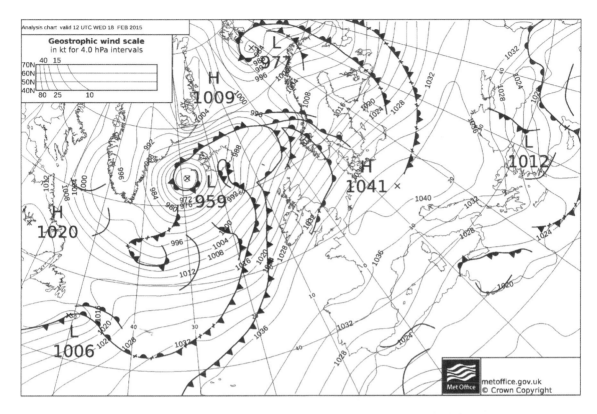

Fig. 77. The UK Met Office surface analysis pressure chart for 1200 GMT on 18 February 2015. This figure contains public sector information licensed under the Open Government Licence v1.0.

the meteorologist to locate the isobars and rain-bearing fronts. The plotting of these 'station plots' is described in a useful Met Office document.[48]

Isobars on an analysis chart give a very good indication of the wind speed and direction. Air might be expected to flow from areas of high pressure to ones of low pressure – much as river water flows from high ground to low ground. However, due to the rotation of the earth, the air is deflected and to a reasonable approximation flows almost parallel to the isobars. Due to friction, caused by the presence of the ground as the air runs over it, the air in fact flows slightly across the isobars towards the direction of lower pressure.

Dutch meteorologist Buys Ballot found in 1857 that, in the northern hemisphere, if you stand with your back to the wind then the pressure is lower to your left than to the right. This implies that the wind

tends to blow anticlockwise around an area of low pressure and clockwise around an area of high pressure – in the northern hemisphere; the converse of this is true in the southern hemisphere.

Thus over the UK in Fig. 77 the wind is blowing from the southwest towards the northeast, while over Iceland the wind is blowing from a southerly direction. Moreover, the closer together the isobars, the stronger the wind. Thus the winds are quite light over central Europe whereas it is windy over the ocean close to southeast Greenland.

Often, the weather conditions are strongly influenced by the wind direction (the direction from which the wind is blowing). Thus winds blowing from the polar regions (a northerly wind in the UK) are more likely to bring cooler conditions that those blowing from the tropics (a southerly wind in the UK). Winds blowing from over a large area of water may contain more moisture than those blowing from a land mass.

Where two air masses with different characteristics meet, meteorologists often draw a front on their weather charts. Thus in Fig. 77 three distinct types of front can be readily seen – namely cold, warm and occluded fronts. In addition, a few trough lines are also shown.

The meeting of cold and warm air along a front tends to result in the cold air sinking below the warm air, leading to the formation of cloud and often precipitation – *see the section on clouds and depressions in Chapter 5.*

WARM FRONTS

A front moving so that the warm air is advancing to replace cooler air is called a warm front. These are marked using semicircular symbols pointing in the direction in which the warmer air is moving. On a surface pressure chart the marked front shows the position of the front at the surface. Higher up in the atmosphere, the position of the front is often ahead of the surface frontal position, so the imminent arrival of the surface front is marked, first, by the appearance of high (cirrus and cirrostratus) cloud.

As the warm front approaches, the cloud thickens and the cloud base lowers before precipitation begins to fall. The precipitation may extend 150–500km ahead of the surface front; it may take several hours after the precipitation commences for the surface front to arrive – at which point there may be a slight rise in temperature.

COLD FRONTS

A cold front is marked using triangular symbols, pointing in the direction in which the colder air is moving to replace warm air. On a surface pressure chart the triangles show the position of the front at the surface – higher in the atmosphere, the front's position usually follows slightly behind the surface frontal position.

As the cold front passes, there is often a drop in temperature – and very often a sudden burst of precipitation. The precipitation may continue as showers behind the cold front if the cold air had been passing over a large expanse of water previously, thereby gathering moisture.

OCCLUDED FRONTS

Cold fronts often move faster than warm fronts, with the result that the cold front catches up with the warm front, creating an occluded front (shown by both semi-circular and triangular symbols side by side). These, too, can be marked by cloud and precipitation.

TROUGH LINES

Trough lines usually mark distinct lines of cloud and showery rain that do not exhibit the full features of a front. They are marked on surface pressure charts by a short, solid black line (without any numbering or symbols).

CORRECTING PRESSURE TO MEAN SEA LEVEL

Air pressure measurements made using a precision instrument that records the station level pressure will need correcting to MSL at each observation.

There are several methods that are used for calculating the height correction,[49, 50] and the one chosen may depend upon the required degree of accuracy. The formula shown below can be easily programmed into a spreadsheet.

PRESSURE CORRECTION FOR STATION ALTITUDES BELOW 50M

A simple correction calculation that can be used is as follows:[49, 50]

Height correction = $p \times h / (29.27 \times (T_v + 273.15))$

Here p is the observed pressure (mb), h is the height of the barometer above sea level (metres) and T_v is the annual mean virtual air temperature (in degrees Celsius, equal to about 1.0 + the annual mean air temperature). Thus for a pressure of 1,000mb observed at a height of 40m where the annual mean air temperature is 10.0°C, the correction is 4.8mb.

The MSL pressure would be 1,004.8 mb in this case. For a specific location only the value of p will vary from reading to reading, so the correction can be pre-computed – and will range in this case from about 4.6mb (for a reading of 950mb) to 5.0mb (when the pressure is 1,050mb).

PRESSURE CORRECTION FOR STATION ALTITUDES OF 50–500M

For stations with an altitude above 50m, then[49] and[50] can again be referred to. Up to 500m altitude the following formula may be used:[51]

Height correction = 1000 × (10ᵐ−1), where
m = h/(18429.1 + 67.53t + 0.003h)

Here, t is the air temperature (°C) and h is the barometer height above sea level (metres). Thus for a barometer at a height of 150m, the corrections range from 20.0mb at an air temperature of −15°C to 16.5mb when the air temperature is 40°C.

The greater the altitude of the barometer, the less accurate is the correction, as the external air temperature may then not apply all the way down to sea level.

PRESSURE CHANGES DURING THE DAY

Atmospheric pressure undergoes a semi-diurnal cycle (rather like the diurnal cycle of surface air temperature). In the British Isles this variation amounts to a range of about 1.5mb (Fig. 78). This means that the time at which the pressure observation is made needs to be noted, along with the pressure observation itself. If observations are made once a day, then this should be done at the same time each day.

Of course, unless the observer is located close to the centre of a large anticyclone that is almost stationary, in the British Isles these semi-diurnal changes are usually masked by the movement of

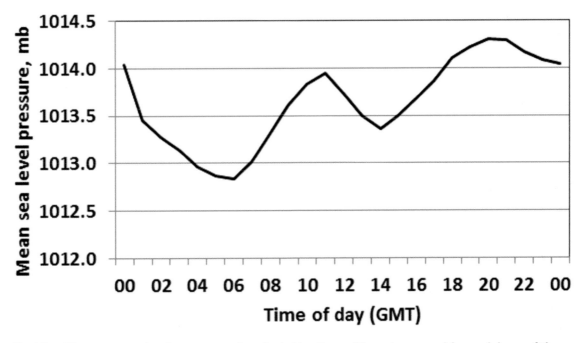

Fig. 78. The mean sea level pressure at London's Heathrow Airport averaged for each hour of the day during the period 1 November 2014–8 February 2015, illustrating the diurnal cycle in pressure.

pressure systems that bring much larger changes to the surface air pressure over the course of a day. This weather-pattern related variation can sometimes be in excess of 25mb over a 24-hour period.

PRESSURE CHANGE AND CHARACTERISTIC

The pressure tendency is used to describe the way in which pressure changes, and is normally comprised of the characteristic of pressure change (for example 'rising', 'falling' or 'steady') and the pressure change itself (for example '−2mb'). The pressure change is the net difference between pressure readings at the end and beginning of a specified interval of time, frequently taken as a period of three hours. So a change of −2mb means a drop in pressure of 2mb.

Unless the observer has access to frequent and accurate measurements of pressure, then this is a quantity not normally reported. However, during a spell of falling pressure ahead of a quickly approaching deep area of low pressure, a barograph may reveal a pressure fall of in excess of 10mb over three hours.

ENTRIES IN THE OBSERVATION REGISTER

Observers making a single pressure measurement at (or close to) 0900 GMT should keep a daily record of that value (converted to mean sea level) at the observation time. A note should also be made of the observation time – due to the small semi-diurnal variation in pressure.

If you have a means of maintaining a continuous record of the pressure using an AWS or a barograph, then it should be possible to extract the MSL pressure at the standard observing hour of 0900 GMT. In addition, the highest and lowest values each day (0000–2400 GMT) can also be determined and noted, along with their times of occurrence.

An AWS whose observations are logged will also enable hourly measurements to be kept – averaging these over a long period of time will enable the semi-diurnal pressure cycle to be seen. An AWS will also allow the pressure change over the three hours prior to the observation time to be recorded.

At the end of each month, the average pressure at each observing time can be determined, along with the highest and lowest monthly values.

10. PRECIPITATION

Precipitation may consist of liquid (including rain or drizzle) or solid (for example snow, hail, ice) aqueous matter from the atmosphere – see the section on hydrometeors in Chapter 3. The total amount of precipitation that falls to the ground over a given period of time is usually expressed in terms of the depth of precipitation (in millimetres in the UK), which also includes any melted solid precipitation. In this chapter 'rainfall' will be used instead of 'precipitation' for simplicity, except where any treatment of solid precipitation is to be handled in a different manner.

Rainfall is measured using a raingauge, which collects the volume of water falling over a known area. By determining the volume of water and knowing the area of the collecting surface of the raingauge, the depth can be found by division of the former by the latter. Many raingauges are sold with a measuring device that has this division process built in. In the UK the oldest design of raingauge still in common use is the Snowdon raingauge, an instrument that dates back over 150 years.

The expectation is that the rainfall that falls in the raingauge is representative of that falling in the wider area around the raingauge – thus the location of the raingauge and its exposure need to be considered carefully. I have known of instances where nearby trees, sheds, washing lines and male dogs are likely to have interfered with the measurements!

Rainfall amounts can often be quite small, maybe just a few tenths of a millimetre. Thus it is important to use an instrument that is able to measure such small quantities of water (or snow).

Prior to the advent of relatively cheap automatic weather stations (AWSs), rainfall measurements were the only instrumental weather measurement made by many observers. This was a reflection of the relative ease of installation and maintenance of a raingauge and also of the usefulness to society of rainfall measurements. In the UK, for example, there were in excess of 5,000 official rainfall stations at one time, as the pages of the publication *British Rainfall* reveal.[52]

TYPES OF RAINGAUGE

Broadly speaking, there are two types of raingauge – the manual gauge and the recording gauge.

The manual gauge, otherwise known as the 'storage' gauge, simply collects rainfall using a funnel and stores it in a container for subsequent measurement. The Snowdon raingauge is an example of this type. The contents are emptied, typically once a day, and measured using a measuring cylinder.

A recording gauge enables a record of the rainfall over time to be determined. Such instruments are often of the 'tipping bucket' or 'tilting siphon' type.

EXPOSURE, RAINGAUGE HEIGHT AND OBSERVATION TIME

EXPOSURE AND OBSTACLES

Any raingauge must be positioned such that its opening is exactly horizontal, as any tilting will mean that the aperture is effectively smaller than its nominal size. Consequently, less rainwater will be collected, which the observer would, erroneously, interpret as a smaller depth of rainfall.

As mentioned in Chapter 2, it is recommended that any obstacle within sight of the raingauge should be at a distance equivalent to at least twice its height away from the raingauge. Moreover, as the raingauge is designed to catch falling raindrops and snowflakes, it is important the surroundings of the instrument do not divert the airflow, and maybe also the rain, away from the funnel of the instrument.

THE SNOWDON RAINGAUGE

The standard raingauge still widely used in the UK is the Snowdon rain-gauge, which dates back to early experiments on the measurement of rainfall carried out in the 1860s and 1870s. The frontispiece of *British Rainfall 1868*,[52] the annual rainfall report of the British Rainfall Organisation, shows one of these experiments involving forty-two raingauges, carried out in the

LEFT: **Fig. 79.   A copper Snowdon raingauge buried in a grass-covered surface with the rim of the funnel 30cm above the ground level.**

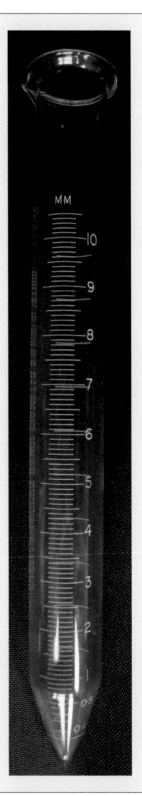

RIGHT: **Fig. 81.   A glass measuring cylinder used with a Snowdon raingauge; the cylinder is about 30cm long. Note the tapered end for measuring small amounts (0.1–0.5mm) accurately.**

Fig. 80.   Component parts of a Snowdon raingauge showing, from left to right, the base buried in the ground; the inner collecting can, into which is placed the glass collecting jar; and the outer funnel, showing the narrow spout that fits inside the collecting jar.

grounds of Stratfield Turgiss Rectory in north Hampshire by the observer, the Reverend Charles Griffith.

The Snowdon raingauge was traditionally made largely of copper, although stainless steel versions are now available. It consists of a collecting funnel, 5in (12.7cm) in diameter and about 5in deep, usually sited with the rim 12in (30cm) above ground level. A similar instrument also exists with a splayed base – where the diameter of the base of the instrument, located under the soil, is greater than 5in to provide an extra level of stability, preventing the instrument from tipping over slightly in the soil.

The funnel directs rainwater into a glass collecting jar with a narrow neck – the narrow neck designed to minimize any evaporation of the contents. The jar itself sits inside a collecting can, which makes only slight contact with the outer case of the instrument, thereby insulating the contents to reduce the risks of freezing in winter and evaporation in summer.

The deep funnel minimizes rainfall loss that may result from drops splashing out in the event of heavy rainfall and, in the case of snowfall, also minimizes the loss of precipitation due to snow being blown out of the funnel. Note that nowadays some 5in copper raingauges are constructed with only a shallow funnel and should be avoided for these reasons.

The instrument comes with a measuring cylinder; the water in the collecting jar should be carefully emptied into this cylinder, which allows the depth of rainfall to be determined to the nearest 0.1mm.

Fig. 82. **A splayed base version of the copper Snowdon gauge, standing above the ground to reveal the widened base.**

EXTREME RAINFALL

Table 19 shows some extreme rainfall totals for the UK, the Republic of Ireland and around the world. In the UK a 24-hour fall of 100mm is rarely recorded in non-mountainous areas, while the annual rainfall total across the British Isles ranges from over 4,000mm over the higher peaks in parts of northwest Scotland to under 600mm in the drier parts of East Anglia and in a few places in north Kent – close to the Thames Estuary, for example.

Table 19 Extreme rainfall totals for the UK,[53] the Republic of Ireland[54] and around the world[55]

Location	Time period	Greatest fall, mm	Place	Date
England	1 day	279	Martinstown, Dorset	18 July 1955
	1 day	341	Honister Pass, Cumbria	6 December 2015
Wales	1 day	211	Lluest Wen Reservoir, Mid-Glamorgan	11 November 1929
Scotland	1 day	238	Sloy Main Adit, Argyll and Bute	17 January 1974
Northern Ireland	1 day	159	Tollymore Forest, Co. Down	31 October 1968
Republic of Ireland	1 day	243	Cloone Lake, Co. Kerry	18 September 1993
Worldwide	1 minute	31.2	Unionville, Maryland, USA	4 July 1956
Worldwide	1 hour	305	Holt, Missouri, USA	22 June 1947
Worldwide	1 day	1825	Foc-Foc, La Réunion	7–8 January 1966
Worldwide	12 months	26.47m	Cherrapunji, India	August 1860–July 1861

If the raingauge is to be positioned close to ground level (standard practice in the UK) then it should not be mounted on a hard surface such as tarmac or concrete, as this may cause raindrops to splash up off the surface and into the raingauge. A surface of short-cut grass is recommended.

If the raingauge is designed to be mounted on a post above ground level then do not mount it along the line of a fence; the fence may, depending upon the wind direction, deflect the air away from the raingauge, which could affect the amount of rain collected.

The nature of any obstruction can also be important. Trees and hedges will have a considerable sheltering effect while a mesh fence will have much less impact at the same height and distance from the raingauge as a hedge. Try to site the raingauge with as good an exposure as possible towards the direction from where the prevailing rain-bearing winds arrive.

THE HEIGHT OF THE RAINGAUGE

The standard height at which the raingauge should be exposed varies by country. A raingauge close to the ground will be less affected by turbulent wind eddies, which might blow air around and out of the raingauge, than one mounted on a post, for example. But having a raingauge with a rim 30cm above the ground is of little use if the typical snow depth each winter will frequently exceed 30cm. In the latter case a raingauge mounted on a post might be more appropriate.

In the UK, at some windy sites, a surrounding turf wall of diameter 3m and height 30cm used to be constructed to shield the raingauge from the extreme effects of strong winds.

Raingauges mounted at ground level (Fig. 83) are usually surrounded by a mesh-covered pit to minimize the likelihood of drops splashing off the nearby ground into the raingauge, while those at greater heights are usually equipped with a

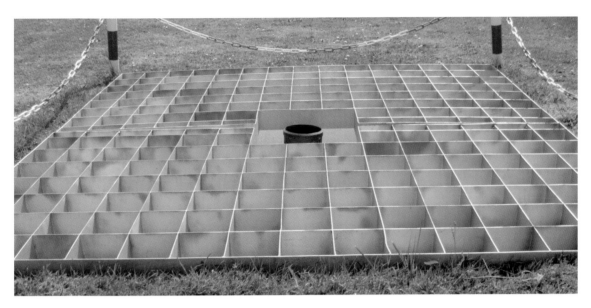

Fig. 83. A ground-level Snowdon raingauge at the University of Reading.

Fig. 84. A Snowdon gauge with an Alter shield at the University of Reading. The rim of the raingauge stands about 1m above the ground.

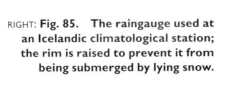

RIGHT: Fig. 85. The raingauge used at an Icelandic climatological station; the rim is raised to prevent it from being submerged by lying snow.

surrounding wind shield (Figs 84 and 85); this helps to dampen any wind turbulence that may affect the amount of rain collected.

Many entry-level AWSs are designed in such a way that all their measuring sensors have to be located close to each other, due to the short lengths of wiring used to link them to a logger or transmitter. In this case the observer will need to decide which of the measurements, for example wind or rainfall or temperature, are of greater importance and maybe locate the raingauge at the relevant height for that required measurement.

HOW MUCH RAIN SHOULD A RAINGAUGE HOLD?

If the raingauge is a storage gauge, then it needs to be able to hold any water accumulated over the time between visits by the observer. In the UK and Republic of Ireland any manual gauge should be able to hold at least 150mm of rainfall if the gauge is not emptied daily (remember that if you are away for a fortnight's holiday then this amount of rain might be collected in that time). Falls in excess of 100mm have been recorded in some parts of the British Isles in just a few hours – so even with a 150mm capacity it might be necessary to empty the gauge more than once a day on occasion.

For observers intending to measure rainfall in areas where larger falls are more common, for example over high ground, then larger capacity raingauges are available. Such gauges also lend themselves to being emptied at weekly or monthly intervals.

RAINFALL OBSERVATION TIMES

In order easily to compare observations with those made by other observers in the same country, it is important for observers to make their observations at the same time.

Throwing Back the Rainfall when Measured before Midday

In the UK the standard 24-hour rainfall period is 0900 GMT to 0900 GMT. In the summer this equates to 1000 BST to 1000 BST. Measurements made at 0900 GMT are 'thrown back' to the previous day (as most of the twenty-four hours prior to the observation time will have occurred on the previous day – and hence we might expect most of the rain to have fallen 'yesterday'). Thus if daily measurements are made at 0900 GMT and 15mm of rain is measured on the third of the month, this is marked in the register as having fallen on the second. This applies even if you know that all the rain fell in the early hours of the third.

Observing the Rainfall at Non-Standard Times

In practice, not all amateurs can make the observation at 0900 GMT due to work constraints. The Climatological Observers Link therefore recommends a regular daily observation between 0600 GMT and 0900 GMT. Should it only be possible to make an observation in the evening, then the measured total should be assigned to the day of observation as most of the preceding twenty-four hours will have been during the day on which the measurement was made. Note, however, that such an observation time will make it difficult to compare rainfall totals directly with those at most other sites.

Observers in other countries should consult documentation from their national meteorological services for guidance upon the timing of daily observations.

ICE, SNOW OR HAIL IN THE RAINGAUGE

Hail, Light Snow or Ice

As a rough guide, 10cm of snowfall will produce about 10mm of liquid equivalent rainfall. However, this is only a rough guide – light and fluffy snow falling at temperatures well below 0°C may give a 15cm to 10mm ratio, while if the snow is wet and compact, then 5cm of snow may equate to 10mm of rain.

As temperatures fall the observer will eventually encounter the problem of trying to determine the 'rainfall' when there is snow or hail in the gauge, or maybe even a layer of ice in the collecting jar of a manual gauge. This will need melting (using the so-called 'warm water method') before any measurement can be made. In the UK the observer should prepare about half a litre of warm (30–40°C) water. If the water is any hotter it may crack the measuring cylinder or make the measuring cylinder too hot to hold. Fill the measuring cylinder with about 10mm equivalent of this warm water and make a note of the amount used. Then carefully pour this water into the funnel of the gauge, ensuring that nothing splashes out of the funnel. This may need to be repeated several times, in which case make a note of all the added warm water. The water content in the raingauge is then measured, and the total amount of added warm water subtracted to give the precipitation total.

Heavy Snow or Snowfall in Strong Winds

In these conditions it is possible that a raingauge close to the ground level may be partially or completely buried in snow, or the snowfall may exceed the funnel capacity. Initially attempt to measure the raingauge and funnel contents using the warm water method, making a note of the results.

Then find an area of level snow, free from any drifting. Press down vertically the inverted raingauge funnel into this snow and try to ensure that all the snow in the area under the funnel is captured by the funnel when you lift it up. Now place the funnel on the raingauge and use the warm water method to measure the snow. Repeat the process two or three times. An average of these measurements can then be taken and used as a measure of the day's precipitation measurement – but make a note in your register that this technique (the 'inverted funnel method') has been used.

If such conditions are likely to persist for the next day then a snowboard might prove useful. Simply place a layer of light-coloured plywood on top of the lying snow and then use the inverted funnel method the following day, extracting snow only down to the level of the snowboard. After completing the measurement, replace the snowboard on top of the lying snow again, having first cleared it of all existing snow, ready for subsequent use.

Snow Depth Measurements

When snow lies on the ground, a measurement of the total snow depth can be made with a ruler in an area that is free from drifting and any scouring of the snow by the wind. Take a note of about ten measurements, discard the highest and lowest, and then take the average. The depth should be noted to the nearest whole centimetre.

RAINGAUGE TYPES

In the UK the Snowdon raingauge is the official standard for a storage raingauge. If measurements are made by an AWS instrument to determine the times and rainfall intensity, then it is recommended that a storage gauge is also used to measure the daily fall. AWS instruments, due to their method of operation, often under-record the daily total – especially during short-lived, intense falls of rain.

CoCoRaHS PLASTIC RAINGAUGE

CoCoRaHS is an acronym for the Community Collaborative Rain, Hail and Snow Network and is a network of volunteers working together to measure and map precipitation across the United States.[56] The network originated with the Colorado Climate Center at Colorado State University in 1998 and now includes thousands of volunteers nationwide.

Observers use low-cost, plastic raingauges and provide measurements of high quality for research, education and monitoring purposes throughout the United States. Their raingauges can be purchased in the UK[57] and are highly recommended for use by any amateur for whom a Snowdon gauge is too expensive, or whose only raingauge is an automatic one. Studies by Stephen Burt[58] have shown that it compares very favourably with the Snowdon gauge.

The raingauge is designed to be mounted on a post – in North America this helps to avoid problems with deep, lying snow in winter and means that it can also be sited in a field of crops. It is made of heavy-duty, UV-resistant polycarbonate. The gauge is about 350mm tall and has a 100mm-diameter funnel opening, affording it greater accuracy than cheap narrow gauges; it is equipped with a 25mm

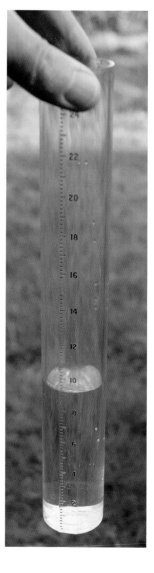

LEFT: **Fig. 86. A CoCoRaHS raingauge mounted on a post.**

RIGHT: **Fig. 87. The measuring cylinder for the CoCoRaHS raingauge showing the rainwater collected after a fall of 9.2mm.**

capacity measuring tube. On the occasions when daily rainfall exceeds 25mm, excess rainfall spills over into, and is retained by, the outer collecting tube, which has an overall capacity of 275mm. Measuring rainfall totals of over 25mm is done by filling the measuring tube with the collected rainfall in 25mm batches until the outer reservoir is emptied.

TILTING SIPHON RAINGAUGE

The rainfall collected in the raingauge funnel (Fig. 88) is fed into a float chamber (the black cylinder

in Fig. 89), causing the float inside the chamber to rise. As the float rises, a pen attached to the float through a lever system records the water level (that is rainfall) on a rotating drum driven by batteries or clockwork. A siphoning mechanism empties the float chamber when this becomes full. If there is no rainfall, the pen traces a horizontal line. Figure 92 shows an example of the type of record obtained.

HELLMANN RAINGAUGE

A useful raingauge for an amateur is the Hellmann raingauge (Fig. 90). This is a siphon raingauge that stands with its 16cm-diameter collecting aperture some 110cm above the ground level so it can be located among plants. It is a recording raingauge, using a seven-day chart (Fig. 91). In the event of the observer being absent, the clockwork recording mechanism of the gauge will run for over ten days.

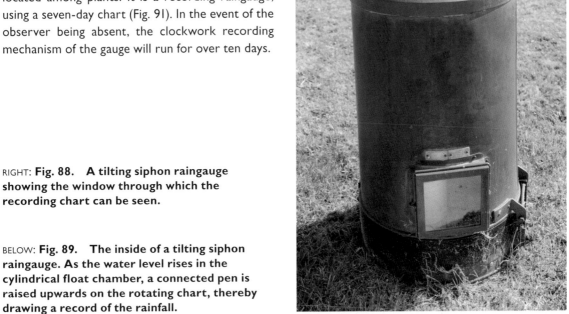

RIGHT: **Fig. 88. A tilting siphon raingauge showing the window through which the recording chart can be seen.**

BELOW: **Fig. 89. The inside of a tilting siphon raingauge. As the water level rises in the cylindrical float chamber, a connected pen is raised upwards on the rotating chart, thereby drawing a record of the rainfall.**

LEFT: **Fig. 90.**
A Hellmann
raingauge.

RIGHT: **Fig. 91.**
The mechanism
inside a Hellmann
raingauge. The
float chamber is
the grey cylinder
on the right, and
allows 10mm
of rain to be
recorded before
siphoning occurs.
A heater can be
seen in the lower
left corner.

WHAT IS A TRACE OF RAINFALL?

Often when the observer empties the contents of the manual raingauge, no water is found in the collecting bottle. Closer inspection of the raingauge may indicate a general wetting of the funnel (perhaps by a heavy overnight dew, fog or hoar frost). Sometimes there may be signs of one of two spots of wetness in the funnel, possibly caused either by a recent and very short shower of rain or a spell of rain or drizzle. Possibly the observer knows that a few spots of rain fell during the period since the raingauge was last examined but knows that this fall would have been insufficient to drop into the collecting jar inside the raingauge.

In each of these cases a 'trace' of rainfall is to be noted in the register as the rainfall total – some precipitation has occurred but it was of such a small quantity that it could not be measured. If a standard Snowdon raingauge and its accompanying measure are used, then any measurement less than 0.05mm (or 0.005in if the measure is marked in imperial units) should be also recorded as a trace.

When totalling up the rainfall over a period of time, any 'trace' should be counted as a fall of 0.0mm (or inches) – unless it is the only fall in that period, in which case the total is a 'trace'.

Fig. 96.   The type of raingauge often used in entry-level AWS kits. The horizontal dimensions are about 10cm by 5cm, and the funnel is only about 1cm in depth.

ENTRY-LEVEL AUTOMATIC RAINGAUGES

Figure 96 shows the type of raingauge employed in many entry-level AWSs. These are rather small with a very shallow funnel, the result being that much of the falling rain can bounce out of the funnel and not be recorded. In addition these often do not use a 0.2mm tip – so small falls over two to three days may be merged into one tip.

Such raingauges are also often combined into a weather station in which all the measuring devices are installed close to one another. The result is that the raingauge can be partially sheltered by the other instruments, reducing the rainfall catch still further.

While such an instrument can give an indication of when rainfall occurs, the actual rainfall would be better measured by a Snowdon or a CoCoRaHS raingauge.

DAVIS INSTRUMENT RAINGAUGES

Popular AWSs used by many observers of the Climatological Observers Link include the Davis Vantage Pro2 (see Chapter 12) and Davis Vue models.

For Davis Vantage Pro models, the raingauge rim will be at a height of about 140cm if the temperature sensor is mounted at the standard 125cm height above the ground. In both this and the Vantage Vue model, the temperature/humidity and rainfall sensors are located together in a single assembly. Studies by Stephen Burt[60, 61] have shown that while the instruments give a good indication of the timings of rainfall, the total collected rainfalls were often poor. Again, a Snowdon or a CoCoRaHS raingauge might be better suited to provide daily and monthly totals.

ENTRIES IN THE OBSERVATION REGISTER

It is suggested that the rainfall record in the weather register should contain the following four entries for each day:

A.   The rainfall total in millimetres (ideally for 0900–0900 GMT in the UK)
B.   The presence of a rain day (1); else 0
C.   The presence of a wet day (1); else 0
D.   The presence of a very wet day (1); else 0

At the end of each month the values of each of these four entries should be totalled, with a note also being made of the greatest daily rainfall total for the month.

If measurements of rainfall duration are available via a recording raingauge, then a daily record (thrown back for the period 0900–0900 GMT) of the rainfall duration can be noted – either the measured rainfall duration or a count of the number of wet hours. Again, both these should totalled at the end of the month.

A note may also be made of any peak rainfall intensities and of any droughts.

11. THERMOMETER SCREENS

WHY USE A THERMOMETER SCREEN?

Once you have decided to measure the air temperature, you will need to answer the question 'where should I place the thermometer?' Here, the use of the word 'thermometer' covers both thermometers of the traditional kind (filled with mercury or spirit) and those that come with an automatic weather station (AWS). The latter equipment may or may not have some kind of thermometer screen as part of the package.

The thermometer should be placed in a screen to protect it from incoming solar radiation (for example, sunshine) during the day and from terrestrial radiation during both day and the night. The screen should prevent the thermometer from being either heated or cooled by radiation, which would cause a false reading of the air temperature.

The thermometer should also be kept out of the rain and snow; clearly if the thermometer becomes covered in snow it will report the temperature of the snow; one exposed to rainfall may record the temperature of the falling raindrops, or else act as a wet bulb thermometer (see Chapter 12) and thereby under-read due to evaporative cooling of the raindrops.

LOCATION OF THE SCREEN

The screen should be sited away from obstructions such as buildings and walls (which may heat up in sunshine and therefore affect the temperature measurements), hedges and fences. Walls and tarmac can also store heat during the day and release it at night – akin to the urban heat island effect (see Chapter 17). Be careful, too, of large walled areas or expansive windows, which can both lead to additional reflection of radiation that may warm your screen. The screen should be located at least twice the height of the obstacle from any obstacle (as mentioned in Chapter 2) – and preferably at a greater distance, especially if that obstacle is a heated building.

In the UK and Republic of Ireland the screen should be installed so that the thermometers inside have their bulbs 1.25m above the ground; in other parts of the world a height of up to 2m is used. The screen should also be located over a surface of short grass wherever possible.

TYPES OF THERMOMETER SCREEN

STEVENSON SCREEN

Traditionally, meteorologists have used a Stevenson screen or similar instrument shelter to shield meteorological instruments from precipitation and radiation from outside sources, while still allowing air to circulate freely around them. In the UK there are two types of screen. The smaller Stevenson screen can be used to hold typically four thermometers that record the dry and wet bulb temperatures, as well as the maximum and minimum temperatures. Nowadays these four thermometers are often replaced by two sensors to record the air temperature and relative humidity – forming part of an AWS.

A large screen may be used to hold additional instruments such as thermographs and thermohygrographs (see Chapter 12).

The screen was designed by Thomas Stevenson (1818–87), a Scottish civil engineer and father of the author Robert Louis Stevenson. Stevenson's original design appeared in the *Journal of the Scottish Meteorological Society* in 1864. The original design was subsequently modified to include walls comprising double louvred slats and a sloping, double

Fig. 97.   A modern MetSpec Stevenson screen as used in the UK. It is constructed of plastic and aluminium, and is mounted on a stand so that the sensors are at a height of 1.25m above the ground. The side panel used as a door to gain access to the interior faces due north to prevent direct sunlight from reaching the sensors when it is opened. In the southern hemisphere the screen door should face south.

roof before becoming the standard screen in the UK. Identical or very similar screens are now used worldwide.

Figure 97 shows a modern thermometer screen manufactured from plastic and aluminium. Due to its durability and low maintenance – the use of plastic removes the need for regular painting and repairs – this design is gradually replacing the traditional wooden Stevenson screen. Figure 98 shows a type of thermometer screen employed by the Icelandic Met Office. Here, and in many countries, the screen is mounted slightly higher than in the UK.

In addition to small screens based on Stevenson's design, some official automatic weather stations now use a smaller screen such as the one on Lihou Island in the Bailiwick of Guernsey (Fig. 99).

Fig. 98. An Icelandic thermometer screen. The steps enable the instruments to be located at a height of 2m above the ground.

LARGE THERMOMETER SCREEN

The large Stevenson thermometer screen (Fig. 100) is about twice the size of the small version, allowing it to house additional instruments. I use my screen (of the traditional wooden type) to house a thermohygrograph, a Piche evaporimeter and additional air temperature sensors – along with the traditional mercury and alcohol-based thermometers. Again, the tendency is increasingly for these screens to be manufactured from plastic rather than from wood.

DIY AND SIMPLE TYPES OF SCREENS

Some budget-level AWS units will not contain any form of thermometer screen. Provided such systems are of the wireless type then it should be possible to place the temperature sensor inside an inexpensive self-assembly wooden screen. These cost (January 2015) about £100–120 (maybe slightly less if purchased as a self-assembly kit) and need to be mounted in such a way that air can move freely in and around the screen.

Such a low-cost screen is ideal for beginners

Fig. 99. The weather station at Lihou, the most westerly weather station in the Channel Islands. This weather station is unmanned and the temperature sensors are contained in the white, ribbed cylindrical screen.

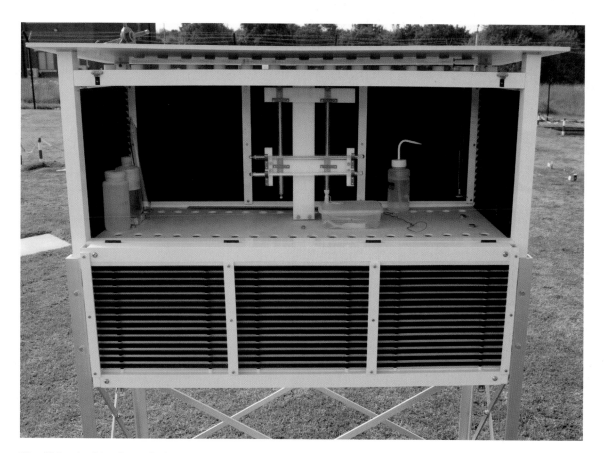

Fig. 100.   Inside view of a large MetSpec Stevenson screen at the University of Reading. At the centre can be seen the four conventional thermometers (measuring the dry and wet bulb temperatures, and the maximum and minimum temperatures). The bottles contain purified water and are used to ensure the water reservoir feeding the wick of the wet bulb thermometer (the right-hand vertical thermometer) is kept wet. Also just visible are the raingauge measuring cylinder and the Piche evaporimeter.

and for school sites, although it should be mounted on some form of sturdy stand rather than being secured to a wall using the back panel. A small screen might be ideal if just a digital thermometer is to be used.

Any weather observer who is adept at wood-work or who access to a workshop may find some of the designs on the Weather for Schools website of use.[64]

North-Facing Wall-Mounted Screens

Before the advent of thermometer screen, thermometers were often exposed on north-facing walls, the reasoning being that this side of the wall would never be exposed to direct sunlight. In fact, there was a time when some thermometers would be exposed inside buildings in a room that was never heated! Nowadays, neither exposure is acceptable for official stations.

For the newcomer to weather observing, if the garden is not a suitable place for installing a thermometer screen – or if you have no garden – then a small screen might be mounted on a north-facing wall. Such a wall should not form part of a building due to likely errors in the thermometer readings caused by heat emitted by the building itself.

Fig. 101. An inexpensive, self-assembly wooden screen. This model comes without a stand and, in this case, has been mounted on a small post. Note that the rear of the screen is solid; there are small holes in the side panels while only the door is louvred in style. GRAHAM WEBSTER

North-Facing Wall-Mounted Thermometers

As a last resort, should a thermometer screen be unavailable, then the thermometers could be mounted on a north-facing wall. In order to prevent the thermometer temperature rising due to contact with a wall that may often be warmer than the surrounding air, a compromise would be to mount the instrument on a bracket at 20–25cm from the wall. The bracket could also be used to carry some form of roof to shelter the thermometer from rain, snow and overhead sunshine.

Using an unheated north wall location without a screen can cause problems around the summer sol-stice, particularly at more northern latitudes such as those of northern Scotland; care needs to be taken to shield the thermometers from sunshine in early morning and late evening when there is an unobstructed view of the sun to the northeast or northwest, respectively.

AUTOMATIC WEATHER STATION SCREENS

Most budget and mid-range AWS systems come with some form of screen – the entry-level ones often of the type shown in Fig. 102. This screen is coloured grey – not a good colour at all! Ideally the screen should be white to reflect incoming solar radiation. In addition it is quite small in size, raising the question of whether there is a tendency for the air to stagnate inside the screen – rather than flowing freely through the screen and over the instruments. During the summer of 2014 I performed a simple experiment to see how such a screen performed.

It was assumed that long spells of sunshine and hot conditions during 17–20 July 2014 would be an ideal time to examine how much the small, grey AWS screen contributed to the heating of the AWS temperature sensor, previous experiments having shown that when the sensor was placed in a Stevenson screen it did agree very closely with the traditional thermometers. Table 20 shows temperature observations made using the liquid-in-glass thermometers in the Stevenson screen along with the readings made using the AWS sensor.

When the sensor was in the Stevenson screen (on the 17th – which was quite a sunny day) there was very little difference between the thermometers and the sensor (typically 0.1 degrees C). However, placing the AWS sensor inside its grey screen in the open air (see Fig. 102) resulted in readings that were up to about 2 degrees C warmer during the day (the maximum temperature) and about 0.5 degrees C cooler by night (the minimum temperature). Note that the 18th was another sunny day while the 19th was rather cloudy for much of the day – yet the spurious heating was quite similar on both days.

Fig. 102. An entry-level AWS system. Shown are the raingauge (left), wind vane and anemometer (centre) and screen (right), containing temperature and humidity sensors. The rather dubious exposure is due to the wiring together of these components with relatively short wires. Note that such screens should be white, not grey.

Table 20 The maximum and minimum temperatures measured during an experiment in July 2014 in Maidenhead to evaluate a grey, budget-level AWS screen

Date	Liquid-in-glass thermometers in Stevenson screen		AWS sensor in Stevenson screen		AWS sensor in grey plastic screen	
July 2014	Max. temp (°C)	Min. temp (°C)	Max. temp (°C)	Min. temp (°C)	Max. temp (°C)	Min. temp (°C)
17th	29.4	15.5	29.5	15.6		
18th	29.3	17.3			31.1	16.9
19th	28.1	18.7			30.2	18.2
20th		18.7				16.4

Further discussion of the issues surrounding screens and temperature sensors can be found in two useful articles written by Simon Bell and colleagues of Aston University[65, 66] on citizen weather stations.

A good, purpose-built AWS screen should be white on the outside, as shown in Fig. 99. Even, then, these come in many shapes and sizes, although they all generally appear to be of the form of a pile of inverted saucers, each separated by a small depth. They are small because electrical sensors used in such screens are small and there is no requirement for the sensors to be read by opening up the screen.

Small screens may allow only limited airflow in and out of the vents and may overheat in strong sunshine. Unfortunately, it is quite difficult to tell good screens from bad – as the results obtained may also depend upon the actual temperature sensors employed within. Very few such screens have been independently evaluated – the Davis Vantage Pro2 is an exception to this[67] – and it is worth consulting weather-related newsgroups or fellow observers (*see* Chapter 18) for their opinions before purchasing an AWS screen.

ASPIRATED SCREENS

The screens described so far (both the Stevenson and AWS types) are passively ventilated – they rely on the wind to blow air in and out the screen. When the wind at screen height is low or calm, there will be little or no flow of air through the screen, thereby increasing the chances of the screen overheating due to solar radiation – especially if it is a small AWS one. Aspirated screens, in which an electrically driven fan is used to draw air continuously through the screen, overcome this problem – and the continually renewed supply of air results in a more varying temperature record. Smaller sites (in back gardens) are obviously prone to reduced wind speeds and this is one reason why such sites tend to be too warm on sunny days with light winds.

AND FINALLY...

When you have purchased your screen make sure that it is well anchored to the ground and to any supports. I know more than one screen that has taken flight in strong winds. At very windy sites, the screen should be held down with guy ropes.

Fig. 103. An aspirated screen made by RM Young in use at the University of Reading. Air is drawn through the opening at the bottom of the tube and expelled out through the vent (from where the cabling protrudes).

12. AIR TEMPERATURE AND HUMIDITY

Along with rainfall, temperature is probably the weather element whose measurement will be of highest priority for any observer; it is one of the elements whose effects can be felt day in, day out. In this chapter the instruments used to measure temperature and humidity are introduced, along with the calculations that can be used to derive various related measures of the moisture content of the atmosphere. Temperature is measured by a thermometer, the latter being taken (at least in this chapter) to mean any device capable of measuring the temperature (and not just a conventional liquid-in-glass sensor).

WHAT IS TEMPERATURE?

Temperature is a measurement of the average kinetic energy of the atoms or molecules in an object or system. Temperature is different from heat, although the two are linked. Temperature is a measure of the internal energy of the system, while heat is a measure of how energy is transferred from one system (or body) to another.

Temperature is measured using fixed scales that are defined in terms of the physical changes of state of various substances. In day-to-day meteorology the Celsius and (older) Fahrenheit scales are used – the units being degrees Celsius (°C) or degrees Fahrenheit (°F), respectively. Temperature differences are given in terms of Celsius degrees (degrees C) or Fahrenheit degrees (degrees F).

In meteorology the air temperature as measured by a surface weather station is sometimes termed the 'dry bulb temperature', to distinguish it from the 'wet bulb temperature' – a measurement used to determine the humidity of the air.

Table 21 Extremes of air temperature for the United Kingdom,[68] the Republic of Ireland[69] and around the world[70]

Country		Reading	Date and location
England	Highest	38.5°C	10 August 2003, Faversham (Kent); this is quite a sheltered site – at Kew 38.1°C was recorded on the same day
	Lowest	−26.1°C	10 January 1982, Newport (Shropshire)
Wales	Highest	35.2°C	2 August 1990, Hawarden Bridge (Flintshire)
	Lowest	−23.3°C	21 January 1940, Rhayader (Powys)
Scotland	Highest	32.9°C	9 August 2003, Greycrook (Borders)
	Lowest	−27.2°C	11 February 1895 and 10 January 1982, Braemar (Aberdeenshire); 30 December 1995, Altnaharra (Highlands)
Northern Ireland	Highest	30.8°C	30 June 1976, Knockarevan (Fermanagh); 12 July 1983, Shaw's Bridge, Belfast (Antrim)
	Lowest	−18.7°C	24 December 2010, Castlederg (Tyrone)
Republic of Ireland	Highest	33.3°C	26 June 1887, Kilkenny Castle (Kilkenny)
	Lowest	−19.1°C	16 January 1881, Marktree Castle (Sligo)
Worldwide	Highest	56.7°C	10 July 1913, Furnace Creek, California, USA
	Lowest	−89.2°C	21 July 1983, Vostok, Antarctica

CELSIUS AND FAHRENHEIT TEMPERATURE SCALES

The Celsius scale, historically known as centigrade and named after the Swedish astronomer Anders Celsius (1701–44), is used by meteorologists worldwide to report temperature measurements. In a few countries (notably the United States and a few Caribbean countries) the Fahrenheit scale, developed by Danzig-born scientist Daniel Gabriel Fahrenheit (1686–1736), is still used.

Nowadays, the thermodynamic temperature (T), having units of kelvin (K), is the fundamental temperature scale. The kelvin is the fraction 1/273.16 of the thermodynamic temperature of the triple point of water – measurements are expressed as differences from absolute zero (0K), the temperature at which the molecules of any substance possess no kinetic energy. The triple point of water is the temperature at which solid, liquid and vapour forms of water (at a pressure of 6.11 millibars) can co-exist.

For meteorological purposes the temperature (C), in degrees Celsius, is given by C = T – 273.15.

Mathematically, to obtain the Celsius equivalent of a Fahrenheit reading (F), use the formula C = (F – 32)/1.8; conversely, F = (1.8 × C) + 32.

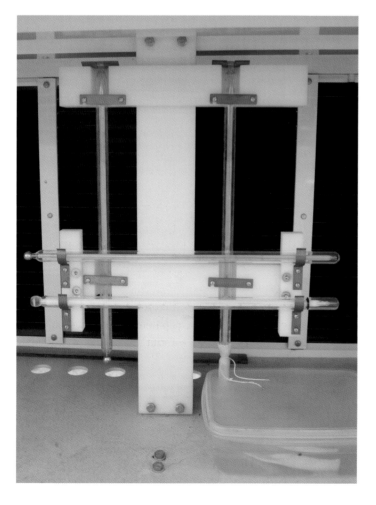

TEMPERATURE EXTREMES

Table 21 shows the officially accepted extremes of air temperature (as recorded in a thermometer screen). In the British Isles temperatures outside the range −15°C to +30°C are rare; in some places worldwide, however, temperatures of −25°C or +40°C are commonplace at some times of the year.

Fig. 104. Illustrating the four thermometers usually found in an official thermometer screen at a weather station where observations are still made manually. Hanging vertically are the dry bulb (left) and wet bulb (right) thermometers, while the horizontal ones are the maximum (upper) and minimum (lower) thermometers. At the bottom right can be seen the reservoir of distilled water that feeds the wet bulb thermometer.

WHAT IS HUMIDITY?

Humidity refers to the amount of water vapour in the air. Hot air can hold more water vapour than cold air before it becomes saturated; the water-holding capacity of air near the ground increases by about a factor of two for every 10 degrees C increase in temperature. This is why in hot climates the air can feel humid or 'sticky' without mist, fog or low cloud forming – and why cold air tends to be quite dry.

Meteorologists often use one of two terms to denote this wetness of the air, the 'dew point' or the 'relative humidity'. Both can be easily determined, often by using a pair of thermometers – the dry and wet bulb thermometers (Fig. 104).

WET BULB TEMPERATURE

The wet bulb temperature is measured by covering a thermometer in a thin muslin sleeve that is kept wet by feeding it from a supply of distilled water. As the humidity of the air falls, the difference between the readings of the dry and wet bulb thermometers (called the 'wet bulb depression') increases. This cooling of the wet bulb thermometer is caused by the evaporation of the water from the muslin sleeve, in much the same way as your wet skin would cool if you let it evaporate to dryness.

The operation of the instruments depends on there being sufficient air movement in the vicinity of the wet bulb to prevent a localized increase in humidity around the bulbs caused by the evaporation. Both thermometers need to be capable of being read to a resolution of 0.1 degrees C in order to determine the relative humidity to within 1 per cent and should ideally be housed in a suitable thermometer screen.

DEW POINT

The dew point is the temperature to which air must be cooled (without changing its pressure or water vapour content) in order for saturation to occur. When this temperature is below 0°C, it is sometimes called the frost point. The dew point depression is the (positive) difference between the dry bulb temperature and the dew point.

The dew point can be measured directly by several kinds of dew point hygrometers or it can (more commonly) be determined indirectly from a psychrometer (that is a dry and wet bulb thermometer pair) – see Table 22.

In thick mist or fog there will be little difference between the dew point, wet bulb and dry bulb temperatures. Since the dew point is a measure of the amount of water vapour in the air, it is often relatively high when the air feels humid.

VAPOUR PRESSURE

In meteorology, the vapour pressure refers to the partial pressure of water vapour in the air, usually expressed in units of millibars (mb) or hectopascals (hPa). At any given temperature there is an upper limit to the amount of water vapour that the air can hold, and hence an upper limit to its vapour pressure – termed the 'saturation vapour pressure'.

Both the vapour pressure and the dew point are indicators of the amount of water vapour that the air holds and, as such, are useful indicators of the air mass type. Unlike the dry bulb temperature, which usually follows a diurnal cycle (cool at dawn and warmer around midday), the vapour pressure and dew point may remain relatively constant during the day unless there is a change of air mass.

RELATIVE HUMIDITY

The relative humidity is the ratio of the amount of water vapour that air holds to the maximum amount that it could hold at its actual temperature and pressure, expressed as a percentage. When the two values are the same, the air is said to be saturated and the relative humidity is 100 per cent. With AWS equipment the relative humidity can be measured without the use of a wet bulb thermometer/sensor.

SETTING UP THE THERMOMETERS

EXPOSURE OF THERMOMETER

Note that the use of the term 'thermometer'

HUMIDITY VARIATIONS DURING THE DAY

On a day with unbroken sunshine the air temperature will, typically, rise from a minimum value close to dawn and reach a maximum value in mid-afternoon, after the sun has reached its highest point in the sky.

If the air mass is unchanged during the day, then the moisture content (and hence the dew point and vapour pressure) of the atmosphere near the surface will vary little at a land-based weather station.

Raising the temperature of the air during the day will mean that it can hold more water vapour before becoming saturated – consequently, the relative humidity (the ratio between the moisture it holds and what it could hold if saturated) will decrease as the temperature rises, and then rise again in the late afternoon and into the evening.

In fact, the relative humidity may reach a peak of about 90 per cent around dawn (unless there is early morning fog – in which case it will be nearer to 100 per cent) and on occasions will fall to 30–50 per cent during mid-afternoon.

This variation in relative humidity is a reason why it is important to observe the humidity at the same time each day (if only one measurement is to be made daily).

HUMIDITY VARIATIONS DURING THE YEAR

Figure 105 shows the variation of temperature and relative humidity averaged over thirty years at 0900 GMT, as recorded at the University of Reading. The dry bulb temperature shows the expected annual variation – warm in summer, cooler in winter. As the air becomes warmer in the summer, more evaporation occurs off nearby seas and so the air tends to hold more water vapour; consequently the dew point also shows an increase towards the summer months.

Since the air tends to be most saturated close to dawn, and since dawn tends to be quite early relative to 0900 GMT in summer (by comparison with winter), the relative humidity tends to be lower in summer at this time. This is also the reason why the number of fogs at this time (and persisting into mid-morning) tends to be much less in summer – the air is relatively drier.

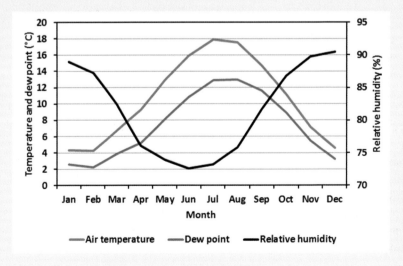

Fig. 105. Illustrating the changes over the year of the 0900 GMT average temperature and humidity elements for the period 1981–2010 at the University of Reading.

here is because, traditionally, both the value of the temperature and the humidity were derived using thermometers. However, the term should be taken to mean whatever instruments are in use at your weather station, be they traditional thermometers or electronic sensors, for measuring temperature and humidity.

Chapter 11 discusses the importance of using a thermometer screen to protect the thermometer from the direct effects of sunshine (and short-wave solar radiation in general) and terrestrial (long-wave) radiation, and from rain and snow.

Significant obstructions, for example buildings, trees and walls, need to be located (ideally) at least twice their height from the thermometer as these can often lead to artificially high readings. Since the air temperature changes with height above the ground, in the UK the thermometer should always be placed in a screen such that the bulb is 1.25m above the ground, while the ground surface underneath the screen should be one of short-cut grass and not bare soil or any form of hardstanding.

URBAN/SUBURBAN SITES

Official weather stations tend to be located in places such as airports or airfields, with the measurements being made in the centre of a large, grass-covered area. Clearly the majority of amateur sites are likely to be in urban or suburban areas, and it is known that urban areas tend to be warmer than rural, greenfield sites.

Indeed, the warming effects of built-up areas have been known for some time[71] – the so-called urban heat island effect. However, it can be argued that a well-exposed back garden site might be more representative of the conditions and climate of that particular town or suburb, and of conditions actually felt by most people. So the enthusiast should not be put off making weather measurements simply because the site is contained within a back garden. More information about urban heat islands can be found on an interesting webpage provided by the Royal Meteorological Society.[72]

WHAT OBSERVATIONS SHOULD BE MADE?

For most amateur observers making a set of observations once (or even a few times) a day, the useful quantities to determine are the daily maximum and minimum temperatures and maybe the air temperature and relative humidity at the observation time. Other quantities can then be derived from these readings. If observations are made once each day, then ideally this should be as close to 0900 GMT (in the UK) as possible, to

---

AIR FROSTS AND ICE DAYS

In addition to keeping a record of the air temperatures, it is interesting to keep a record of the days when the temperature extremes lie within certain ranges. Two useful such measures are those of 'air frost' and 'ice days'.

An air frost is a 24-hour period when the minimum air temperature in the screen falls to $-0.1°C$ or below, while an ice day occurs when the 24-hour period has a maximum air temperature of no more than $-0.1°C$. Ideally these periods should begin at 0900 GMT.

The number of hours of air frost is also a useful quantity to measure – I keep a record of the number of hours each day when the air temperature remains at $-0.1°C$ or below. This can be easily extracted from AWS records or manually from (thermograph) paper chart records.

Other useful daily counts that I keep a record of are those when the minimum temperature remains at 15.0°C or above (a warm night), when the maximum temperature is above 25.0°C (a hot day) or above 30.0°C (a very hot day).

THROWING BACK THE MAXIMUM TEMPERATURE

In the UK, where climatological (once daily) observations are made at 0900 GMT, the maximum temperature reading is 'thrown back' to the previous day. Thus the maximum temperature reading noted on the second of the month is recorded as having occurred on the first. Why?

On most days we would expect the highest temperature to occur in the afternoon, shortly after the sun reaches its peak elevation (and therefore its peak warming capability) in the sky. But this peak temperature value will not be read on the thermometer until the next morning – hence the 'throwing back' to the day on which it probably occurred.

Note the use of the word 'probably' here – in winter a change in air mass type (perhaps from a cold northerly one to a mild southwesterly type) may occur during the hours of darkness, in which case the highest temperature in the twenty-four hours before 0900 GMT may have occurred in the early hours of the current day. Nevertheless, the maximum temperature reading is still thrown back for consistency. To enable comparisons of records to be made it is important that the same convention is used everywhere.

Following a similar argument, the minimum temperature usually occurs shortly after dawn in the UK – so the value as read a few hours later at 0900 GMT is assigned to the day of the reading. In winter, a change in air mass type might mean that the temperature keeps rising overnight and that the 24-hour minimum occurred yesterday. Nevertheless, the minimum temperature is always assigned to the current day.

What if I Make my Daily Observations Later in the Day?
Such a practice is not recommended. Assuming that your observations are made at about the same time each day, decide when the most recent occurrences of 1400 GMT and 'dawn' will have occurred. Then assign your maximum and minimum temperatures to the (possibly different) dates containing these times.

enable comparisons to be made with other stations, both past and present.

If continuous (automatic observations) are made, then values of the air temperature and relative humidity can be found at hourly intervals – or maybe even more frequently.

INSTRUMENTS

Ideally, whatever thermometer you choose to use should be capable of giving you a measurement to a resolution of 0.1 degrees C; if it is a traditional thermometer that means the stem should be graduated every 0.5 degrees C. Two useful concepts to bear in mind when deciding which of a myriad of instruments might suit your purpose are accuracy and precision.

Accuracy is a measure of the overall uncertainty of the value of the quantity being measured. Thus even if a digital thermometer screen provides a measurement to a resolution of 0.1 degrees C, it may still only be accurate to 2 degrees C.

Precision is a guide to the repeatability of the provided measurement for the same real conditions. A precise instrument is one that gives a very similar reading when the same value of the quantity is measured. But a precise instrument can still be inaccurate.

Details of instrument suppliers mentioned in this chapter can be found in the Appendix.

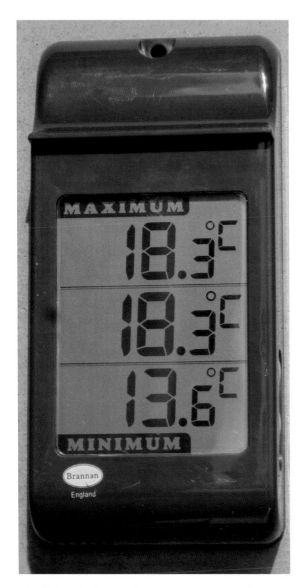

Fig. 106. A simple digital thermometer (from Brannan and Sons), suitable for use with the small, entry-level screen or as a substitute for traditional mercury thermometers.

STAND-ALONE DIGITAL THERMOMETER

Figure 106 shows a simple digital thermometer purchased from Brannan and Sons. The company claims this has an accuracy of 1 degrees C, while the temperature is shown to a resolution of 0.1 degrees C.

Such an instrument would be ideal for the simple, entry-level type of waterproof screen (*see* Chapter 11). The display shows the current temperature, along with the highest and lowest values since the instrument was last reset.

If you have an imperfect exposure for your thermometer, or live in a colder area of the world, make sure that the thermometer will cope with the expected temperature range. The instrument shown in Fig. 106 has a measurement range of −10°C to +40°C and I found that it agrees very well with my traditional thermometer measurements. The company also sells a similar device for measuring relative humidity and temperature.

MINDSETS MINI TEMPERATURE LOGGER

The neat, compact temperature sensor and logger shown in Fig. 107 is available from Mindsets online. This cheap data logger comes in the form of a USB stick, so once the measurements have been made it can be plugged into a computer without the need for cables. The sensor, memory and battery are all enclosed in a single unit, so no additional hardware is required. Mindsets estimate the replaceable battery life at two to three years. The sampling rate can be set between once per second and once every hour; hence the 8,192 sample-size memory can store from two hours to almost a year of data! It is easy to program and comes with free software to enable plotting and archiving of the data.

Figure 108 shows the air temperature recorded by the logger in a large thermometer screen on a hot summer's day in Maidenhead. As can be seen, the agreement with the site's maximum and minimum temperatures (as recorded by traditional thermometers) is very good. Setting the sensor to record every five minutes will give twenty-eight days of data – perfectly adequate to give holiday cover if you are away from your weather station without any other method of recording the extremes of temperature each day.

An interesting study using this instrument can also be found in a 2015 *Weather* article.[73]

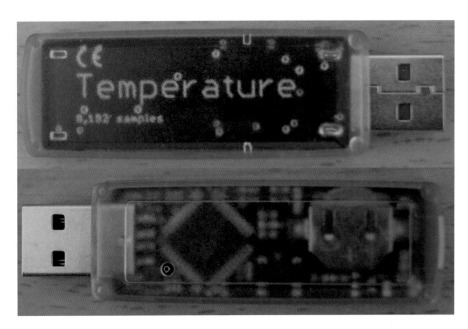

Fig. 107. Illustrating the two sides of a USB-based temperature sensor and logger from Mindsets online.

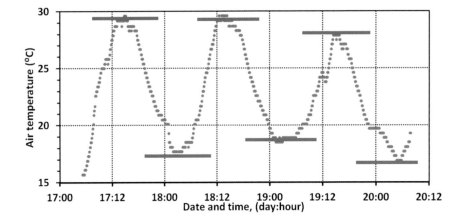

Fig. 108. Shown in red is the air temperature recorded in Maidenhead by a Mindsets temperature sensor and logger every seven minutes during 17–20 July 2014 in a large thermometer screen, with the blue lines showing the limits of the daily air temperature as recorded by standard mercury and alcohol thermometers.

TRADITIONAL DRY AND WET BULB THERMOMETERS

The two vertically hung thermometers in Fig. 104 are the traditional dry and wet bulb thermometers used in the UK. These are mercury thermometers and, consequently, are currently being phased out at official weather stations as observations at such stations are increasingly being automated. Such instruments are known as sheathed thermometers, as the central mercury stem is encased in an outer sheath, except at the bulb.

MAXIMUM AND MINIMUM THERMOMETERS

Sheathed thermometers (the two horizontal thermometers in Fig. 104) are still standard thermometers at non-AWS sites in the UK for recording maximum and minimum air temperatures.

The maximum thermometer is similar to the dry bulb thermometer in that it contains mercury. To the right of the bulb in Fig. 104 there is a small constriction in the stem of the thermometer – this allows the mercury to pass upwards as the temperature rises and the mercury in the thermometer bulb expands; but when the temperature falls, the constriction prevents the mercury from returning back into the bulb – so that the instrument always reads the highest temperature since the instrument was reset.

WIND CHILL

The wind chill or wind chill factor is the apparent temperature felt by humans as a result of wind and low temperatures. Many factors contribute to the level of discomfort felt apart from the meteorological conditions, including the clothing being worn, the body temperature, and the physical fitness and metabolic rate of the person experiencing the chill.

Wind chill is more commonly presented in weather forecasts in North America than in the UK, due to the much lower temperatures that occur there. Wind blowing over the skin causes heat loss and evaporation of any moisture on the skin. Bright sunshine can raise the wind chill temperature.

Several formulae have been proposed to calculate the wind chill. The National Weather Service of the United States currently uses this formula[74] (given in spreadsheet notation):

Chill (°F) = 35.74 + 0.6215 * T – 35.75 * (V^0.16) + 0.4275 * T * (V^0.16)

Here T is the air temperature in °F, V the wind speed in mph. Also, X^Y denotes X raised to the power of Y.

If T is converted to degrees Celsius then the formula becomes:

Chill (°C) = 13.127 + 0.6215 * T – 12.2611 * (V^0.16) + 0.4275 * T * (V^0.16)

Thus, at a temperature of –10°C and a wind speed of 10mph, the wind chill (or 'feels like') temperature is –17°C.

Once the reading of the thermometer has been recorded, it is reset by firmly grasping the instrument (away from the bulb) and swinging it through about 90 degrees vertically. This action (which needs to be carried out carefully to avoid hitting anything and possibly breaking the thermometer) forces the mercury back through the constriction and into the bulb.

The minimum thermometer is identical to the grass minimum sheathed thermometer (see Chapter 13). It is filled with alcohol and is reset by gently tilting the bulb upwards, thereby allowing the index to come to rest against the upper end of the alcohol thread (and not inside the thermometer bulb).

A Quick Thermometer Check

Should the four thermometers shown in Fig. 104 be working correctly, then after being reset the maximum, minimum and dry bulb thermometers should register the same temperature, while the dry bulb and wet bulb thermometers should also agree if the sleeve over the wet bulb is temporarily removed and the bulb allowed to dry. In practice there may be a discrepancy in either case of up to 0.2 degrees C, owing to a combination of instrument errors and/or a slower response time of one thermometer.

SIX'S THERMOMETER

This basic maximum-minimum thermometer consists of a single U-shaped tube (see Chapter 1), the tubes usually being labelled 'min' and 'max'. The bulb at the top of the minimum ('min') reading arm is filled with alcohol; the other contains low-pressure alcohol vapour. In between these two is a column of mercury, although modern versions of the instrument use a mercury substitute.

The minimum and maximum temperatures recorded since the instrument was last reset can be found by noting the value of the temperature scale at the lower end of each of the small magnetic, grey markers.

Before a new maximum or minimum temperature reading can be taken, the thermometer must be reset by moving the magnetic markers so they make contact with the mercury, usually with a small magnet. Any change in temperature after that will move one of the markers. If the temperature rises, the maximum scale marker will be pushed upwards; if it falls, the minimum scale marker will be raised.

A downside of most Six's thermometers purchased in garden centres is that the temperature extremes can only be determined to the nearest 0.5 degrees C rather than the 0.1 degrees C used by professional meteorologists, as the instruments are often designed to operate between −50°C and +50°C. Such temperatures are never approached in the UK in a thermometer screen, in which the instrument should be housed if used for weather observing. Before purchasing the instrument, make sure that both branches of the thermometer show the same temperature.

MASON'S HYGROMETER

Mason's wet and dry bulb hygrometer (see Chapter 1) consists of a dry bulb and a wet bulb thermometer pair (a psychrometer) mounted as one instrument. Humidity is determined in the same manner as with traditional dry and wet bulb thermometers.

If you purchase an instrument of this type, make sure that both thermometers show the same temperature when the wick is dry and the instrument is still in its packaging in the shop. Hopefully, these readings will also agree with those of other identical instruments on the same shop shelf.

Note that a hygrometer is an instrument that is used to measure the moisture content of the air, one such instrument being the dry and wet bulb thermometer pair − otherwise known as a psychrometer.

THERMOHYGROGRAPH, THERMOGRAPH AND HYGROGRAPH

There are several autographic (that is self-recording) instruments that have been (and still are) used by meteorologists to obtain a continuous record of the temperature and relative humidity, namely the thermograph, hygrograph and thermohygrograph (the latter being a combination of the previous two).

Such instruments will generally require housing in a large thermometer screen (see Chapter 11).

A thermohygrograph (see Fig. 109) has instruments and a chart recorder that allow both temperature and relative humidity to be recorded. The temperature sensor consists of a bimetallic strip, fixed at one end to the instrument case, with the other end free to move as the temperature changes and the two metals of the strip expand at different rates. This free end is connected via a system of levers to a pen that draws a trace of the temperature variation on a chart mounted on a drum that rotates, usually once a week.

The humidity sensor operates in a similar way, except that a bundle of human hair is used instead

INSTRUMENT RESPONSE TIMES

Different types of temperature sensor react at different rates to changes in air temperature. In particular, any temperature sensors housed in a screen will also be affected by the amount of air blowing through the screen (the ventilation). The recommendation of the World Meteorological Organization[75] is that temperatures be reported as averages over a one-minute period; such a time period is similar to the response time of a mercury thermometer.

Electrical sensors may respond more rapidly than this, unless they are sheltered inside small, compact AWS screens of the type bought on the high street. Such screens usually contain electrical equipment that provides the wireless transmission of data to an indoor console.

The slower the response time of an instrument-screen system, the lower will be the maximum temperatures recorded and the higher will be the minimum temperatures. One way to minimize such effects is to employ an aspirated screen − see Chapter 11.

Fig. 109. A thermohygrograph showing the relative humidity (red) and temperature (black) pen arms.

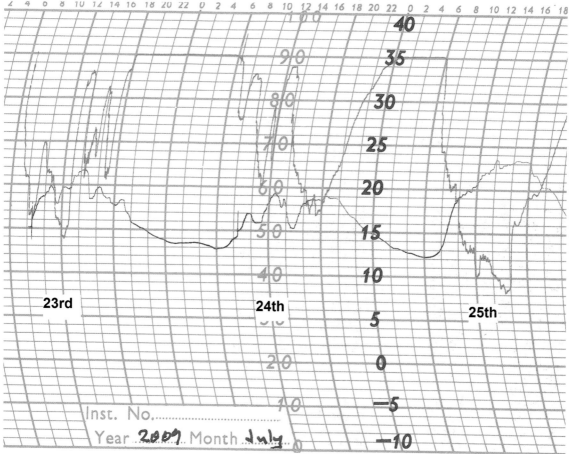

Fig. 110. The Maidenhead thermohygrograph chart for 23–25 July 2009. The red trace (and numerical scale) shows the relative humidity and the black trace (and scale) the air temperature. Note how the humidity peaks at 90 per cent – such instruments are known to have problems in accurately recording saturated or near-saturated air. During both the 23rd and 24th the temperature can be seen to fall sharply by as much as 4 degrees C quite quickly during some heavy and, at times, thundery showers, with the relative humidity rising by up to 40 per cent at the same time.

of the bimetallic strip. Both ends of the bundle are fixed, and any stretching due to humidity changes is amplified by a set of levers and passed to a pen that again draws a trace on the revolving chart. The hairs need to be kept clean from salt, soot and other dirt – and may need replacing at intervals. In any case, they should be cleaned at regular intervals with distilled water.

Unfortunately, the response of the humidity sensor is not particularly accurate at high humidities, while the nature of the hair-based sensor, the small scale of the charts and the backlash in the gearing of the clockwork drum mean that pinpoint measurements are difficult to achieve. In addition, the instrument needs to be kept clean and the clockwork mechanism checked for any fast or slow running (as with any wind-up watch).

MODERN AWS SENSORS

Figure 111 shows the inside of an official UK Met Office screen, containing two sensors that are used to measure the air temperature and relative humidity. These are gradually replacing the manual in-screen observations across the UK, and similar temperature sensors are also being installed (see Chapter 13) to measure surface and soil temperatures. For example, at climatological stations that once provided observations once daily at 0900 GMT, data measurement and collection is now done by the MMS (Meteorological Monitoring System), which uses local data loggers to feed observations into a database at the Met Office's headquarters.

The white probe on the left in Fig. 111 is a capacitor-based humidity sensor, which measures the capacitance of a hygroscopic dielectric material placed between two electrodes. The electrical impedance of the capacitor in a circuit can be measured and this gives, in conjunction with knowledge of the air temperature, the relative humidity. Once saturated, such sensors can take a while to dry out and thus they tend to over-record the incidence of humid conditions.

The silver probe on the right in Fig. 111 is a platinum resistance thermometer used to measure air temperature. The resistance of the platinum sensor varies in a linear way with temperature, meaning that it is quite easy to infer the temperature if the resistance is known very accurately; this variation can be used to generate a voltage that varies with temperature

Fig. 111. The modern AWS probes used at a typical Met Office climatological station to measure relative humidity (on the left) and air temperature (on the right).

in a known way, so measuring the voltage generated by the electrical circuit provides an accurate measure of the air temperature.

DAVIS INSTRUMENTS AUTOMATIC WEATHER STATIONS

Among the Climatological Observers Link amateur observing community, the most popular AWS systems are arguably those manufactured by Davis Instruments, of California. Figure 112 shows a Davis Vantage Pro2 weather station (VP2), which, according to Stephen Burt's review,[76] provides a good measurement of air temperature and adequate measurement of relative humidity.

The VP2, according to the Prodata website,[77] consists of three main components: the indoor console on which all the weather readings are displayed; the anemometer for measuring wind speed and direction; and an assembly known as the Integrated Sensor Suite (ISS) that contains all the other outside sensors, such as those for temperature, humidity, rainfall and so on.

The VP2 uses a naturally ventilated white plastic radiation screen consisting of five 'inverted saucers', inside which are placed the temperature and humidity sensors. This screen is larger in size than many entry-level AWS screens. The sensors are mounted directly below the raingauge but, perhaps surprisingly, this does not appear to affect their performance to any great extent. The output from all the sensors can be displayed on an indoor console, either via cabling or a wireless link.

TINYTAG DATA LOGGERS

Gemini Data Loggers sell a very compact series of data loggers that measure temperature and relative humidity (see also Chapter 13). These need installing in a thermometer screen when used to measure air temperature and/or relative humidity, and come supplied with software to enable downloading of the observations at intervals. Their 'View' range of data loggers includes a small screen to enable viewing of the 'current conditions' – again the data logger contents can be downloaded to a computer at intervals.

Fig. 112.   A Davis Instruments Vantage Pro2 weather station. Note that the black raingauge sits directly above the screen housing the temperature sensor. STEPHEN BURT/CLOUDBANK IMAGES LTD

HUMIDITY CALCULATORS

Nowadays there are several online humidity calculators available, such as the one on Vaisala's website.[78] Alternatively, try programming the formulae on page 132 into your spreadsheet; the uppercase letters/number pairs refer to cells within the spreadsheet, while EXP and LN are the exponential and natural logarithm functions, respectively.

By convention in the UK the relative humidity is calculated with respect to the saturated vapour pressure above a water surface. In addition, the vapour pressure depends upon the latent heat of evaporation of water when the wet bulb temperature is above freezing, but upon the latent heat of sublimation of ice when the wet bulb temperature is below freezing. The relative humidity and dew point should be saved as integers, the vapour pressure (if required) to one decimal place. Goff and Gratch's paper for the American Society of Heating and Ventilating Engineers[79] gives in-depth details.

WET BULB TEMPERATURE 0.0°C OR HIGHER

A1: Dry bulb temperature

A2: Wet bulb temperature

A3: Saturated vapour pressure at the dry bulb temperature = $6.112*EXP((17.67*A1)/(A1+243.5))$

A4: Saturated vapour pressure at the wet bulb temperature = $6.112*EXP((17.67*A2)/(A2+243.5))$

A5: Vapour pressure = $A4-0.799*(A1-A2)$

A6: Dew point = $237.3*(LN(A5/6.11)/17.27)/(1-LN(A5/6.11)/17.27)$

A7: Relative humidity = $100*A5/A3$

WET BULB TEMPERATURE −0.1°C OR LOWER

A1: Dry bulb temperature

A2: Wet bulb temperature

A3: Saturated vapour pressure at the dry bulb temperature = $6.112*EXP((21.87*A1)/(A1+265.5))$

A4: Saturated vapour pressure at the wet bulb temperature = $6.112*EXP((21.87*A2)/(A2+265.5))$

A5: Vapour pressure = $A4-0.720*(A1-A2)$

A6: Dew point = $237.3*(LN(A5/6.11)/17.27)/(1-LN(A5/6.11)/17.27)$

A7: Relative humidity = $100*A5/(6.112*EXP((17.67*A1)/(A1+243.5)))$

DEW POINT LOOKUP TABLE

Table 22 is a quick lookup table for determining the dew point, using measurements of the dry and wet bulb temperature.

Table 22 Dew point temperature (°C) as determined from the dry bulb temperature and the wet bulb depression

The wet bulb depression is how far below the dry bulb temperature the wet bulb temperature lies.

Dew point (°C)

Dry bulb °C	Depression of the wet bulb (degrees C)													
	0.0	0.5	1.0	1.5	2.0	2.5	3.0	4	5	6	7	8	9	10
35	35	34	34	33	32	32	31	30	28	27	25	24	22	20
30	30	29	29	28	27	27	26	24	23	21	19	18	16	13
25	25	24	24	23	22	21	20	19	17	15	13	11	8	6
20	20	19	18	18	17	16	15	13	11	9	6	3	0	−5
15	15	14	13	12	11	10	9	7	4	1	−2	−7	−13	−26
10	10	9	8	7	6	4	3	0	−3	−8	−15	−27		
5	5	4	3	1	0	−2	−4	−8	−14	−19	−43			
0	0	−1	−3	−5	−7	−9	−11	−18	−32					
-5	−6	−7	−10	−12	−15	−18	−23							
-10	−11	−14	−17	−21	−26	−36								

If the dry bulb temperature is 30.0°C and the wet bulb temperature is 28.0°C, then the depression of the wet bulb is 2 degrees C and the dew point is 27°C. To determine intermediate values, simply interpolate between four adjacent boxes. Thus if the dry bulb temperature is 22.0°C and the wet bulb temperature is 17.5°C, then the wet bulb depression is 4.5 degrees C. Looking at the row labelled with a dry bulb reading of 25.0°C, a wet bulb depression of 4.5 degrees C returns a dew point of about 18°C. Likewise, for a dry bulb reading of 20.0°C and a wet bulb depression of 4.5 degrees C, the dew point is about 12°C. Interpolating between these two dew points gives a dew point of about 15°C for a dry bulb temperature of 22.0°C and a wet bulb depression of 4.5 degrees C.

Table 23   Relative humidity as determined from the dry bulb temperature and the wet bulb temperature

The wet bulb depression is how far below the dry bulb temperature the wet bulb temperature lies.

Relative humidity (%)

Dry bulb °C	Depression of the wet bulb (degrees C)													
	0.0	0.5	1.0	1.5	2.0	2.5	3.0	4	5	6	7	8	9	10
35	100	97	93	90	87	83	80	74	68	63	57	52	47	42
30	100	96	93	89	85	82	78	72	65	59	53	47	42	36
25	100	96	92	88	84	80	76	68	61	54	47	41	35	29
20	100	95	91	86	81	77	73	64	56	48	40	33	25	18
15	100	94	89	84	78	73	68	58	49	39	30	21	13	4
10	100	93	87	81	74	68	62	50	39	27	16	5		
5	100	92	84	76	69	61	53	39	24	15	2			
0	100	90	80	71	61	52	43	24	7					
−5	95	83	70	58	46	34	22							
−10	91	74	58	42	25	10								

See Table 22 for an explanation of how to use this table.

RELATIVE HUMIDITY LOOKUP TABLE

The relative humidity can also be determined from the dry and wet bulb temperatures – see Table 23.

ENTRIES IN THE OBSERVATION REGISTER

If single, daily, observations are made then the following columns relating to the air temperature and humidity may appear in the register of observations:

A. Maximum temperature (thrown back if read around 0900 GMT)
B. Minimum temperature
C. Mean temperature: the average of (A) and (B)
D. Diurnal temperature range: (A) − (B)
E. Dry bulb temperature at the daily observation time
F. Wet bulb temperature at the daily observation time
G. Dew point at the daily observation time
H. (Optional) Vapour pressure at the daily observation time
I. Relative humidity at the daily observation time

J. Air frost: enter 1 if (B) is −0.1°C or less; else enter 0
K. Warm nights: enter 1 if (B) is 15.0°C or more; else enter 0
L. Ice days: enter 1 if (A) is −0.1°C or less; else enter 0
M. Hot days: enter 1 if (A) is 25.0°C or more; else enter 0
N. Very hot days: enter 1 if (A) is 30.0°C or more; else enter 0
O. Hours of air frost: the number of hours during 0000–2400 GMT when the air temperature remained below 0.0°C

Note that for (C) and (D) the maximum and minimum values are for each calendar date – and are read on two consecutive days due to the 'throwing back of the maximum value.

At the end of each month, determine the highest, lowest and average of (A) to (I), along with the totals of each of the entries (J) to (O).

If continuous observations are available via an AWS, then a record of the hourly temperature and relative humidity would make a useful addition to the entries listed above. Again, the highest, lowest and average hourly values for the month as a whole could then be determined at the end of the month.

13. SOIL AND SURFACE TEMPERATURES

In addition to measuring air temperatures, many weather stations also record the minimum temperature of the soil surface or at grass-tip level. At official sites the minimum temperature at the centre of a concrete slab is also sometimes recorded.

Why measure these temperatures? Soil temperatures can be related to the growth of plants, the minimum temperature near the surface often being much lower than the minimum air temperature. On a clear night, it is the surface of the ground (or the top of a vegetation layer) that will most rapidly lose its heat, and this cooling is then transferred to the atmosphere in contact with the ground. This loss of surface heat will, partially, also be replaced during the night by heat from the upper layers of the soil (or concrete).

In the case of grass temperatures, the air trapped between the blades of grass will act as a partial insulator to this upward movement of heat. Thus the lowest temperature reached at grass tip level will be lower than that on a bare soil patch or concrete slab.

As with all observations, if a single daily observation is being made then this should be done as close to 0900 GMT as possible. Any minimum temperature measurement should be made after the temperature has fallen to its lowest value, which will usually be close to dawn.

In addition to surface temperature measurements, measurement of the sub-surface soil temperature is also carried out at some weather stations. In the UK, measurements at depths of 5cm, 10cm, 20cm, 30cm, 50cm and 100cm are made at a few sites, while many more sites observe nowadays only at depths of 10cm, 30cm and 100cm. Measurements at depths shallower than 30cm are normally made under a surface of bare soil and are termed 'soil temperatures'; at depths of 30cm and greater the measurements are made under a short, cropped grass surface and are termed 'earth temperatures'. However, for simplicity, both are often called simply 'soil temperatures'.

Ideally soil temperatures should be measured to the nearest 0.1 degrees C for meteorological purposes. This generally means that the thermometer should be marked at 0.5 degrees C intervals.

THE USE OF MERCURY THERMOMETERS

Traditional thermometers used for measuring soil temperatures contain a small amount of mercury and, due to legislation, are generally no longer available for the amateur weather observer to purchase. As a result, nowadays many amateurs are increasingly turning to electronic probes (electrical platinum resistance thermometers, or PRTs) to measure soil temperature, although a few glass stem-type thermometers containing alcohol or other spirit are available. However, the alcohol or spirit thread of such thermometers can break very easily and the thread can then be difficult to re-join.

Minimum temperature thermometers contain alcohol and are not subject to the same restrictions.

SURFACE TEMPERATURE

TERMINAL HOURS

Ground surface temperatures normally fall to their lowest overnight, reaching a minimum close to dawn. Measurements during the day are not representative of conditions at the surface – they may simply be an indication of the fact that the sensor (being made largely of glass or metal) is itself being heated up by the sunshine.

The minimum thermometers are reset at the morning observation time at most amateur sites –

that is close to 0900 GMT. This may mean that, should a very cold night be followed by a mild one in winter, then two consecutive 'nights with ground frost' may be recorded as the grass (and soil) may still be covered by a hoar frost at the earlier obser-

vation time. For this reason, if possible, the surface temperature thermometers should be reset just before the time of the earliest winter sunset – as otherwise early minima just after sunset may go unrecorded.

GROUND FROSTS – GARDENERS BEWARE!

In the British Isles a ground frost is said to occur when the grass minimum temperature falls below 0.0°C. Since the grass minimum temperature is almost always lower than the air temperature, this means that over a year many more ground frosts than air frosts are recorded.

Soil surface and concrete surface frosts occur when the temperature on these surfaces falls below 0.0°C. Table 24 shows the annual statistics of air and surface frosts during the period 1981–2010 recorded at the University of Reading's climatological station in Berkshire. Note that a ground frost was observed in each month of the year during this period, while the months of June to September were entirely free of any air frost. In any autumn–winter–spring period, ground frosts tend to occur earlier in the autumn and later in the spring than air frosts.

The possibility of large differences between the air and grass minimum temperatures needs to be borne in mind by any gardener intent on transplanting seedlings too early in spring. For example, in Reading on 17 March 2003, the minimum air temperature was 4.4°C while that at grass tip level was −10.8°C, a difference of 15.2 degrees C; differences in excess of 5 degrees C are quite common, although extremely large differences are less likely in an urban garden due to the heat from buildings and the shading effect of trees.

Table 24   The variation of minimum temperatures and the incidence of frosts at the University of Reading, Berkshire, 1981–2010

The thermometers used in these observations are reset at 0900 GMT every day of the year.

Month	Average number of air frosts	Lowest air temperature (°C)	Average number of ground frosts	Lowest grass minimum temperature (°C)	Average number of soil surface frosts	Average number of concrete surface frosts
January	9.1	−14.5	19.8	−20.1	16.0	15.2
February	9.3	−11.6	18.0	−16.5	15.2	14.2
March	4.8	−6.4	16.6	−13.2	12.3	10.9
April	2.2	−3.5	14.7	−12.5	8.4	6.2
May	0.2	−2.0	7.2	−9.1	2.9	1.2
June	0	1.5	2.1	−5.7	0.5	0.1
July	0	4.9	0.3	−2.2	0	0
August	0	3.4	0.5	−2.6	0	0
September	0	0.8	3.5	−7.6	0.8	0.2
October	1.1	−4.4	8.4	−12.1	4.1	3.3
November	4.4	−8.3	14.2	−12.7	9.8	8.9
December	9.8	−13.4	18.2	−16.1	15.6	14.9
Year	40.9	−14.5	123.5	−20.1	85.6	75.1

ANTI-CONDENSATION SHIELDS

If alcohol-based surface minimum thermometers are used and are kept outdoors during the day in the sunshine, as is the case at many weather stations, then the temperature recorded can exceed 40°C and an anti-condensation shield should be fitted. Such a temperature represents the temperature of the glass stem of the thermometer rather than anything meteorological. However, it does mean that the thermometer should be capable of measuring temperatures from around −30°C to +50°C.

An anti-condensation shield is a black metal covering that is placed around the high-temperature end of the thermometer, with a cotton sleeve between the thermometer and the shield. This shield will absorb more heat from the sun than the low-temperature end of the thermometer, meaning that any alcohol vapour that may have been evaporated off the alcohol thread is prevented from condensing here − instead it will (hopefully) condense back on to the alcohol thread.

GRASS MINIMUM TEMPERATURE

Traditional, Sheathed Thermometer

In the UK the grass minimum temperature is traditionally measured using a thermometer with a thread comprised of alcohol, rather than mercury. The thermometer (Fig. 113) is contained within a glass sheath and has a small, dumb-bell shaped index inside the alcohol thread that is used to record the minimum temperature (Fig. 114). As the temperature falls, the index is pushed down towards the bulb, remaining at its lowest position as the temperature later rises. The position of the index further from the bulb indicates the lowest temperature reached. After noting the minimum temperature, the thermometer is reset by tilting the bulb upwards, thereby allowing the index to come to rest against the upper end of the alcohol thread once more.

To prevent the thermometer from being disturbed, and also to prevent the index from sliding

Fig. 113. **Grass minimum thermometer. This is placed with the bulb slightly raised above the level of the grass tips. The black cover at the high temperature end of the thermometer is an anti-condensation shield that must be fitted if the instrument is to be kept in the sunshine all day. Except for the shield, the thermometer is identical to the one used to record air temperatures inside a thermometer screen.**

Fig. 114. **A close-up view of a sheathed grass minimum thermometer. The actual thermometer is held inside a glass jacket sheath and the contraction of the alcohol column**

on cooling overnight causes the small, black index within the stem of the thermometer to descend (to the left as shown). The current reading of the thermometer is 4.5°C while the minimum temperature since the instrument was last reset is 2.6°C.

back down away from the bulb, the instrument is normally placed upon a couple of wooden pegs or a rubber rest so that the thermometer tilts at an angle of about 2 degrees down towards the bulb.

The same type of thermometer, without any anti-condensation shield, is used inside a thermometer screen to measure the minimum air temperature (Chapter 12).

Modern Grass Minimum Sensor

In the UK, when modern AWS systems are in use, the observation of the grass (and other surface) temperatures is made by means of an electrical sensor probe (Fig. 115). These are exposed throughout the day, with the minimum temperature being that observed during the period 1800–0900 GMT at official weather stations.

BARE SOIL AND CONCRETE MINIMUM THERMOMETERS

Concrete minimum temperatures are recorded at official weather stations as they give an indication of the incidence of freezing conditions on roads or pavements.

Identical instruments to those in use for grass minimum temperatures are used to measure the minimum temperatures reached on a bare soil surface or a concrete surface. Again, the thermometers should be placed with a 2-degree tilt, being held in place by rubber or wooden mounts.

In practice, few amateur observers measure concrete minimum temperatures, although if these are measured then the concrete slab should measure about 90cm by 60cm, and be 5cm thick. The surface should lie level with the adjacent ground. Bare soil temperatures should be recorded on a plot of bare soil that is sufficiently large that the effects of any neighbouring grassed areas will not affect your measurements – ideally in a square of bare soil with sides of at least 2m in length.

SURFACE MINIMUM TEMPERATURE AND FALLS OF SNOW

When snow covers the grass minimum thermometer, it should be placed above the snow (but not in contact with it) by placing wooden pegs or rubber supports beneath it (but not touching the bulb). This should be done as soon as the snowfall has ceased or, at the very least, at the morning observation time.

When snow covers the bare soil surface, the soil minimum thermometer should be set on top of the snow layer as soon as possible after the snow covers the thermometer.

Fig. 115. The grass minimum temperature probe used at the University of Reading as part of the Met Office's set of instruments for climatological observations.

If snow falls and covers the concrete slab, then the slab should be swept clear of the snow (without disturbing the index of the thermometer) – and the concrete minimum thermometer replaced on the slab. At the very least this procedure should be carried out at the observation time.

If any of the thermometers is found to be buried under lying snow at the observation time then it should be read as normal, re-laid as indicated above, and a note made in the observation register.

SOIL TEMPERATURES

SEASONAL AND DIURNAL VARIATION OF SOIL TEMPERATURE

At weather stations on land, the daytime solar radiation is absorbed by the soil surface; some of this heat is then conducted downwards into the soil. During the night, under clear skies, the surface of the soil cools, and heat is then conducted upwards from the deeper soil.

A result of this is that the soil temperature varies most at, and just below, the surface (for example at a depth of 5cm), while at greater depths (30cm, for example) the variation is much less.

Figure 116 shows the monthly averaged soil temperature in Maidenhead at 0700 GMT; at a depth of 5cm the mean temperature varies by about 13 degrees C through the year, but at 100cm the variation is only 10.6 degrees C. The figure also shows that although the longest and shortest periods of daylight occur in June and December, the highest and lowest soil temperatures occur about two months later – in late July–August and February.

On a sunny summer's day, the temperature at a depth of 5cm under bare soil can vary by 30 degrees C or more during the day, while at 100cm depth the variation is normally less than 0.2 degrees C. On such a day the 5cm temperature reaches a maximum during mid- to late afternoon, while the temperature at a depth of 30cm will peak much closer to midnight; at 50cm the highest temperature will be reached early the following morning as the some of the heat from the sunshine of the previous day finally conducts down to that depth. At a depth of 100cm the diurnal cycle is barely discernible. An example of some of these variations (in this case under grass) can be seen in Fig. 117.

Unless an AWS is used to measure the soil temperature, in which case the temperature may be determined at specific times of day (along with

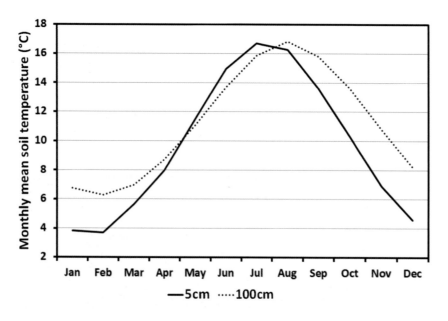

Fig. 116. The annual cycle of monthly mean soil temperatures at 0700 GMT recorded in Maidenhead during 1981–2010. The temperature at a depth of 100cm (dotted line) varies less than that at a depth of 5cm. However, at this time of day the temperature at a depth of 5cm is close to its minimum value – later in the day the differences between the two curves would be much larger.

Fig. 117. Illustrating the diurnal variation of soil temperature at 10, 20, 30, 50 and 100cm at the University of Reading during a sunny day in late May 2015. All measurements were made by electronic probes under a grass-covered surface and observations are shown every five minutes.

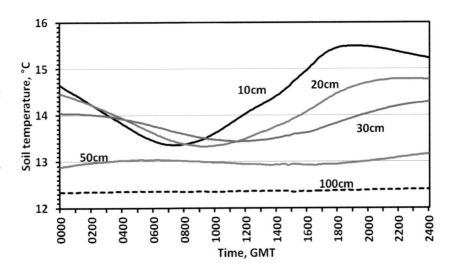

maximum and minimum values), it is important to measure the soil temperature as close as possible to the same time each morning. This is especially true for temperatures measured at depths of less than 20cm under bare soil: shortly after dawn, the temperature here can change quickly as the soil begins to warm up in the sunshine after cooling down during the night.

THERMOMETERS FOR USE AT DEPTHS OF LESS THAN 30CM

The traditional instrument used for measuring the soil temperature at depths of 5cm, 10cm and 20cm in the UK is shown in Fig. 118. This is an ordinary thermometer (without any surrounding glass sheath) with a 90 degree bend in the stem. The length of the short, vertical part of the thermometer corresponds to the depth at which the temperature is

measured while the horizontal part lies flat on the ground surface so that the temperature scale along it can be read.

These thermometers are installed in a plot of bare soil. Any cracks in the soil around the thermometer should be removed, while the surface soil is still crumbly, by pushing soil into the cracks. This will prevent water draining into cracks close to the bulb, which might lead to spurious readings. Care should be taken in this procedure, as the thermometers are very fragile at the 90 degree bend.

In addition, it is advisable to insert a couple of wooden pegs into the ground either side of the thermometer at the high-temperature end of the thermometer stem. This will prevent the thermometer from rotating over the soil about the 90 degree bend – something which can lead to the thermometer breaking here, at its weakest point.

Fig. 118. A right-angled soil thermometer used to measure the temperature at a depth of 5cm.

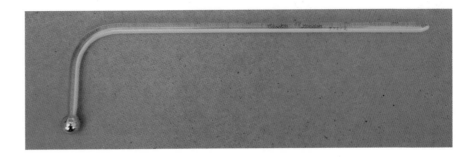

THERMOMETERS FOR USE AT DEPTHS OF 30CM OR MORE

In the UK soil temperatures are also measured at depths of 30cm, 50cm and 100cm, using so-called earth thermometers as shown in Fig. 119, which are suspended in steel tubes buried under a grass surface. The thermometers are enclosed in a glass sheath with their bulbs embedded in wax to prevent them from being affected by sudden external temperature changes – as might occur when they are lifted out of their tubes at observation times into bright sunshine. Temperatures at these depths only change slowly and the presence of the wax does not affect the response of the thermometer to changes in temperature.

Water must be kept out of the tubes by using a cap, as shown in Fig. 119, secured to the top of the thermometer; these caps then fit over the top of the steel tubes when the thermometer is inserted. These thermometers are named Symons-pattern earth thermometers as they are based on a design first proposed by George Symons in the 1870s.[80] Nowadays there is a trend towards replacing the steel tubes with plastic ones, for use with the 30cm depth thermometers, at official sites. This is because a metal tube may conduct heat from the surface on

ABOVE: **Fig. 120. Close-up of the lower end of an earth thermometer showing the wax that covers the thermometer bulb.**

LEFT: **Fig. 119. The soil thermometers and the type of steel tube used by for recording temperatures at a depth of 30cm. To measure the temperature at depths of 50cm and 100cm, longer tubes are used and the thermometers are suspended from their caps on longer chains. Note the flange on the metal tube, which ensures that the required depth is obtained, provided that the flange rests tightly on the grass surface.**

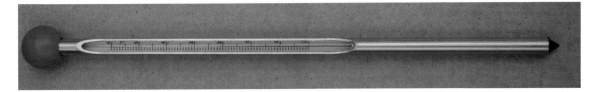

Fig. 121.   A red spirit thermometer suitable for immersion at 10cm depth – that is, the distance from the black tip to the visible glass thermometer stem is 10cm.

a sunny day, downwards to the thermometer bulb, and give a spuriously high temperature reading.

When installing a Symons-pattern steel tube into the ground, care needs to be taken to ensure that the soil is disturbed as little as possible. Try to insert the tube by removing a small-diameter column of soil from the ground, into which the tube is then inserted vertically, before replacing any of the soil around the tube in the reverse order to which it was extracted. This process is quite easy if you are installing a 30cm tube but rather more difficult for a 100cm one. Using an auger may help (available at some hire shops) to avoid disturbing too much of the surrounding soil – as may be done if you dig a hole with a spade.

ALTERNATIVE INSTRUMENTS FOR MEASURING SOIL TEMPERATURES

Figures 121 and 122 show a non-mercury (red spirit) thermometer available from Russell Scientific, suitable for use at depths of up to 30cm. These are reasonably priced and are designed to be read while still inserted into the soil, but the stem temperatures are marked only every 1 degree C.

Care needs to be taken to ensure that the immersion depth into the soil is maintained as there is no flange along the stem to prevent it from sinking further into wet or muddy soil. The stem does protrude some 5–10cm above the ground, so at shallow depths it is possible that the weight of this part of the thermometer may cause the whole thermometer to tilt slightly away from the vertical should the soil become soft after rain. Since much of the stem is made of metal, this also begs the question as to whether the readings of the soil temperature will be on the high side, due to the conduction of heat down the stem – particularly as the upper part will become very warm in strong sunshine.

Fig. 122.   A red spirit thermometer inserted in the ground to a depth of 10cm.

AUTOMATIC WEATHER STATIONS AND PLATINUM RESISTANCE THERMOMETERS

Entry-level AWS systems usually do not allow the user to measure surface and soil temperatures although the Davis Vantage Pro2 does offer this option. However, one of the problems in using electrical probes is that they may need replacing at intervals of a few years and this will mean disturbing the soil layers. With traditional earth thermometers the thermometer tubes will last for at least a couple of decades and a faulty thermometer can be replaced without digging up the metal containing tube.

In addition, care needs to be taken when digging a trench to install deep soil instruments – if the soil is disturbed too much then it may well be unrepresentative of the surrounding soil layers, and any significant disturbance may mean it could take several days (at least) for the soil temperature profile to settle down to 'normal' values.

For the user who is interested in measuring soil temperatures at depth, or even surface temperatures (such as the grass minimum temperature), then a Gemini Data Loggers Tinytag data logger and temperature probe (Fig. 123) might be a solution. However, the data logger needs to be protected from the elements, as for both types of measurements it will need to be located outdoors and outside of the thermometer screen. One option for earth temperatures is to install the probe in a conventional metal thermometer tube and to protect the logger from the surface elements[80] – although heat will be conducted down the tube (as is the

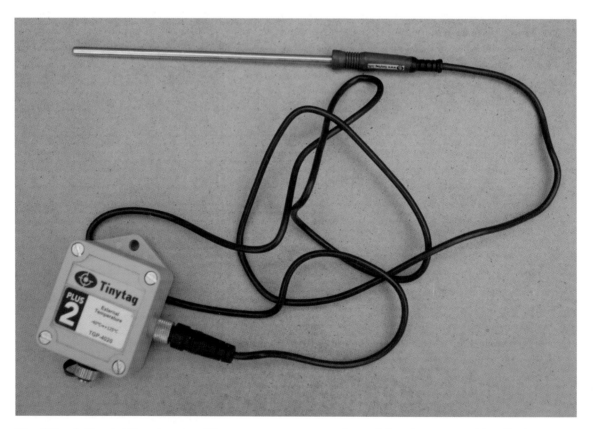

Fig. 123.   A Gemini Data Loggers Tinytag temperature probe and data logger capable of being used to measure either surface minimum temperatures or soil temperatures down to a depth of 30cm (by virtue of the length of the cable).

case with traditional earth thermometers) leading to temperatures being lower in winter and higher in summer.

ENTRIES IN THE OBSERVATION REGISTER

If surface temperature measurements are made of the grass, concrete or bare soil, then the daily minimum values of these readings (made as close as possible to 0900 GMT) should be recorded.

In addition, a single column for each of these measurements should be filled with either '1' or '0', indicating the presence or absence of 'frost' (ground, concrete or bare soil), respectively. Note that such indicators should only be used when the corresponding surface minimum temperature is recorded; do not simply count the number of mornings with 'hoar frost seen' as a proxy for ground frost, as the former may be dependent, for example, upon the presence of early-morning sunshine prior to the observation time.

The in-soil measurements to be recorded in the weather register simply consist of (ideally) the 0900 GMT values (or the values at the morning observation time) of the temperatures at depths of 5cm, 10cm, 20cm under a bare soil surface, and at depths of 30cm, 50cm and 100cm under a grass-covered surface. Of course, not all these measurements will be made at all sites; indeed, at some sites the ground may be too rocky and the surface soil too shallow to permit measurements at any great depth.

At the end of the month, the daily average of all surface minimum and in-soil temperatures, along with the highest and lowest values of the daily readings, should be determined. The number of frosts can also be calculated.

Records made with an AWS might include hourly values each day, along with the daily maximum and minimum values. Then each of these hour-specific values can be averaged at the end of the month to give an interesting illustration of the variation in the diurnal temperature cycle with depth.

14. EVAPORATION

Evaporation is an important process in the global water cycle. Solar radiation passes downwards through the atmosphere and reaches the earth's surface, where it warms the surface of the water or land, resulting in evaporation of water into the atmosphere.

As the air temperature increases so does the process of evaporation; warming the air enables it to hold more water vapour than cooler air. Clearly the humidity of the air adjacent to the earth's surface will also have an effect on the evaporation rate – if the air is dry (less humid) then it is able to accept a greater quantity of water vapour before becoming saturated, and the evaporation rate may consequently be higher.

An increase in wind speed at the surface can also lead to an increase in evaporation as the wind removes evaporated liquid away from the earth's surface – thereby reducing the water content of the lowest layer of the atmosphere and allowing further evaporation to occur.

There are two instruments that are sometimes used to measure evaporation at weather stations, namely the Piché evaporimeter and the evaporation tank. The former is kept inside a thermometer screen while the latter is buried into the earth's surface.

Consequently, the former gives an indication of the dryness (or humidity) of the air at head height over a period of time, while the latter gives an idea of the evaporation occurring off a body of water such as a lake or pond. Neither of these is the same as the evapotranspiration – which is the process by which water is transferred from the land to the atmosphere, both by evaporation from the soil and by transpiration from plants.

DETERMINING EVAPOTRANSPIRATION

Evapotranspiration can be determined by direct measurement or by calculation. To measure evapotranspiration directly a lysimeter is used, in which

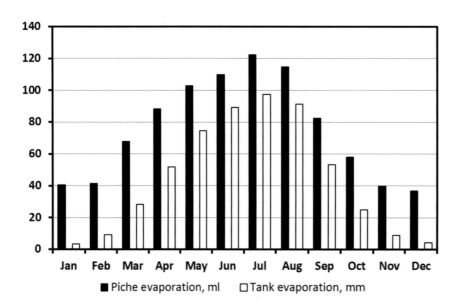

Fig. 124. Average evaporation totals recorded over thirty years at the University of Reading's weather station. White bars show the evaporation (mm) as measured by an evaporation tank while the black bars show the evaporation (ml) as measured by a Piche evaporimeter.

a crop grows in an isolated tank filled with soil. By weighing the tank and accounting for any rainfall and water drainage out of the tank, the amount of water lost by evapotranspiration can be determined.

Owing to the difficulty of obtaining accurate field measurements, evapotranspiration is commonly computed from observed weather data, using a formula. Nowadays the Penman-Monteith method[81] is often recommended as the standard method for the definition and computation of the potential evapotranspiration – that is the evapotranspiration that would occur in ideal conditions if the supply of water was not restricted in any way. Clearly, if the soil is dry then the actual evapotranspiration will be less than this potential value. Some AWS systems are programmed to determine potential evapotranspiration using this method (for example the Davis Vantage Pro2[82]).

Evaporation from an open water surface provides a measure of the combined effects of radiation, air temperature, air humidity and wind on evaporation. However, differences between a water surface and a cropped ground surface mean that there are significant differences in the water loss from an open water surface and a crop.

VARIATIONS IN THE ANNUAL EVAPORATION CYCLE

How much evaporation might be expected to occur? Figure 124 shows the average monthly evaporation measured in Reading over a period of thirty years. Both the tank and evaporimeter water losses reach a peak in the summer months when the air is warmer and the relative humidity tends to be lower. Given that the rainfall in Reading tends to average about 50–55mm in each month of the year, the tank evaporation rate tends to exceed the rainfall from late April to early September.

There is a large variation in the evaporation total for any particular month from year to year. During a very warm summer month Reading might be expected to lose as much as 150mm of water due to evaporation from the tank (or about three times the expected rainfall); daily evaporation rates in

the summer in Reading have occasionally exceeded 10mm in a single day.

Northern parts of the UK will, by virtue of their lower temperatures, experience less evaporation than Reading. During cold spells, when a layer of ice might form on the evaporation tank and then persist for several days, the evaporation rate will be almost nothing.

INSTRUMENTS FOR MEASURING EVAPORATION

PICHE EVAPORIMETER

According to Donald Perkins, the Piche evaporimeter was invented by Albert Piche, an administrative official in the Prefecture de Pau.[83] He carried out various scientific experiments in his spare time and his evaporimeter was one of several instruments that he invented.

The Piche evaporimeter consists of an inverted, graduated cylinder that is open at the lower end when installed in the thermometer screen. It is filled with distilled or purified water (to prevent the build-up, over time, of impurities dissolved in the water). The lower, open end of the cylinder is closed with a 2cm diameter sheet of filter paper held in place by a metal clip. The water in the cylinder evaporates from the filter paper and the level of the water in the cylinder therefore falls over time.

Daily measurements of the level of the water in the cylinder are made at the same time each day (ideally at or close to 0900 GMT in the UK). The difference in the water levels between two consecutive days is noted – this is the daily evaporation amount, and is credited to the earlier of the two days.

When the water level in the tube becomes low, the tube must be refilled and a note made of the water level after refilling. The occurrence of air frost may freeze the water in the tube, pushing the paper and the clip off the tube. When frozen, the filter paper may dry out as the 'water supply' turns to ice. If water in the glass tube starts to freeze then it is best to remove the instrument and discard

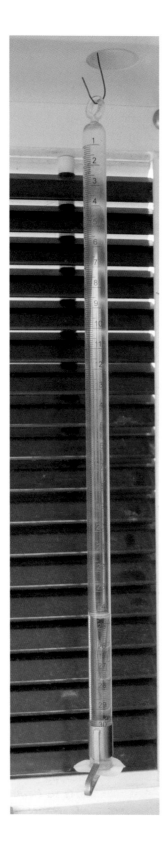

Fig. 125. A Piche evaporimeter inside a thermometer screen.

the reading for that day – to prevent the glass tube from cracking, as may happen in a severe frost.

STANDARD EVAPORATION TANK

The UK British Standard tank consists of a large metal tank, sunk into the ground so that the water level is at about the same level as the ground surface (Fig. 126). The water level is measured each day at 0900 GMT using a hook gauge (Fig. 127) and the difference between the readings over twenty-four hours (after making allowance for any rainfall over this period) gives the evaporation for the earlier of the two days.

If the water level drops then it may become necessary to partially fill the tank with water. Care must also be taken not to overfill it as a heavy fall of rain may cause the tank to overflow and an evaporation calculation will then be impossible; during periods of heavy rainfall it may become necessary to empty the tank partially.

If the water surface freezes then daily measurements become impossible. However, once the surface turns to liquid water again the evaporation over the intervening (frozen) period can be determined.

Fig. 126. The British Standard evaporation tank at the University of Reading, showing the hook gauge, in the foreground, resting on the still well. The tank measures 1.8m along each side, making it too large for many weather stations.

ENTRIES IN THE
OBSERVATION REGISTER

If a Piche evaporimeter is used, then keep a note of the actual reading of the instrument (along with the level after any refilling) and also the calculated 24-hour evaporation.

If evaporation is measured using a tank, then keep a note of the actual reading, the rainfall since the previous reading, and the calculated 24-hour evaporation.

If evapotranspiration is derived using AWS software, then a note should be kept of the daily values, and perhaps also the hourly evapotranspiration values.

At the end of each month, the daily values should be summed to give a monthly total (along with the monthly totals of the evapotranspiration amounts for each hour of the day if these are available).

Fig. 127. A hook gauge of the type used to measure the water level in an evaporation tank. The three arms support the instrument on the still well. The hook is lowered to below the water surface and then raised so that the tip of the hook just breaks the water surface, before the depth measurement is taken using a scale on the stem.

15. INSTRUMENTAL OBSERVATIONS OF THE WIND

Accurate and representative instrumental observations of wind using an anemometer are particularly difficult for the amateur meteorologist to achieve, chiefly because wind is the most variable of those weather elements that an amateur observer might wish to measure. This variation is largely due to turbulent nature of the wind itself; the speed of the wind can halve or double within a few seconds while the direction can change by 180 degrees (for example from southeast to northwest) within a minute.

The World Meteorological Organization[84] specifies that wind measurements should be made at a height of 10m above the ground, in an open, level location. At official sites wind measurements are normally made on a mast or tower. The turbulent effects of upwind obstacles (trees or buildings, for example) can be felt as much as fifteen times the height of the obstacle downwind – meaning that there should ideally be no significant obstacles within at least 100m of the wind mast.

Part of the variation in the wind can be due to the exposure of the recording instruments. As a student in London with the college wind vane perched on the top of a ten-storey tower, I remember how, under windy conditions, the turbulence caused by the presence of this tower rising into the atmosphere above the roofline of the adjacent buildings caused the wind vane to continue to spin through a full 360 degrees, time after time, in windy conditions. Only by recording the observations on a chart could any true direction be determined.

At official weather stations an anemometer will be specified as having an 'effective height' – which might indicate that the instrument exposure falls short of being ideal. Wind speed measurements made at a non-standard height can be corrected to a standard height using a simplified form of the Hellmann equation;[85] this indicates, for example, that the mean wind speeds at heights of 1m, 2m and 5m are, respectively, 0.73, 0.78 and 0.88 times the wind speed at a height of 10m. It must be stressed that these heights are 'effective heights'; an anemometer in a back garden just 2m above the ground might record even lower speeds due to the surrounding urban housing and tall garden trees: the effective height will be lower than 2m in this case.

In view of this difficulty, many amateur observers opt to estimate measurements of wind speed following the guidelines shown in Chapter 4.

SOME DEFINITIONS

As a consequence of the rapidly changing nature of the wind, any measurement will depend upon the period of time over which it is made. In particular, in the UK the wind speed and direction are usually taken as the vector average values over a ten-minute period.

The value of a gust, according to the World Meteorological Organization.[84] is the running mean of the observed wind speed over three seconds. This means that rapid sampling of AWS wind equipment is needed to measure gust values. Wind gusts should never be corrected for height.

In determining a vector average, the magnitude of the vector is represented by the wind speed observation, while the direction observations are used for the orientation. The vectors are broken down into two perpendicular components, which are then averaged separately over a period of time. The resulting average speed and direction are then calculated from these averaged components.

MEASUREMENTS

Typically, wind measuring instruments used by amateur observers comprise of one or more of the following:

- A wind vane for determining the wind direction
- A cup anemometer mounted on a mast for measuring the wind speed
- A hand-held wind speed measuring device

Wind measurements will include one or more of the following:

- Wind speed
- Wind direction
- Wind gust

At most amateur sites these observations will refer to the time at which observations are made; where automatic logging equipment is available, then, say, an hourly record for each calendar day (the 24-hour period commencing 0000 GMT) may also be kept – as all three of these wind measurements can vary considerably during the day (see Fig. 128). In particular, the wind speed often reaches a minimum around dawn and a maximum during mid-afternoon – typically, winds are also gustier during the day than at night.

Both these variations are due to the role played by the sun's heating during the day, which causes increased vertical motion in the lowest part of the atmosphere and can also bring down higher speed air from aloft. Winds are usually strongest in the winter, when high and low pressure systems are strongest and horizontal pressure gradients are greatest.

STARTING SPEEDS

Wind speed is normally measured by a cup anemometer consisting of three or four cups, conical or hemispherical in shape, mounted symmetrically about a vertical spindle. As the wind blows into the cups the spindle rotates. In standard instruments the design of the cups is such that the rate of rotation is very close to being proportional to the speed of the wind.

Modern instruments tend to be quite light and a wind speed of about 1 knot (see Chapter 4 for an explanation of the units) is usually sufficient to cause the cups to rotate. Older instruments (for example, see Fig. 129) tended to be of a heavier, more solid,

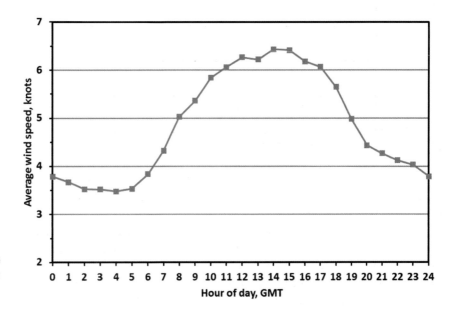

Fig. 128. The average variation in wind speed during the day at a height of 10m at the University of Reading during 2013.

Fig. 129. An older type of anemometer. The cups of the instrument and movement of the wind vane each produce an electrical signal, which are then passed down a cable to a dial (not shown) on which the wind speed and direction are indicated. The wind vane measures about 1m from tip to tip and the equipment has to be mounted on a sturdy steel pole.

design and sometimes required a wind speed of 5 knots or more before the cups rotated. This can have a significant effect upon the resulting winds recorded over a period of time, as in the not-so-windy parts of the UK such values are often close to the prevailing speed – see Fig. 130, for example.

In addition, these older, heavier cup anemometers had a large inertia that made them slow to respond when the wind speed either increased or decreased.

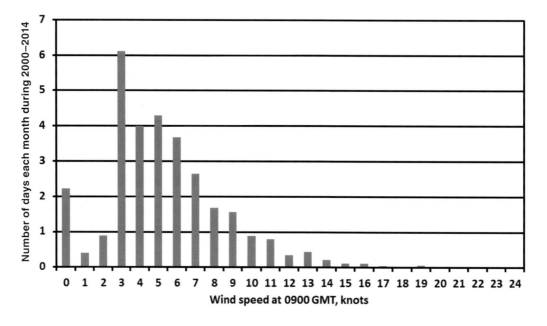

Fig. 130. The wind speed distribution at the University of Reading during 2000–2014 at 0900 GMT. Winds at this time are most frequently observed to be in the range 4–6 knots (on about fourteen days each month) while speeds in excess of 12 knots are rare (occurring one day each month on average at this time). Reading is an inland site – at weather stations close to the coast in exposed locations wind speeds will be higher.

INSTRUMENTS

WIND VANE

Wind direction (that is the direction from which the wind blows) is measured by a vane consisting of a thin horizontal arm carrying a vertical flat plate at one end with its edge to the wind, and at the other end a balancing weight that also serves as a pointer. The arm is carried on a vertical spindle mounted on bearings, which allows it to turn freely in the wind.

Any wind vane must be sensitive so that it correctly shows the direction of all but the very lightest winds and it must be accurately balanced so that it does not have a preferential direction. The vane must be located so that it is not affected by eddies caused by nearby buildings, trees and obstacles; nor must it be influenced by channelling of the wind, as may occur between adjacent buildings.

Any wind vane used to determine the wind direction must be aligned to true north, and not to magnetic north.

HAND-HELD CUP ANEMOMETER

Wind vanes are normally mounted in a permanent position, while wind speed is sometimes measured using a hand-held instrument. The problem with hand-held instruments is that the instrument must be held above head height when the wind speed is measured, meaning that the measurements are taken at heights well below the 'effective' 10m height – especially so if the instruments are used in a sheltered back garden site.

Fig. 131. A hand-held cup anemometer. The current speed is shown on a series of scales found inside the plastic cover. The observer must watch one of these scales and mentally average the wind speed over the observing period, which is usually between 30 and 60 seconds.

Figure 131 shows an example of a hand-held cup anemometer. This needs to be held above head height with the speed scale visible to the observer. With practice an observer can determine the average wind speed over a period of 1–2 minutes – but it becomes tiring if the instrument is held for longer than this.

HAND-HELD VANE ANEMOMETER

The Kestrel vane-type anemometer shown in Fig. 132 is another type of portable instrument that must be held above head height when used. It is quite sensitive in light wind speeds and can be set to show the current, average or maximum wind speed. The latter cannot be taken to be the maximum wind gust; nevertheless the calculation of the average speed by the instrument is more accurate than watching a dial for a period of time and then mentally averaging the observed speeds.

Fig. 133. A cup counter anemometer. As the cups of the anemometer rotate, the run of wind (a distance measurement) is displayed by the counter in a window at the bottom of the instrument.

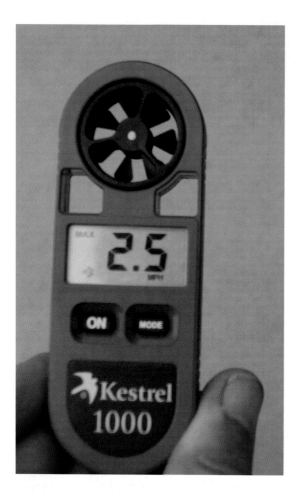

Fig. 132. A Kestrel 1000 vane-type anemometer. To obtain accurate readings the anemometer must be aimed so that the wind blows perpendicularly into the vane. An advantage is that the average wind speeds can be displayed on the small screen.

RUN OF THE WIND

An alternative measure of the wind speed (used by a 'cup counter anemometer', Fig. 133) is the 'run of wind'. Over twenty-four hours, the mean wind speed (in metres per second) is the run of wind (in kilometres) divided by 86,400 (the number of seconds in a day) and then multiplied by 1,000 (to convert km/s into m/s).

TEN-METRE (OR ROOFTOP) WINDS

At amateur weather stations it is rare to be able to mount wind vanes or anemometers at a height of 10m. A glance at Fig. 134 reveals how much of an eyesore such a tower could be in an urban environment! In practice, amateur anemometers will be mounted just 1–2m above the roof ridge of the observer's house, with (nowadays) a wireless connection to an indoor console display and data logger.

Burt[86] provides some guidance on the installation of masts and anemometers, including advice on planning permission, which may be required for masts or towers.

In fact many modern AWSs designed for the amateur are made with short cables connecting all the measuring devices, so that the anemometer has

Fig. 134. An example of a 10m-tall wind tower, this one being at the University of Reading, with a cup anemometer and wind vane at the top. Also shown are cup anemometers at heights of 5m and 2m.

to be sited close to the raingauge or thermometer screen (see Fig. 102 in Chapter 11). If the site exposure is sufficiently good (for example a large garden without hedges or solid fences) then the anemometer may be used to derive a 2m run of wind type of measurement. But a better approach would be to buy a system where the anemometer observations are transmitted, wirelessly, to a data logger and console – as can be done with the Davis Vantage Pro2 system, for example.

Fig. 135. A Vector Instruments lightweight A101M anemometer. The third cup is hidden behind the spindle.

Modern AWS cup anemometers (Fig. 135) and wind vanes (Fig. 136) are lightweight and have a low starting speed.

These cup anemometers convert the rotation of the shaft of the instrument into a pulse count for processing by a data logger. Older, heavier instruments contained a small dynamo that generated a continually varying voltage or, as in the case of the 'run of wind' indicator shown in Fig. 133, used a system of mechanical gears to produce a distance count – rather like the odometer in a car. It was these internal workings that made for a rather heavy instrument and one that was slow to start moving at low wind speeds.

Modern wind vanes are very light due to their use of modern electronics. An electrical potentiometer grid located under the vane allows the direction of the pointer to be accurately sensed and converted into a digital signal.

For the amateur a light wind vane and cup anemometer also has practical advantages; it need not be mounted on a sturdy, vertical steel pole and, should it be mounted above the rooftop and suddenly develop a fault, then taking it down should be an easy task – as long as somebody holds the ladder for you!

Fig. 136.   The wind-measuring equipment of a Davis Vantage Pro2 weather station.
STEPHEN BURT/CLOUDBANK IMAGES LTD

ENTRIES IN THE OBSERVATION REGISTER

At weather stations where a single daily observation is made, the following can be noted each day if they are available:

A. Wind direction (degrees) at the observation time; a calm is registered as 0 degrees
B. Wind speed (knots) at the observation time
C. Maximum wind gust (knots) for the period 0000–2400 GMT of the previous day
D. The mean daily wind speed converted from a 'run of the wind' measurement. This usually covers the 24-hour period between successive morning observation times.

In addition, a note can be made of wind speed and direction at hourly intervals (or even more frequently) if automatic weather observations are available, as these will reveal the diurnal cycle of the wind, for example.

At the end of the month the average of each of (B), (C) and (D) can be calculated, along with the highest and lowest values of these observations. The monthly wind direction can be summarized by counting the number of observations with particular wind directions, as shown in Table 25. Such an analysis might explain why the month was mild (lots of southerly winds) or cool (more northerly winds than normal) in the UK.

Table 25 Converting wind direction (degrees) into the eight main compass points	
Direction range (degrees)	**Wind direction (compass point)**
Calm	Calm
23–67	Northeast
68–112	East
113–157	Southeast
158–202	South
203–247	Southwest
248–292	West
293–337	Northwest
338–360 and 1–22	North

16. SUNSHINE AND SOLAR RADIATION

Sunshine, or solar radiation, is rarely measured by amateur weather observers. For example, during 2014 only about one-quarter of the amateur sites reporting to the Climatological Observers Link (COL) measured sunshine. There are perhaps two reasons for this. First, the traditional instrument used to record sunshine, the Campbell-Stokes sunshine recorder, uses a piece of card into which the sun burns a thin trace and this has to be changed every day by the observer.

Second, while modern instruments can now record the sunshine electronically without the need for a daily visit to the instrument, even a modern instrument requires a clear view down to the horizon. This is between the directions of northeast through south to the northwest in London, but between about northeast by north through south to northwest by north in northern Shetland.

Consequently, a sunshine recorder is best mounted on a roof or mast, provided that safe access is available. Sunshine can be recorded when the sun rises about 3 degrees above the horizon – below that level its intensity is usually too low to register with standard sunshine recorders.

However, given the importance of solar radiation and sunshine of everyday life, from the growth of plants to human health and the planning of summer holidays, including sunshine recorders in a book of this nature seems justified.

Observations of sunshine have been made for about 150 years – in 1853 John Francis Campbell described a method of measuring sunshine by using a glass sphere, filled with water, mounted in a wooden bowl. More recently the trend has been for the development and deployment of instruments that are capable of measuring the whole solar radiation spectrum – that is more than just the visible part of the radiation emitted by the sun.

SOLAR RADIATION

Solar radiation, meaning the electromagnetic output from the sun, covers a wide range of wavelengths. Of the solar radiation arriving at the top of the earth's atmosphere, some 97 per cent is contained within the range of wavelengths from 290 to 3,000 nanometres, encompassing the ultraviolet, visible and near infrared (or short wavelengths).[87] One nanometre (nm) is equivalent to 1 metre divided by 1,000,000,000.

Part of this solar radiation penetrates through the entire atmosphere to reach the earth's surface, while part of it is scattered and/or absorbed by the gas molecules, aerosol particles, water droplets and ice crystals in the atmosphere.

Light is the radiation visible to the human eye, and covers the wavelength range from about 400nm to 780nm. Thus much of the solar radiation lies within the visible band of wavelengths.

The radiation of wavelengths in the range 10–400nm is called ultraviolet (UV), while infrared radiation is that in the range 780nm–1mm. The infrared range reaching the ground can be divided into the near infrared and far infrared ranges, while that UVB reaching the ground is sometimes divided into three sub-ranges, UV-A, UV-B and UV-C:

- UV-A lies in the wavelength range 315–400nm. Most of this reaches the ground but it is less biologically active than the higher-energy (shorter-wavelength) UV-B and UV-C radiation.
- UV-B has wavelengths in the range 280–315nm. Although about 90–95 per cent of this is absorbed by the atmosphere, it is biologically active and it is this type of UV radiation that is the main cause of sunburn and skin cancer.

- UV-C, with wavelengths of 100–280nm, is almost completely absorbed by the earth's atmosphere before it reaches the ground.

TERRESTRIAL RADIATION

Wien's Law tells us that objects of different temperature emit radiation spectra that peak at different wavelengths. Because the earth is cooler than the sun, the radiation emitted by the earth (the so-called terrestrial radiation) has a longer wavelength and lies typically in the far infrared wavelength range of 3,000–50,000nm; this lies outside the visible wavelength band. Most of the infrared radiation from the sun has a wavelength of typically 780–3,000nm.

For the purposes of this chapter it is solar radiation that is of interest.

UNITS OF MEASUREMENT

Solar radiation intensity, or irradiance, over all the wavelengths is measured in units of watts per square metre (W/m^2), which corresponds to units of power per unit area. Over a period of time, this can be integrated to give daily totals of energy per unit area, expressed using the unit of joule per square metre (J/m^2). This is a very small quantity in terms of solar radiation reaching the ground and meteorologists often use units of MJ/m^2 instead: 1MJ equals 1,000,000 joules. Typical daily values in the UK lie in the range of about 0.5–6MJ/m^2 in midwinter and about 5–30MJ/m^2 in midsummer.

GLOBAL (OR TOTAL), DIRECT AND DIFFUSE RADIATION

By the time it reaches the ground, some solar radiation will have been scattered or reflected by the constituents of the atmosphere. This gives rise to two main components of solar radiation that can be measured near the ground, namely the direct and diffuse components.

The direct component is that received directly from the sun's disk alone, while the diffuse component is that received from all other parts of sky due to the scattering and reflections occurring in the atmosphere. The total (or global) solar radiation is the sum of these two components. On a day with very thick cloud the direct component will be nil, while on a sunny day as much as 80–85 per cent of the solar radiation is from the direct component. Some useful explanations can be found on the Australian Bureau of Meteorology website.[88]

Fig. 137.   A Kipp & Zonen CM11 pyranometer used to measure solar radiation at the University of Reading. A pyranometer consists of a thermopile (a set of thermocouples) mounted on a black carbon disc, which generates electricity according to how hot it gets (that is how much solar radiation falls on it). The double glass dome eliminates air movements and dirt, rain or snow that might affect the measurements.

Few amateur weather observers measure global solar radiation intensity or irradiance – again, observations made by the observers of COL would suggest that only one observer in sixteen makes such observations. The majority of these use either an optional sensor available with the Davis Vantage Pro2 AWS.[89] while one or two use a Kipp & Zonen CMP3 sensor.[90] Those readers wishing to learn more about the subject of solar radiation measurements are referred to *The Weather Observer's Handbook*.[91]

WHAT IS SUNSHINE?

According to the World Meteorological Organization, sunshine duration during a given period is defined as the time during that period when the direct solar irradiance exceeds $120W/m^2$.[92] Thus a

sunshine recorder is a member of a subset of solar radiation sensors that measure the intensity of visible radiation.

This direct solar irradiance intensity is equivalent to the level of solar irradiance shortly after sunrise or shortly before sunset in cloud-free conditions. To the human eye, this may be taken as the duration of the appearance of sunshine shadows and maybe it is for this reason that sunshine, rather than solar irradiance per se, is more commonly measured in an amateur weather station.

SUNSHINE

There are two principal sunshine sensors that are used nowadays to determine the duration of solar radiation – the manual Campbell-Stokes and electronic Kipp & Zonen CSD sunshine recorders – while another favourite among UK amateurs

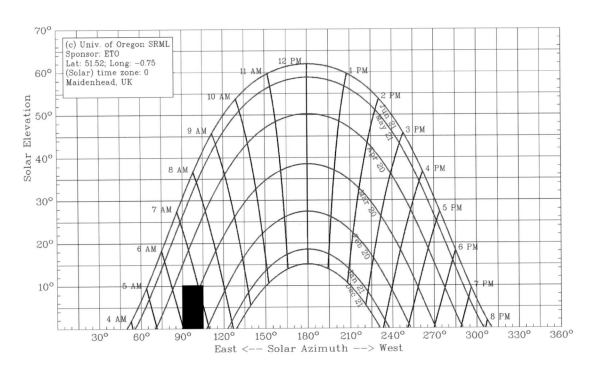

Fig. 138. Illustrating the path of the sun through the sky in Maidenhead from 21 December to 21 June. The blackened area shows the location of a hypothetical obstruction to illustrate when sunshine would be missing owing to such an obstruction. The diagram was created using software provided by the University of Oregon Solar Radiation Monitoring Laboratory.[94] The software can also be used to generate a similar image for the latter half of the year.

is the Instromet sunshine sensor. Of historical interest only, these days, is the Jordan sunshine recorder, while the Blake-Larsen recorder is under development as this book is written. Stephen Burt has written a good comparison of a selection of sunshine recorders, based on their technical specifications and cost.[93]

SUNSHINE INSTRUMENTATION

SITE REQUIREMENTS

As mentioned above, ideally an unbroken horizon between about northeast through south to northwest is required in much of the UK in order to obtain a good record of the daily duration of bright sunshine. In mid-latitudes any sunshine (even under clear skies) during the first 20–30 minutes after sunrise and the final 20–30 minutes before sunset will not normally be strong enough to be recorded by a sunshine recorder.

The University of Oregon Solar Radiation Monitoring Laboratory website[94] is a useful source of information concerning the bearing and alti-tude of the sun at your weather station. Using the coordinates of my own weather station resulted in Fig. 138, on which I superimposed a hypothetical obstruction (maybe a tall building) extending 10 degrees into the air between bearings of 90 and 105 degrees. The diagram shows that such an obstruction would cause the sunshine record to be lost, assuming it is only recorded at 3 degrees or more above the horizon, from about 26 February to 11 April (and on the corresponding dates in autumn) until as late as about 7.05am (when sunrise is close to 6.00am). Dates earlier in the year would be unaffected as the sun rises closer to the southeast, as would dates later in the spring and early summer as the sun would be seen to rise above the obstruction.

Since trees grow, obstructions in Fig. 138 should be redrawn every two to three years. In addition, since deciduous and coniferous trees provide differing canopy cover at different times of the year, care should be taken when analysing the timings of any obstructions. Using Fig. 138 it is fairly straightforward to ascertain the amounts of sunshine likely to go unrecorded over a year – before purchasing

Table 26 A guide to the purchase price and running costs of various sunshine recorders (as at January 2015) and the pros and cons of using the instruments

Type	Purchase price (new)	Annual running cost (excluding any electrical supply)	Advantages	Disadvantages
Campbell-Stokes	£1,300	£80	No moving parts	Cannot be mounted on a mast; needs daily attention; cost of the cards
Instromet	£360	Nil	Small and light; can be mounted on a mast; hourly values available	Threshold not accurately calibrated
Jordan	£100–£150 (auction price)	Cost of photographic paper	None	Measurements very dependent upon type of paper used
Kipp & Zonen CSD	£1,800	Nil	Can be mounted on a mast; hourly values available	Expensive for the amateur
Blake-Larsen	£385	Nil	Can be mounted on a mast	Non-standard and variable threshold

any instrument. If more than, say, 10 per cent of the total is likely to be lost then it may not be worth making any measurements.

SUNSHINE SENSORS
Measuring sunshine can be an expensive task, as can be seem in Table 26, and is probably not an observation to be made by a newcomer to weather observing, unless they happen to acquire a cheap, second-hand instrument – as I did many years ago.

ESTIMATING SUNSHINE DURATION USING CLOUD COVER AMOUNTS
Given the cost of a traditional manual sunshine recorder and the difficulty of measuring sunshine in general, the observer may be tempted to estimate the duration of sunshine according to the cloud cover. However, the problems with this approach – which I cannot recommend – are several.

The method assumes that an overcast sky results in no sunshine and a clear sky in unbroken sunshine. However, the location, height and type of cloud can have an effect on the results – as can the frequency at which the cloud observations are made. Thus, while shortly after dawn the cloud cover may be 50 per cent (4 oktas), the hourly sunshine duration at this time might vary between one hour, if the cloud lies in the west, to nothing if the cloud lies to the east (that is hiding the sun at sunrise). Low cloud will tend to reduce the sunshine duration more than high cloud, the latter tending to be thin and semi-transparent. Sunshine can be quite difficult to estimate on days with variable cloud, or under cloudy skies with an occasional break. How many observers can maintain a frequent observation of the varying amount and type of cloud from sunrise to sunset, day after day?

So observers should avoid this method of estimating sunshine.

CAMPBELL-STOKES SUNSHINE RECORDER
John Francis Campbell designed his first sunshine recorder in 1853, and the modern-day instrument

Fig. 139. An old-style Campbell-Stokes sunshine recorder. This dates back over seventy years and is still in perfect working order. Note that the glass sphere sits on a small support, and is not anchored in place.

Fig. 140. The University of Reading's Campbell-Stokes sunshine recorder with the glass sphere anchored in place. The card was just about to be removed and shows the burn trace from the previous day's sunshine.

Fig. 141. Rear view of a Campbell-Stokes sunshine recorder showing the anchoring points and supporting arm that, on modern versions, helps to keep the glass sphere in place.

owes much to his work and to subsequent modifications made by George Gabriel Stokes in 1880. The latter consisted of substituting a metallic ring to hold the cards, rather than a wooden bowl, a new platform to support the metal ring and the use of three different cards for the equinoctial, winter and summer seasons. The resulting instrument then became the standard instrument for measuring sunshine across the UK until the early years of the twenty-first century.

The Campbell-Stokes sunshine recorder (Figs 139–141) concentrates sunlight through a glass sphere onto a recording card placed at its focal distance. The length of the burn trace left on the card represents the sunshine duration.

For exact measurement, the sunshine recorder must be accurately adjusted for horizontal levelling, meridional direction (the instrument sits with its sphere facing south in the northern hemisphere and the metal bowl facing north) and latitude.

Three different recording cards are used, depending on the season (Fig. 142). One of the problems with the recorder is that the determination of the duration of sunshine is slightly subjective. Moreover, even on a sunny day it is possible for sunshine not to be recorded, as ice or frost can cover the glass sphere; lying snow can also be blown onto the green cards and on a snowy day the instrument can easily become encased in snow. In addition, if the card becomes wet following rainfall it is quite likely that the burn threshold will differ to that before the rain, while different meteorological services use cards with different surface characteristics that may affect the amount of card burn that takes place.

The card can be changed by the observer during daylight hours, as long as a note is made of the time of the change. The burn mark is then apportioned to both the current and previous day as appropriate.

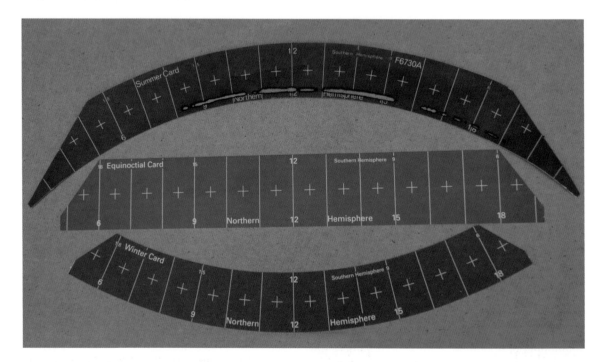

Fig. 142.   The three charts are (from top to bottom) for use in the summer, around the equinoxes and during the winter months in the UK with a Campbell-Stokes recorder. Each chart is marked with the hours of the day. The upper chart has been used and shows burn marks denoting eight hours of sunshine.

Fig. 143. An older version of the Instromet sunshine sensor showing the photosensitive detectors.

BELOW: **Fig. 144. The Instromet sunshine sensor indoor display unit.**

Fire Warning

If you keep the glass sphere of the Campbell-Stokes sunshine recorder indoors before you install it outside, be careful. The sphere has quite a short focal length – as can been seen by the distance between the sphere and the sunshine charts in the figures. This means the sphere could focus the sun's rays onto nearby objects – and set them alight. If this happens you will not be the first person requiring the services of the fire brigade in such circumstances!

INSTROMET SUNSHINE RECORDER

The Instromet sunshine recorder works by comparing the output of several photosensitive detectors. A small post under the glass dome (see Fig. 143) casts a shadow when the sun shines, causing a differential voltage, which triggers an output signal or a timer increment. A stand-alone display module means the instrument can be run without a data logger. The instrument is reasonably priced and easy to install.

Fig. 145.   A Jordan sunshine recorder, installed with a clear view of the horizon. One of the slits that enable sunlight to be received by the photographic card inside the instrument can be seen on the side of the black drum. JONATHAN DANCASTER

THE JORDAN RECORDER

The Jordan sunshine recorder is an old-fashioned instrument and is not recommended nowadays for serious recording of sunshine duration. The instrument (Fig. 145) lets in sunlight through a small hole in a cylinder on to photosensitized paper, set inside the cylinder, on which traces are recorded. Sunshine duration is ascertained by measuring the length of time the paper was exposed to sunlight.

KIPP & ZONEN CSD RECORDER

In the UK the Campbell-Stokes instrument is steadily being replaced at Met Office sites by the Kipp & Zonen CSD recorder (Fig. 146), although the records obtained from the two instruments are not directly comparable. Perhaps the main reason for their introduction is the fact that they can record

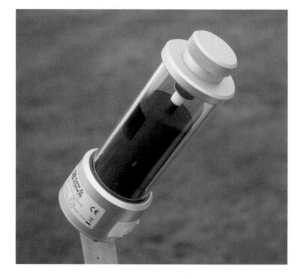

Fig. 146.   A Kipp & Zonen CSD sunshine recorder.

the sunshine without a daily site visit by an observer. However, for the amateur they are expensive pieces of equipment and so cannot be recommended for use by a newcomer to weather observing.

The Kipp & Zonen CSD recorder is a solar cell type of sunshine recorder that uses the contrast method to determine the sunshine duration. The device is equipped with three solar cells on a triangular prism oriented toward the celestial North Pole – one on top and one on each of the southeast and southwest faces. The output of the solar cells on each of the southeast and southwest faces includes both direct and diffuse solar irradiances. As the solar cell on the top is shaded from direct sunlight, its output can be considered as giving a measure of the diffuse radiation. By taking the difference between these outputs, an output value equivalent to the level of direct solar irradiance can be obtained.

BLAKE-LARSEN RECORDER

The Blake-Larsen sunshine recorder[95] (Fig. 147) is the result of a long collaboration between Alan Blake in Cornwall and Ole Jul Larsen in Denmark. It was created in 2011 and uses a sensitive photocell that measures full-sky solar radiation. Sensor output is compared with a calculated threshold value to determine 'sunshine/no sunshine' output, with the sunshine duration then being calculated by sophisticated computer-based software.

ENTRIES IN THE OBSERVATION REGISTER

Unless observations are made electronically, then it is suggested that just the total daily sunshine duration between the hours of midnight and midnight be recorded, along with two additional columns in the weather register that are used as follows:

A. An indicator of sunless days: enter a 'I' if no sunshine was recorded, else enter a '0'. This should only be based on an instrumental record – not on visual inspection of the sky by eye at intervals during the day.
B. An indicator of sunny days: enter a 'I' if, say, at least twelve hours of sunshine were recorded, else enter a '0'.

At the end of the month, total up the daily sunshine amounts to give a monthly total and determine the maximum sunshine duration. In addition, total up the counts of the sunless and sunny days.

If electronic instruments are used, then keeping a note of the sunshine duration for each hour of the day (GMT time, so for 0000–0100, 0100–0200 and so on up to 2300–2400 GMT) throughout the month is well worth doing in order to keep a record of the diurnal variation of sunshine amount. These individual hourly totals can be totalled at the end of each month.

Fig. 147. The Blake-Larsen sunshine recorder. OLE JUL LARSEN

17. LOCAL WEATHER AND CLIMATE

Weather observations vary from site to site – the observations that you make will never be the same as those from a different site, no matter how close the two sites.

Differences between two neighbouring sites may reflect the use of different instruments or slight differences between the two locations. Perhaps your thermometer screen is not quite so close to a building or tree; in a garden site, nearby buildings may emit different amounts of heat or provide different degrees of shading.

Your weather observations will depend upon the large-scale weather patterns and the conditions that they bring, and they will also reflect any peculiarities in the local weather due to geographical features of the area. The local weather might include effects due to sea breezes, an urban heat island, local topography or surface water.

Areas of low-lying land can often lead to the formation of local fog and frost, as cold air drains into such places, particularly in the early hours of the day. The presence of hills can cause local intensification of precipitation as approaching air is forced to rise – possibly leading to cloud and precipitation where none might otherwise have occurred. Further downwind, precipitation amounts may also be affected as a result.

Local lakes and rivers can also be instrumental in the formation of local fog patches – due to the supply of moisture at the surface leading to a dampening of the air.

In time, even non-meteorologists will spot such vagaries of their local weather.

Differences in observations between two locations in the same town may be due to urbanization. Imagine two sites, one on the southwestern edge of a large town, and the other in the town centre. Let's suppose that this town is surrounded by agricultural countryside and that a river runs through this countryside to the southwest of the town.

If the prevailing winds arise from the southwest (as they tend to do in the British Isles), then the site in the southwest may often be cooler than the town centre site, because air blowing over the town will be warmed by the urban heat island effect. In addition, when the air is cool it is quite possible that fog patches will be more likely to form in areas close to rivers and hence the site in the southwest may often record slightly higher values of humidity and more days with fog. Indeed, most keen observers will be aware of localities around their home towns where fog tends to form or persist – maybe along only certain parts of the daily route to work each morning.

HOW DO WEATHER AND CLIMATE DIFFER?

'Climate is what we expect, weather is what we get' is a succinct way of describing the difference between climate and weather. Part of the difference is due to the timescales involved. Weather can be highly variable from day to day – one particular day of the year may have snowfall in one year but have temperatures of 20°C the following year.

Climate is the average weather (or more exactly, a statistical description of the weather in terms of the average and variability of the weather patterns and weather types) in a place, averaged over typically thirty years or longer.

THE URBAN HEAT ISLAND

An urban heat island[96] is a man-made area that's significantly warmer than the surrounding area, typically a town that is warmer than the surrounding countryside. This difference occurs particularly at night.

The differences occur because the buildings and ground surfaces in towns and cities are formed of materials such as concrete and tarmac. These materials absorb and store heat so their temperatures are raised – more so than those of the vegetation and wet ground in the countryside. As the air cools (as happens at night) this heat is slowly released back into the air in the town. In addition, the population density is greatest in towns and the lifestyle of human beings leads to additional heating resulting from their use of energy. In the countryside cooling can be relatively higher due to the effects of wind; many people will have experienced being windswept on the hills while wind at street level in towns was calmer.

In the UK, towns are warmer than the countryside for much of the winter season; the incidence of frosts will be lower here than in the countryside.

SEA BREEZES

Sea breezes are local winds that are caused by the different heating rates of land and sea. During the day the land surface heats up more rapidly than the sea surface because the land has a lower specific heat capacity than water – so the land requires less heat than water to raise the temperature by the same amount. In addition, any heating can be spread out over a greater depth in the sea because of the motion of water.

This surface heat is then passed into the air; consequently the air over the land will be warmer than that over the sea and will have a greater tendency to rise – drawing in air from the sea to replace it. A sea breeze circulation is established as the air over the sea subsides and air from over the land moves towards the sea (at upper levels) to take its place.

Similar circulations, called lake breezes, can also be formed around large inland areas of water.

At night the circulation is reversed; the land cools down faster than the sea and so the surface winds tend to blow from the land to the sea – forming a land breeze.

Sea breezes can move a large distance inland. At Maidenhead in Berkshire the sea breeze has been observed moving northwards from the south coast of England – some 80km to the south. Signs of a passing sea breeze may include a fall in temperature and rise in humidity as the cooler air from the sea arrives, a change in wind direction or a band of cumulus-type cloud marking the arrival of the rising branch of air of the sea breeze circulation pattern.

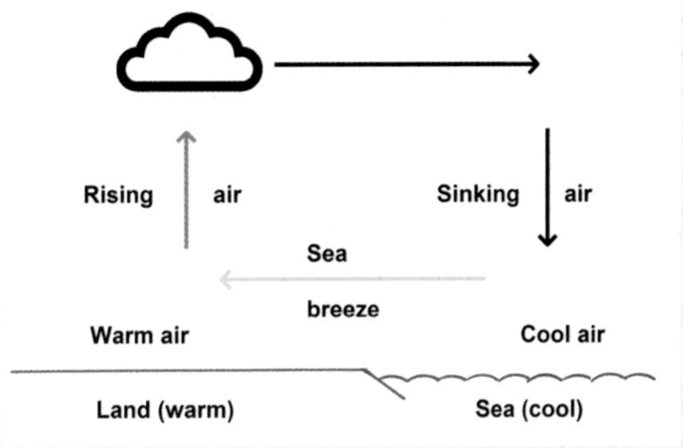

Rising air   Sinking air

Sea breeze

Warm air   Cool air

Land (warm)   Sea (cool)

Fig. 148. Schematic diagram of a sea breeze.

CREATING CLIMATOLOGICAL AVERAGES

Once you have spent a few years observing the daily weather, you might ask how these observations compare to the long-term climatology. Due to site differences, any long-period averages that may have been calculated for a neighbouring site may not be applicable to your site. Such variations should be borne in mind should you move house (and weather station) from one part of the town to another.

In order that one extreme event in one month does not overly influence the climatological statistics, the latter are normally calculated, by international agreement, over a period of thirty years. Currently, climatological averages tend to cover the period 1981–2010, being updated every ten years. If your weather station has been in operation for this period and there are no missing data, then simple arithmetic will allow you to determine the average monthly temperatures and rainfall, and also the averages of other quantities (for example, the average number of days with air frost or thunder each month). Averages for the British Isles can be found in a publication by the Climatological Observers Link (COL).[97]

Of course, most amateurs do not have an unbroken set of weather observations from their own site for a complete thirty-year period. In that case it may be interesting to attempt to compile averages over the final ten years of the thirty-year period, for example 2001–2010. At stations with missing observations in a given period of time, missing monthly data can be estimated using data from suitable neighbouring stations. In all cases, missing data should, ideally, amount to no more than 30 per cent of the averaging period. Thus for decadal averages, no more than three years of missing data should be estimated.

ESTIMATING MISSING DATA

Suppose there are two neighbouring weather stations, A and B. These should be close enough that the weather conditions might be expected to be similar at both sites.

To estimate missing temperature observations a 'difference method' is used. For example, if the average daily temperature at station A in January is 0.1 degrees C higher than that at station B over a particular period, then 0.1 degrees C should be added to the values at station B for the years when records were not available at station A, to give estimated values at station A. Note that such a calculation may not be valid if there are any significant observational changes at either site over the averaging period.

Suppose that the monthly mean temperatures in January at A and B are the values shown in the second and third columns of Table 27; site A has no observations for 2001–2003. Comparing the observed mean temperatures at the two sites for 2004–2010 we see that A is 0.1 degrees C warmer than B (the correction, DIFF). So if site A is this much warmer than B during 2001–2003, we can estimate that the mean temperatures for these years at A are 3.9°C, 5.7°C and 4.9°C. Combining these estimates with the actual values for later in the decade (the final column) gives an average temperature at A for the decade of 5.2°C.

This calculation should be done separately for each month of the year as it is possible that the site exposures or the geographical differences between the two sites might mean that the measurement differences vary during the year.

To estimate missing values of rainfall and sunshine, monthly values for missing intervals should be estimated using a 'ratio method'. For example, suppose station A had 475mm of rainfall in January over a particular period of time, and station B had 500mm over the same period. The monthly values of rainfall at station B, for the years when values were not available at station A, are then multiplied by the ratio 475/500 to give the probable values at station A.

Monthly totals of the number of rain days and wet days, and the number of days with certain weather types, can be estimated using the difference method. However, in many cases it might be inadvisable to estimate the number of days with certain types of weather since these can be very dependent upon altitude and the exact nature of the surrounding environment.

Table 27   **Illustrating the method of estimating average temperatures for a site A in which there are missing observations, assuming that there are years when observations for both A and B are available, and that B has observations for the period when A has no records**

See the text for an explanation of the calculations.

Year	Site A actual mean temperature (°C)	Site B mean temperature (°C)	Site A – Site B = DIFF (degrees C)	Site B + DIFF = Site A estimate (°C)	Site A estimated or actual (°C)
2001		3.8		3.9	3.9
2002		5.6		5.7	5.7
2003		4.9		4.9	4.9
2004	5.8	5.8	0.0		5.8
2005	6.2	6.3	–0.1		6.2
2006	5.2	4.9	0.3		5.2
2007	7.7	7.6	0.1		7.7
2008	7.2	7.2	0.0		7.2
2009	3.2	3.0	0.2		3.2
2010	1.9	1.7	0.2		1.9
2001–2010		5.1			5.2
2004–2010 average			0.1		

WHERE TO FIND PAST WEATHER INFORMATION FOR YOUR AREA

Having identified the need to use observations for a nearby weather station when determining the climate of your site, you then need to discover where such monthly observations could be found. Obvious sources are the members of the COL (see Chapter 1). COL members have observed from over 1,500 weather stations between 1970 and 2015.

In the UK the Met Office has sets of monthly data available for about thirty-five sites covering 50–100 years in the UK.[98] Other national meteorological services provide similar summaries – either listed by site or by month (for example under 'Past Weather' on the Met Éireann website[99]

for Ireland and on the KNMI website[100] for the Netherlands). In the USA, historical station observations can be obtained from the National Climate Data Center.[101]

LOCAL WEATHER AND CLIMATE BOOKS

There are several good books about local weather that have been published in the British Isles over the years. Some of these are listed here; the list is by no means exhaustive and your local library may be aware of other, similar, publications.

Brazell, J.H., *London Weather* (HMSO, 1968)
Brugge, R. and Burt, S., *One Hundred Years of Reading Weather* (The Climatological Observers Link, 2015)

Davison, M. and Currie, I., *The Surrey Weather Book* (Frosted Earth, 1990). Similar books, which each contain many photographs, have been written for the counties of Berkshire, Dorset, Essex, Sussex, Hampshire and the Isle of Wight, Norfolk and Suffolk, and Kent.

Foggitt, W. and Markham, L., *The Yorkshire Weather Book* (Countryside Books, 1993)

Glenn, A., *Weather Patterns of East Anglia* (Dalton, 1987)

Johnson, P., *Cumbria's Weather – Your Complete Guide* (Cinderbarrow Publishing, 2009)

Manton, P., *Jersey Weather and Tides* (Seaflower Books, 1995)

Rohan, P.K., *The Climate of Ireland* (The Stationery Office of Ireland, 1986)

HISTORICAL WEATHER NEWS STORIES AND DATA

Many weather observers, having made their own observations over a period of time, see their own records being broken and, rather than only being able to say (for example) 'yesterday brought the highest temperature since my records began six years ago' begin to wonder how this temperature compares with observations in the locality over earlier years. But how can you find out about past weather events of my home town/village?

One place to start is the local library. Their collection of local newspapers may contain news stories about notable past weather events and possibly weekly or monthly summaries from a previous weather observer living in the town. Their local history archives might contain copies of observations from such an observer. They may also have information about the availability of similar observations in the local county archive. Your local librarian might also be a good source of information about local history society websites containing local news stories about the weather.

PAST WEATHER SUMMARIES FOR THE UNITED KINGDOM

Over the past century and a half there have been numerous official publications covering the weather of the UK. Increasingly, these are being digitized and put online – some hardcopy versions may be available in the libraries of large towns.

National Meteorological Library and Archive

The National Meteorological Library and Archive[102] is located in Exeter; it is part of the UK Met Office and holds the country's most comprehensive collection on meteorology. The library contains copies of all the printed weather summaries and reports published in the UK over the years, along with journals and periodicals from the UK and abroad. Many original daily and monthly returns of weather observations from UK weather stations are stored in the archives.

Daily Weather Report

The *Daily Weather Report* of the Met Office provides a daily summary of the observed weather for a selection of stations, with charts and tables detailing the weather of the day. It was produced between 1860 and 1980. The format and content varied over the lifetime of the publication and some digitized versions are available.[103] More recently, these have been replaced by the *Daily Weather Summary*, issues of which are available on the Met Office website.[104]

British Rainfall *(and Similar Titles)*

This was an annual publication giving monthly and annual totals of rainfall for the UK over the period 1860–1991. In early volumes, monthly totals are available for a selection of the stations while, from 1961, monthly information from all stations was included. Typically, each volume from 1961 contains data from several thousand rainfall stations – so there is probably one close to your own site. The complete volumes have been digitized by the Met Office.[105]

Monthly Weather Report

Covering the UK, this monthly periodical (with additional annual issues) gave detailed monthly summaries from official stations over the period

1884–1993. Information on temperature, rainfall, sunshine, air pressure, days with certain types of weather and other weather statistics were included in these reports.

Currently (July 2015), the cover pages (containing a written summary of the weather that month) have been digitized by the Met Office and can be seen on their website.[106] The Met Office has also provided an online monthly summary of the weather in the UK since 2001.[107]

Snow Survey of Great Britain

Between 1946/1947 and 1952/1953 an annual snow survey of Great Britain was published by the British Glaciological Society. The Met Office then published snow surveys for the winters of 1953/1954 to 1991/1992. Observers reported details of the days on which snow or sleet fell and also information about lying snow. These surveys have been digitized by the Met Office.[108]

Climatological Observers Link Monthly Bulletin

The monthly and annual bulletins of COL contain statistical summaries and station notes from many (mostly amateur) weather stations across the British Isles. The bulletins are available from May 1970 onwards.[109]

Monthly Hydrological Summary for the UK

The National Hydrological Monitoring Programme produces the *Monthly Hydrological Summary for the UK*. According to their website.[110] this report describes the hydrological conditions during the preceding month, using the data holdings of the National River Flow Archive and National Groundwater Level Archive. Focusing on rainfall, river flows, groundwater levels and reservoir stocks, it places the events of each month, and the conditions at the end of the month, in a historical context. It is available online for December 1988 onwards from the Centre for Ecology and Hydrology.

PAST WEATHER DATA FROM OUTSIDE THE UNITED KINGDOM

Republic of Ireland: Monthly Weather Bulletin (and Monthly Weather Summary)

Copies of the *Monthly Weather Bulletin* of Met Éireann for 1986 onwards are available online.[99] At the beginning of each month the *Monthly Weather Summary* is also produced, providing an initial view of the weather of the previous month.

Monthly Climatic Data for the World

Worldwide monthly weather summaries for weather stations are provided by the National Climate Data Center of the USA[111] for 1948 onwards. This publication contains mean temperature, pressure, precipitation and sunshine data for approximately 2,000 stations.

CLIMATOLOGICAL AVERAGES

In addition to month-by-month or daily statistical summaries, most countries publish climatological averages – typically month-by-month averages (and extreme values) of weather elements covering thirty-year periods. Current averages can usually be obtained from national meteorological services – often online.

The Met Office Book of the British Weather[112] contains monthly, seasonal and annual average maps for a variety of weather elements. The Met Office also provides climatological averages online,[113] while Met Éireann has a website[114] that provides information, including statistical data, on the climate of the Republic of Ireland.

Worldwide averages are published by the World Meteorological Organization for 1961–1990.[115] This includes tables of monthly and annual climatological averages of atmospheric pressure, air temperature (mean, maximum and minimum), relative humidity, sunshine duration and precipitation amounts – and much more.

18. SHARING YOUR OBSERVATIONS AND FURTHER LEARNING

Having set up your weather station and made some observations, you've probably already started comparing your observations with those made by other observers – if only to check that your instruments are working correctly.

Maybe you'd like to share your observations with a wider audience, receive feedback and advice, or meet fellow observers? Perhaps this involvement with meteorology is a new hobby for you and you would like to learn some more about the subject in general? Of course nowadays there are many sources of information on the internet. This chapter aims to give you some ideas and pointers to some of these sites from the perspective of a new weather observer and also to some of the many organizations that exist to promote meteorology.

YOUR OWN WEATHER WEBSITE

If you have purchased popular AWS equipment, other than a very basic one, then it is quite possible that the equipment will contain software and connections to enable you to create and publish your own station website, using some basic templates and minimal programming effort.

Alternatively, it is possible to create your own website from scratch, including whatever weather data from your observations that you wish to upload. This may, for example, be just a summary of last month's weather or, perhaps, just the most recent observations.

Some of the types of AWS website software currently available are briefly mentioned here – see the Appendix for contact details. Before purchasing

Fig. 149. Motorway fog in Yorkshire, England. Visibility was close to 200m but the fog was not very deep; earlier, a white image of the sun had been visible in the fog.

software, find out if it allows you a free trial for a short period of time – something that is always advisable if you are a newcomer to manipulating weather observations in this way.

CUMULUS

Cumulus, written by Steve Loft of Orkney, is freely available although Steve asks for a small donation in order to help development work. It allows you to store downloaded data from your AWS and to upload/display them to a web server; it runs on a variety of computer platforms and supports most popular AWSs.

VIRTUAL WEATHER

Virtual Weather, from Ambient Weather of Chandler (Arizona), also offers the user the ability to plot, store and display AWS observations and to upload these observations to a website. A variety of home computer platforms is supported.

WEATHER DISPLAY

Weather Display is written by Brian Hamilton from New Zealand and can also be used with many AWSs. At time of writing, Weather Display includes multi-language support. As well as allowing you to upload your own observations to a webpage, it can be used with Weather Display Live, an add-on for Weather Display, which allows you to view live weather data over the internet from your weather station in near real time.

WEATHERLINK

WeatherLink software comes from Davis Instruments and provides good display and download abilities. Related software – WeatherLinkIP for Vantage weather stations – allows you to upload your weather data directly to the internet using a plug-in data logger. This allows you to create webpages that can be viewed by anyone.

WEATHERUNDERGROUND

This is a website designed to provide access to weather observations from around the world. Free interfacing software for a variety of AWSs is available, allowing observations to be uploaded to regional maps. You can search for a specific location and examine observations from other sites close to yours. Go to www.wunderground.com/ for more details.

METEOBRIDGE

Meteobridge is a device that allows your AWS to connect to public weather websites like WeatherUnderground. This allows you to feed your observations into the internet and to have them visible from wherever you are.

LOCAL PRESS AND LIBRARIES

If you are a meteorologist for whom weather observing is a new activity, you might wish to share your observations locally. For many years I wrote a weekly column in my local paper, which included daily reports of the highest and lowest temperature and the rainfall and sunshine amounts.

Nowadays I tend to provide interesting statistical snippets when some unusual weather is experienced. With many professional weather stations now being unmanned, newspaper editors are often keen to find a local weather observer who is happy to share their news. Newcomers to weather observing might find this easier than maintaining a regular weekly column – although an end-of-month summary might not take up too much time.

Many libraries have a local history archive and may be pleased to receive monthly summary reports from your weather station. A chat with the local history librarian might reveal a collection of local weather observations (and maybe old weather-related photographs) for your town or village – perhaps a way of putting your own observations into a longer, historical context.

You might be surprised to discover just how many local weather observers have lived in and around your town over the years. Some 150 years ago these tended to be members of the landed gentry and clergy, as these were the people with some spare time who could afford to indulge in activities other than the task of daily work – they were also often

Fig. 150.   **Weather forecasts need observations from all levels in the atmosphere, and one way to make such measurements is by means of a radiosonde. A red parachute can be seen below the balloon – deployed when the balloon bursts (often around 20km above the ground) – while the white package beneath the parachute contains the instruments that measure pressure, temperature and humidity.**

rich enough to purchase scientific observing instruments and maybe employ somebody to maintain daily observations. An exercise in collecting old rainfall records from within about a 10km radius of my home led to the discovery of over 125 rain-gauges that had been reporting their observations in a 100-year period, enabling me to build a good picture of how rainfall had varied locally over the years.

WEATHER ORGANIZATIONS

There are several weather organizations in Europe and North America to which observers can send observations. Much of the information in this section is extracted from the websites of the relevant organizations – from where further details may be obtained. This listing is by no means exhaustive and readers from other countries should enquire about similar organizations via their national meteorological service or learned meteorological society.

CLIMATOLOGICAL OBSERVERS LINK (UK)

The Climatological Observers Link (COL, www.colweather.org.uk/index.php) is an organization of people who are interested in the weather. Its members are mainly amateur meteorologists, but many professionals and observers from schools, universities and research establishments also belong to COL.

Observations made by contributors are combined into a monthly bulletin, which is circulated within four weeks of the end of each month. COL also runs a forum (www.colweather.org.uk/notes) for those interested in exchanging news and seeking advice.

Fig. 151.   Flooding along the River Thames in Maidenhead. Predicting such events requires knowledge of the rainfall that causes them and an understanding of the local hydrology.

THE TORNADO AND STORM RESEARCH ORGANISATION (UK)

The Tornado and Storm Research Organisation (TORRO, www.torro.org.uk/site/intro.php) is a privately supported research body based in the UK, serving the national and international public interest. The core of TORRO's activity is that of data collection, post-storm site investigations and meteorological research into severe weather events such as tornadoes and thunderstorms.

Data collection is undertaken by some 300–400 observers, investigators and other contributors. Most supporters are British, with a smaller number from elsewhere in Europe and across the world.

VERENIGING VOOR WEERKUNDE EN KLIMATOLOGIE (THE NETHERLANDS)

The Vereniging voor Weerkunde en Klimatologie (VWK, www.vwkweb.nl) is a Dutch association, whose goal is to make the popular scientific study of meteorology accessible to everyone. The activities and interests of its members are diverse – but all are interested in aspects of the weather and climate.

Weather watchers provide observations to their website and their monthly publication, *Weerspiegel*. VWK has close links with the Koninklijk Nederlands Meteorologisch Instituut (KNMI).

RING EUROPÄISCHER HOBBYMETEOROLOGEN (GERMANY)

Ring europäischer Hobbymeteorologen (ReH, www.reh-ev.de) is an organization for weather observers in Germany and other countries in central Europe, although some members live as far afield as the USA. Membership to ReH includes a subscription to the monthly publication, *Laubfrosch*, in which members summarize their weather observations.

CLOUD APPRECIATION SOCIETY (UK)

According to their website, the Cloud Appreciation Society (CAS, http://cloudappreciationsociety.org)

'was set up to encourage an understanding and love of the sky that we all inhabit. ... We also like the fact that clouds sometimes look like dogs, elephants and flying witches'. CAS currently just asks for a one-off payment for membership of the society, so you will not be expected to pay any yearly renewal fees.

CITIZEN WEATHER OBSERVER PROGRAM (USA)

The Citizen Weather Observation Program (CWOP, www.wxqa.com) is a public–private partnership that aims to collect weather data contributed by citizens. CWOP aims to provide feedback to the data contributors so they have the tools to check and improve their data quality. In fact, their web address stands for weather quality assurance.

THE WEATHER OBSERVATIONS WEBSITE (UK)

The Weather Observations Website (WOW, wow.metoffice.gov.uk) is a website that allows observers to share their weather observations. Run by the Met Office, the site is helping to coordinate the growth of the weather observing community in the UK. Observations can be made using all types of equipment.

Despite its UK focus, WOW now has global coverage. A WOW Forum has also been established to enable users to communicate with each other and share hints and tips, and to enable the Met Office to provide useful help and assistance as required.

CoCoRaHS (USA)

CoCoRaHS is an acronym for the Community Collaborative Rain, Hail and Snow Network (www.cocorahs.org). It is a network of volunteers of all ages and backgrounds working together to measure and map precipitation primarily, but not exclusively, in the USA. By using low-cost measurement tools, stressing training and education, and utilizing an interactive website, their aim is to provide the highest-quality data for natural resource, education and research applications.

The network originated with the Colorado Climate Center at Colorado State University in

Fig. 152.   A portable mast used by MSc students in the Department of Meteorology of the University of Reading during their annual field trip in Dorset. Between the cup anemometer and the wind vane is a gold-coloured electrostatic field meter, used to determine the electrical potential gradient of the local atmosphere. Halfway down the mast is a screen to hold the temperature and humidity sensors (left) and equipment to measure the vertical fluxes of heat and radiation (right). A raingauge sits in the foreground.

1998, thanks in part to the Fort Collins flood a year earlier. The CoCoRaHS website notes that the 'only requirements are an enthusiasm for watching and reporting weather conditions and a desire to learn more about how weather can effect and impact our lives'.

REGIONAL WEATHER SUMMARIES IN THE UK

There are two principal amateur regional monthly weather bulletins that are available in the UK, the *Cumbria Weather Report* and *Weather Front*.

Cumbria Weather Report

This is an interesting monthly summary if only because it covers one of the wettest parts of the UK. Each monthly bulletin[116] contains data from about twenty weather stations and gives primarily temperature and rainfall information, but also some details about snow, frost and thunder, and a brief description of the local weather during the month.

Weather Front

This regional weather report[117] covers the weather of the East Midlands – a relatively dry part of the England. Beginning in 1981, it contains data from about a dozen local weather stations, covering mainly rainfall and temperature, along with some details of the number of days with snow, thunder, fog and hail – and a few monthly sunshine totals.

NEWSGROUPS AND BLOGS

There are several newsgroups on the internet that allow you to post messages relating to the weather – these are often a useful way for the amateur weather enthusiast to obtain practical advice and to announce any unusual observations. The only downside to some weather newsgroups and forums is that they occasionally become dominated by those who appear to know little about meteorology. Sometimes totally inappropriate messages are posted, unless the group is moderated or registration is required.

A few words of warning relating to weather forecasts that can sometimes be found on these newsgroups: often forecasts are given by individuals without any forecasting training or an adequate meteorological background. As such, it is often unwise to completely trust such forecasts; they should checked against ones obtained from reputable meteorological services. Indeed, some 'independent forecasting companies' also claim to make weather forecasts that have little scientific backing.

Nevertheless, these groups and blogs are often excellent ways of finding out about the weather as it happens.

uk.sci.weather The uk.sci.weather newsgroup was formed in 1996 and has several regular contributors who post their UK and European weather observations and summaries.

sci.geo.meteorology This newsgroup is rarely used nowadays and tends to be USA-centred.

UKweatherworld (www.ukweatherworld.co.uk) This discussion forum is worth visiting; it covers mainly (but not exclusively) UK weather with many useful links, including to current and recent observations.

The Netweather forum (https://forum.netweather.tv) This is a very active forum covering the weather of the UK and North America.

LEARNING MORE ABOUT METEOROLOGY

So, you have a weather station up and running, maybe with the observations being shared with other members of the observing community. Perhaps this is as far as you wish to take your hobby. Or maybe you have caught the 'weather bug' and wish to find out more about observing in particular or the weather in general?

To learn more about weather observing and weather instrumentation, I would recommend a read of Stephen Burt's excellent *The Weather Observer's Handbook*.[118]

NATIONAL METEOROLOGICAL SOCIETIES

If you wish to become involved with other weather enthusiasts, then contact your national society for meteorologists. Many countries have such a society, which should be able to help you – many of these societies have good contacts with local and amateur weather organizations.

A listing of these societies can be found on the website of the World Meteorological Organization,[119] while Table 28 lists some of the larger, English-speaking, ones.

All these societies should also be able to point you in the direction of suitable magazines and educational information or activities with which they are associated, and will probably be pleased to send you a sample so that you can judge whether they are right for you. Some societies also help in the running of local and national meetings for the non-professional meteorologist.

Possibly they will know of part- or full-time courses that you might be able to attend – anything from a friendly evening class to a complete degree course!

Royal Meteorological Society (UK)

The society (which dates back to 1850) serves not only those in academia and professional meteorologists, but also those whose work is affected in some way or other by the weather or climate, or who simply have a general interest in the weather. The membership includes scientists, practitioners and a broad range of weather enthusiasts.

It publishes the popular *Weather* magazine each month, maintains a host of weather and climate information pages, and also the MetLink pages at www.metlink.org – the educational pages of the society. The society also runs The Weather Club (www.theweatherclub.org.uk), which produces a quarterly newsletter.

Irish Meteorological Society

According to its webpage, the Irish Meteorological Society was founded in 1981. Its main aims are the promotion of an interest in meteorology and the dissemination of meteorological knowledge.

The society includes members not only from Ireland but from all over the world who are interested in weather and weather-related topics. The membership is drawn from those who work in meteorology and aviation, agriculture and shipping, from teachers and lecturers and indeed anyone who is interested in meteorology and the environment.

Table 28 The URLs of some of the national meteorological societies	
Society	**URL**
American Meteorological Society	www.ametsoc.org
Australian Meteorological and Oceanographic Society	www.amos.org.au
Canadian Meteorological and Oceanographic Society	www.cmos.ca
Irish Meteorological Society	www.irishmetsociety.org
Meteorological Society of New Zealand	www.metsoc.org.nz
Royal Meteorological Society	www.rmets.org

GLOSSARY

°C   The unit of temperature on the Celsius scale; i.e. the air temperature is currently 5°C.

AWS   Automatic Weather Station. An AWS typically consists of: a set of sensors mounted outdoors to measure the various elements of the weather; a console unit, usually located indoors, to collate and display the measurements; and a data logger linking the system to a computer to enable the observations to be stored permanently.

BST   British Summer Time, the local civil time in the UK from 01:00 GMT on the last Sunday of March to 01:00 GMT (02:00 BST) on the last Sunday of October. BST is equivalent to GMT plus one hour.

Climate   A reference to a region's long-term weather conditions. It is described in terms of the averages of precipitation, of maximum and minimum temperatures, and of other elements. A description of climate also includes measures of variability and frequency of occurrence of weather conditions.

Climatological averages   The statistics of the weather over a standard period of time, usually thirty years (e.g. 1981–2010).

Data logger   An electronic device that stores data over time.

degree(s)C   Used in this book to denote a temperature difference; i.e. today is 5 degrees C warmer than yesterday.

Electrometeor   A visible or audible manifestation of atmospheric electricity, of which thunderstorms are the most common type.

GMT   Greenwich Mean Time, the local civil time in the UK from 01:00 GMT on the last Sunday of October to 01:00 GMT on the last Sunday of March. Ideally, weather observations made in the UK should always refer to GMT clock times.

Hydrometeor   A meteor consisting of an aggregate of liquid or solid water particles suspended in, or falling through, the atmosphere, blown by the wind from the earth's surface, or deposited on objects on the ground or in free air.

Knot   A unit of speed equal to one nautical mile per hour, approximately 1.151mph. In the UK, and other countries, it is the unit used when reporting wind speeds.

Lithometeor   An ensemble of particles most of which are solid and non-aqueous. The particles are more or less suspended in the air, or lifted by the wind from the ground. Examples include haze and blowing sand.

Meteor   A phenomenon, other than a cloud, observed in the atmosphere or on the surface of the earth, which consists of a precipitation, a suspension or a deposit of aqueous or non-aqueous liquid or solid particles, or a phenomenon of the nature of an optical or electrical manifestation.

Meteorology   The study of the physics, chemistry, and dynamics (motion) of the Earth's atmosphere. It includes the study of atmospheric phenomena and the impact of the atmosphere upon mankind.

Millibar   The unit of atmospheric pressure. The hectopascal is the equivalent SI unit with the same numerical value.

MSL   Mean Sea Level. To enable comparison of air pressure measurements made at different heights at different weather stations, air pressure is (at most weather stations) converted to the value that would exist at mean sea level.

Photometeor   a luminous phenomenon produced by the reflection, refraction, diffraction or interference of light from the sun or the moon.

Precipitation   Any form of solid or liquid water falling from the sky. Precipitation includes rain, drizzle, snow, sleet, hail and phenomena such as ice pellets and diamond dust. Dew and hoar frost are generally not considered to be precipitation as they form on the ground.

Weather   The state of the atmosphere. Weather consists of the short-term (minutes to days) variations of the atmosphere. Weather is often described in terms of temperature, precipitation, cloudiness, visibility, humidity and wind.

INSTRUMENT AND SOFTWARE SUPPLIERS

This list of meteorological equipment and software suppliers shows those that are primarily found in the UK. A brief indication of some of equipment or software sold by each is given, but the reader should visit the company websites for a complete listing of products sold. I have purchased equipment from some, but by no means all, of these suppliers.

This listing is aimed primarily at the amateur observer, but does include some suppliers of specialized equipment that is sometimes purchased by amateur observers. The list is by no means exhaustive. Indeed, there will be other UK websites that sell observing equipment. Any reader seeking to purchase equipment can, however, use the companies and websites listed below as a starting point in their hunt for instruments and software.

All details are correct as of February 2016.

COMPANY LISTINGS

Ambient Weather
www.ambientweather.com
Suppliers of the Virtual Weather Station software for automatic weather stations.

Barometer World Ltd
Quicksilver Barn, Merton, Okehampton
Devon EX20 3DS
www.barometerworld.co.uk
Barometers and barographs sold and repaired; both modern and antique equipment.

Blake Larsen
www.sunrecorder.net
The website for those interested in the Blake Larsen sunshine recorder.

S. Brannan & Sons Ltd
Leconfield Industrial Estate, Cleator Moor
Cumbria CA25 5QE
www.brannan.co.uk/home-garden
Suppliers of hand-held anemometers and digital thermometers.

Campbell Scientific Ltd
Campbell Park
80 Hathern Road
Shepshed
Loughborough LE12 9GX
www.campbellsci.co.uk
Data loggers, data acquisition and measurement systems.

Environmental Measurements Ltd
Business and Innovation Centre
Sunderland Enterprise Park (East)
Wearfield
Sunderland SR5 2TA
www.emltd.net
Instrumentation for meteorological and environmental monitoring.

Equinox Instruments
PO Box 897
Lincoln LN5 5AW
www.equinoxinstruments.co.uk
Equinox Instruments provide instruments for professional meteorologists, including Kipp & Zonen sunshine equipment.

Fairmount Weather Systems
Unit 4, Whitecroft Road
Meldreth
Hertfordshire SG8 6NE
www.fairmountweather.com
General observational equipment.

Fine Offset Electronics Co. Ltd
4/F, Block B3, East Industrial Park
Huaqiaocheng
Shenzhen City
Guangdong Province
China
www.foshk.com
The company manufactures many of the entry-level weather stations sold by Maplin Electronics, Amazon and several high street stores.

Gemini Data Loggers Ltd
Scientific House, Terminus Road, Chichester
West Sussex PO19 8UJ
www.geminidataloggers.com
Tinytag data loggers and related sensors.

Instromet Weather Systems Ltd
10B Folgate Road
Lyngate Industrial Estate
North Walsham
Norfolk NR28 0AJ
www.instromet.co.uk/Index.html
Sunshine recorders and other equipment.

La Crosse Technology
2817 Losey Blvd South
La Crosse
WI 54601
USA
www.lacrossetechnology.com
A range of electronic consumer products including
automatic weather stations suitable for a newcomer
to weather observing.

Meteobridge
www.meteobridge.com./wiki/index.php/Home
Suppliers of Meteobridge, a small device that con-
nects your personal weather station to public
weather networks.

MetSpec
Unit 10–11
Lendal Court
Gamble Street
Nottingham NG7 4EZ
www.metspec.net
MetSpec produce the UK Met Office-standard
plastic and aluminium Stevenson screen as part of a
range of instrument shelters and radiation shields.

Mindsets Online
Mindsets (UK) Ltd
Unit 10
The IO Centre
Lea Road
Waltham Cross
Hertfordshire EN9 1AS
www.mindsetsonline.co.uk/Site/Home
USB thermometers and other scientific gadgets.

Munro Instruments Ltd
Gilbert House, 406 Roding Lane South
Woodford Green
Essex IG8 8EY
www.munroinstruments.com
General observational equipment.

Oregon Scientific Inc.
19861 SW 95th Avenue
Tualatin
OR 97062
USA
http://us.oregonscientific.com
www.oregonscientific.co.uk
Oregon Scientific produces a range of entry-level
weather stations.

Prodata Weather Systems
Unit 7, Espace North Building
181 Wisbech Road
Littleport, Ely
Cambridgeshire CB6 1RA
www.weatherstations.co.uk
Davis Instruments weather stations and the
CoCoRaHS raingauge; also WeatherLink software.

Richard Paul Russell Ltd
The Lodge
Unit 1
Barnes Farm Business Park
Barnes Lane
Milford on Sea
Hampshire SO41 0AP
www.r-p-r.co.uk/kestrel/kestrel.php
UK distributor of Kestrel wind and weather instru-
ments.

RM Young
2801 Aero Park Drive
Traverse City
MI 49686
USA
www.youngusa.com

United Kingdom supplier:
Read Scientific Ltd
32 Brancaster Way, Swaffham
Norfolk PE37 7RY
Weather monitoring instruments and systems.

Russell Scientific Instruments

Rash's Green Industrial Estate
Dereham, Norfolk NR19 1JG
www.russell-scientific.co.uk
General observing equipment, including small screens.

Sandaysoft

http://sandaysoft.com/products/cumulus
Producers of Cumulus – software for retrieving, storing and displaying data from an automatic weather station.

Setra Systems

159 Swanson Road
Boxborough
MA 01719
USA
www.setra.com
Manufacturers of pressure transducers (electronic barometers).

Skyview Systems

9 Church Field Road
Chilton Industrial Estate
Sudbury, Suffolk CO10 2YA
www.skyview.co.uk/acatalog/SkyScan_P5.html
Lightning detectors and observing equipment.

UK Weathershop

Unit 19, Ford Lane Business Park
Ford Lane, Ford, near Arundel
West Sussex BN18 0UZ
www.weathershop.co.uk
Sellers of a wide variety of equipment from many of the suppliers listed here.

Vaisala Ltd

Vaisala House
351 Bristol Road
Birmingham B5 7SW
www.vaisala.com/en/meteorology/Pages/default.aspx
Manufacturers and suppliers of a range of meteorological observing equipment.

Vector Instruments

Windspeed Limited
115 Marsh Road
Rhyl
Denbighshire LL18 2AB
www.windspeed.co.uk
Manufacturers and retailers of wind sensors and automatic weather station equipment.

Weather Display

www.weather-display.com/index.php
Weather Display software for websites.

MAKE YOUR OWN INSTRUMENTS

You can also make some simple instruments yourself – Geoff Jenkins of the Royal Meteorological Society has written a useful document titled *Simple Weather Measurements at School or at Home* that can be found on the society's website at www.rmets.org/sites/default/files/pdf/simweameasurements.pdf.

Note, however, that such instruments should not be used if you wish to set up a weather station whose records can be used for a proper climatological study of your area.

REFERENCES AND FURTHER READING

1. The website www.trafficweather.info/road-Weather/rwisMap.jsp is operated by Vaisala on behalf of their customers, who own networks of weather stations dedicated to improving traffic safety. The website www.trafficweather.info/Index/example/Index.action allows the user to select various regions (some outside the UK) from where observations may be extracted.

2. Burt, S., *The Weather Observer's Handbook* (Cambridge University Press, 2012)

3. Overton, A.K., *A Guide to the Siting, Exposure and Calibration of Automatic Weather Stations for Synoptic and Climatological Observations* (Royal Meteorological Society, 2009). Available online from the Royal Meteorological Society at www.rmets.org/sites/default/files/pdf/guidelines/aws-guide.pdf

4. Oke, T.R., *Initial Guidance to Obtain Representative Meteorological Observations at Urban Sites* (in World Meteorological Organization: *Instruments and Observing Methods*, report no. 81, WMO/TD-No. 1250, 2006). Available online at https://googledrive.com/host/0BwdvoC9AeWjUazhkNTdXRXUzOEU/wmo-td_1250.pdf

5. Meteorological Office, *Observer's Handbook*, 4th edn (HMSO, London, 1982). The *Observer's Handbook* was based largely on guidance provided by the World Meteorological Organization. The fourth edition was the last to be published and was reprinted in 2000. It can be found online at www.metoffice.gov.uk/archive/observers-handbook

6. Meteorological Office, *Meteorological Glossary*, 6th edn (HMSO, London, 1991)

7. World Meteorological Organization, *International Cloud Atlas*, Vol. 1 (WMO, Geneva, 1956)

8. Elsom, D.M., Meaden, G.T., Reynolds, D.J., Rowe, M.J. and Rowe, J.D.C., 'Advances in tornado and storm research in the United Kingdom and Europe: the role of the Tornado and Storm Research Organisation', *Atmospheric Research* (2000, 56, pp. 19–29). Available at www.sciencedirect.com/science/article/pii/S0169809500000084

9. Kirk, P.J., 'An updated tornado climatology for the UK: 1981–2010', *Weather* (2014, 69, pp. 171–5)

10. The Tornado & Storm Research Organisation (TORRO). This is the UK's leading organization for the collection and collation of thunderstorm- and tornado-related reports. Useful information, including how to submit severe weather reports to TORRO, can be found on their website, www.torro.org.uk

11. Meaden, G.T., 'Selsey tornado, the night of 7–8 January 1998', *Journal of Meteorology*, UK (1998, 23, pp. 41–55)

12. World Meteorological Organization, *Manual on Codes – International Codes, Volume I.1: Part A – Alphanumeric Codes* (WMO, Geneva, 2014)

13. Where are the windiest parts of the UK? This is a Met Office website at www.metoffice.gov.uk/learning/wind/windiest-place-in-UK

14. *Beaufort*, National Meteorological Library and Archive Fact sheet 6 — The Beaufort Scale (version 01). Download from www.metoffice.gov.uk/media/pdf/b/7/Fact_sheet_No._6.pdf

15. *Key to Clouds*. This laminated fold-out identification chart by the Royal Meteorological Society contains eight panels, each approximately 15cm × 25cm. The chart features fifteen common types of cloud, with a colour picture and description of each, plus handy hints on cloud identification, and brief information about the processes that bring about cloud formation. Available from www.rmets.org/shop/merchandise/key-clouds

16. *Cloud Types for Observers*. This Met Office online publication can be found at www.metoffice.gov.uk/media/pdf/r/i/Cloud_types_for_observers.pdf. It is a useful primer for those who wish to learn more about clouds and how to identify them.

17. Hamblyn, R., *The Cloud Book* (David & Charles, 2008). There is also a smaller edition by Richard Hamblyn, *The Met Office Pocket Cloud Book* (2010), also published by David & Charles.

18. Pretor-Pinney, G., *The Cloudspotter's Guide* (Sceptre/Hodder & Stoughton, 2006)

[19] The Cloud Appreciation Society, http://clouda preciationsociety.org. As they write on their homepage: 'At The Cloud Appreciation Society we love clouds, we're not ashamed to say it and we've had enough of people moaning about them. Read our manifesto and see how we are fighting the banality of "blue-sky thinking". If you agree with what we stand for, then join the society for a minimal one-off postage and administration fee and receive your very own official membership certificate and badge.'

[20] World Meteorological Organization, *Manual on Codes – International Codes, Volume I.1: part A – Alphanumeric Codes* (WMO, Geneva, 2014)

[21] Meaden, G.T., 'An atmospheric deposition code using observations of the state of the grass', *Weather* (1996, 51, pp. 68–71)

[22] Burt, S.D. and Brugge, R., *Climatological Averages for 1981–2010 and 2001–2010 for Stations Appearing in the Monthly Bulletin of the Climatological Observers Link* (Climatological Observers Link, 2011)

[23] Les Cowley's Atmospheric Optics website at www.atoptics.co.uk has many fascinating photographs of optical phenomena and explanations as to how they were formed. The HaloSim3 software is also available on the site.

[24] World Meteorological Organization, *International Cloud Atlas, Volume I* (WMO, Geneva, 1956)

[25] Meteorological Office, *Meteorological Glossary*, 6th edn (HMSO, London, 1991)

[26] The Space Weather Prediction Centre of the United States has a useful website at www.swpc. noaa.gov that provides a wealth of information, observations and forecasts.

[27] The UK Met Office has a space weather page that provides background information on why space weather is important: www.metoffice.gov. uk/publicsector/emergencies/space-weather

[28] www.skyscancanada.com/manuals. The SkyScan thunderstorm detector is available via many outlets and websites in the UK.

[29] www.sat24.com/en/gb is a useful website for tracking cloud motion across the British Isles and other regions of the earth.

[30] www.metoffice.gov.uk/learning/learn-about-the-weather/thunder-and-lightning/lightning is a useful website giving information about thunder, lightning and the Met Office lightning detection system.

[31] www.blitzortung.org/Webpages/index. php?lang=en&page_0=12 – a useful site for tracking thunderstorm activity; this link is for the British Isles in particular.

[32] The University of Alaska Geophysical Institute webpage at http://elf.gi.alaska.edu details their research into middle and upper atmospheric optical and electrical phenomena.

[33] www.llansadwrn-wx.info/ice/precipitation. html#pad. One of the webpages of weather observer Donald Perkins covering snow and hail with instructions on making a simple hailpad.

[34] www.cocorahs.org/Media/docs/ HowToMakeHailPads_1.0.pdf. This is one of the webpages of the Community Collaborative Rain, Hail and Snow Network (CoCoRaHS) illustrating how to make a hailpad. CoCoRaHS is now the largest provider of daily precipitation observations in the United States and also has observers in most Canadian Provinces.

[35] Burt, S. D., 'Synoptic transport and deposition of Saharan dust to the British Isles' (MSc dissertation thesis, University of Reading, 2014). Stephen Burt has observed and studied Saharan dust falls for many years and this thesis summarizes many of his findings.

[36] www.bgs.ac.uk/discoveringGeology/hazards/ volcanoes/grimsvotn2011.html. This webpage from the British Geological Survey shows some interesting observations made following the Grímsvötn volcanic eruption of May 2011.

[37] www.bgs.ac.uk/research/volcanoes/AshFall WhatYouCanDo.html shows how you can help the British Geological Survey in the collection of volcanic ash for analysis.

[38] www.bgs.ac.uk/myvolcano is a British Geological Survey app that enables people to take photographs as well as enter quantitative observations and take samples.

[39] Middleton, W.E.K., *The History of the Barometer* (The John Hopkins Press, Baltimore, USA, 1964)

[40] www.npl.co.uk/reference/measurement-units. This is a useful webpage from the National Physical Laboratory of the United Kingdom that explains the SI system of units

[41] http://physics.nist.gov/cuu/Units/units.html. This is the SI units page of the American National Institute of Standards and Technology.

[42] http://wmo.asu.edu. This is the World Meteorological Organization Global Weather & Climate Extremes webpage produced in conjunction with Arizona State University.

[43] Martin Rowley maintains an interesting set of webpages detailing past weather in the UK at http://booty.org.uk/booty.weather/climate/wxevents.htm; details of UK pressure extremes were extracted from http://booty.org.uk/booty.weather/climate/1900_1949.htm and http://booty.org.uk/booty.weather/climate/1850_1899.htm

[44] The Met Éireann webpage www.met.ie/climate-ireland/weather-extremes.asp provides records of extreme weather conditions observed in the Republic of Ireland.

[45] Burt, S., 'The Lowest of the Lows ... Extremes of barometric pressure in the British Isles, Part 1 – the deepest depressions', *Weather* (2007, 62, pp. 4–14)

[46] Burt, S., 'The Highest of the Highs ... Extremes of barometric pressure in the British Isles, Part 2 – the most intense anticyclones', *Weather* (2007, 62, pp. 31–41)

[47] www.metoffice.gov.uk/public/weather/observation is the Met Office weather observations website. Enter your postcode, and recent hourly observations from your nearest official weather station should be shown – one of these observations is that of MSL pressure.

[48] National Meteorological Library and Archive (UK), *Fact sheet No. 11 – Interpreting Weather Charts*. Available online at www.metoffice.gov.uk/media/pdf/a/t/No._11_-_Weather_Charts.pdf. This document reveals how we can interpret weather charts and describes the station plotting symbols used to plot weather conditions on such charts.

[49] Burt, S., *The Weather Observer's Handbook* (Cambridge University Press, 2012)

[50] World Meteorological Organization, The *CIMO Guide* (Part 1, Chapter 3) (WMO, Geneva, 2012). Details on the reduction of pressure to mean sea level can be found in the document 'CIMO/ET-Stand-1/Doc. 10', which can be found online at www.wmo.int/pages/prog/www/IMOP/meetings/SI/ET-Stand-1/Doc-10_Pressure-red.pdf

[51] Meteorological Office, *Observer's Handbook*, 4th edn (HMSO, 1982). Available online at https://metoffice.access.preservica.com/archive/ – *see* under 'Publications'.

[52] *British Rainfall* was a publication giving monthly and annual totals of rainfall for the UK from 1860 to 1991, although there were minor name changes to the publication during this time. It has been digitized by the Met Office and can be found at www.metoffice.gov.uk/learning/library/archive-hidden-treasures/british-rainfall

[53] Some extremes of weather in the UK can be found on this Met Office website: www.metoffice.gov.uk/public/weather/climate-extremes/#?tab=climateExtremes

[54] Information about extremes of weather in the Republic of Ireland are available from Met Éireann at www.met.ie/climate-ireland/weather-extremes.asp

[55] Worldwide weather extremes can be found on an Arizona State University website at http://wmo.asu.edu

[56] The CoCoRaHS website can be found at www.cocorahs.org

[57] http://shop.weatherstations.co.uk/cocorahs-manual-rain-gauge-802-p.asp describes the CoCoRaHS manual raingauge.

[58] Burt, S., *Review: the CoCoRaHS Raingauge* (2014). Available online at http://measuringtheweather.com/wp-content/uploads/2012/06/CoCoRAHS-raingauge-review-v1.20-2014-08-c-Stephen-Burt.pdf

[59] Burt, S. D., '"Rainfall duration" versus "hours with rainfall"', *Bulletin of the Climatological Observers Link* (2009, 485, pp. 19–21)

[60] Burt, S., *The Davis Instruments Vantage Pro2 wireless AWS – an Independent Evaluation Against UK-Standard Meteorological Instruments* (2009). Available online at http://measuringtheweather.com/wp-content/uploads/2012/06/Davis-Vantage-Pro2-AWS-review-2009-c-Stephen-Burt.pdf

[61] Burt, S., *Instrument Review: Davis Instruments Vantage Vue AWS* (2013). This review was presented at the Royal Meteorological Society's Second Amateur Meteorologists' Conference and is available at http://measuringthe-weather.com/wp-content/uploads/2012/06/Stephen-Burt-Davis-Instruments-Vantage-Vue-review-Sept-2013-c-Stephen-Burt.pdf

[62] Burt, S.D. and Brugge, R., *Climatological Averages for 1981–2010 and 2001–2010 for Stations Appearing in the Monthly Bulletin of the Climatological Observers Link* (Climatological Observers Link, 2011)

[63] Climatological averages for official weather stations across the UK for the period 1981–2010 can be found at the Met Office website www.metoffice.gov.uk/public/weather/climate/gcvdxj13y

[64] The *Weather for Schools* website has some interesting designs for do-it-yourself screens at www.weatherforschools.me.uk/html/weatherboxes.html

[65] Bell, S., Cornford, D. and Bastin, L., 'The state of automated amateur weather observations', *Weather* (2013, 68, pp. 36–41)

[66] Bell, S., Cornford, D. and Bastin, L., 'How good are citizen weather stations? Addressing a biased opinion', *Weather* (2015, 70, pp. 75–84)

[67] Burt, S., *The Davis Instruments Vantage Pro2 wireless AWS – an Independent Evaluation Against UK-Standard Meteorological Instruments* (2009). Available online at http://measuringtheweather.com/wp-content/uploads/2012/06/Davis-Vantage-Pro2-AWS-review-2009-c-Stephen-Burt.pdf

[68] Some extremes of weather in the United Kingdom can be found on the Met Office website www.metoffice.gov.uk/public/weather/climate-extremes/#?tab=climateExtremes

[69] Information about extremes of weather in the Republic of Ireland are available from Met Éireann at www.met.ie/climate-ireland/weather-extremes.asp

[70] Worldwide weather extremes can be found on an Arizona State University website at http://wmo.asu.edu

[71] Howard, L., *The climate of London, Deduced from Meteorological Observations Made in the Metropolis, and at Various Places Around it* (Harvey and Dalton, London, 1833)

[72] As an introduction to urban heat islands, there is an interesting webpage produced by the Royal Meteorological Society at www.metlink.org/other-weather/urban-heat-islands/urban-heat-island-background, illustrating the physics of the urban heat island, with numerous pointers to the results of local studies.

[73] Jenkins, G., 'Simple investigations of local microclimates using an affordable USB temperature logger', *Weather* (2015, 70, pp. 85–8)

[74] The National Weather Service wind chill chart is available online at www.nws.noaa.gov/om/winter/windchill.shtml

[75] World Meteorological Organization, *Guide to Meteorological Instruments and Methods of Observation, WMO-No. 8* (World Meteorological Organization, 2008). Available online at www.wmo.int/pages/prog/gcos/documents/gruanmanuals/CIMO/CIMO_Guide-7th_Edition-2008.pdf . Chapter 2 describes the measurement of temperature.

[76] Burt, S., *The Davis Instruments Vantage Pro2 wireless AWS – an Independent Evaluation Against UK-Standard Meteorological Instruments* (2009). Available online at http://measuringtheweather.com/wp-content/uploads/2012/06/Davis-Vantage-Pro2-AWS-review-2009-c-Stephen-Burt.pdf

[77] An overview of Vantage Pro2 stations is available on the Prodata website at www.weatherstations.co.uk/vp_main.htm

[78] A useful humidity calculator can be downloaded at www.vaisala.com/en/services/technicalsupport/downloads/humiditycalculator/Pages/default.aspx

[79] Goff, J.A. and Gratch, S., 'Low-pressure properties of water from –160 to 212°F', *Transactions of the American Society of Heating and Ventilating Engineers* (1946, pp. 95–122; presented at the 52nd annual meeting of the American Society of Heating and Ventilating Engineers, New York, 1946)

[80] Burt, S., 'A comparison of traditional and modern methods of measuring earth temperatures', *Weather* (2007, 62 pp. 331–6)

[81] Allen, R.G., Pereira, L.S., Raes, D. and Smith, M., *Crop Evapotranspiration – Guidelines for Computing Crop Water Requirements* (FAO Irrigation and Drainage paper 56, Food and Agriculture Organization of the United Nations, Rome, 1998). See Chapter 2 – FAO Penman-Monteith equation. Available online at www.fao.org/docrep/x0490e/x0490e06.htm

[82] www.weatherstations.co.uk/vp_accessories.htm is the website of Prodata, suppliers of Davis Instruments AWS equipment in the UK.

[83] www.llansadwrn-wx.co.uk/evap/albertpiche.html. Donald Perkins' website Measuring

Evaporation using Monsieur Albert Piche's Evaporimeter provides information on the history and usage of the Piche evaporimeter.

[84] World Meteorological Organization, *Guide to Meteorological Instruments and Methods of Observation, WMO-No. 8* (World Meteorological Organization, 2008). Available online at www.wmo.int/pages/prog/gcos/documents/gruanmanuals/CIMO/CIMO_Guide-7th_Edition-2008.pdf

[85] Meteorological Office, *Observer's Handbook*, 4th edn (HMSO, London, 1982). The *Observer's Handbook* was based largely on guidance provided by the World Meteorological Organization. The fourth edition was the last to be published in 1982 and was reprinted in 2000. It can be found online at www.metoffice.gov.uk/archive/observers-handbook

[86] Burt, S., *The Weather Observer's Handbook* (Cambridge University Press, 2012). This is worth reading (especially Chapter 9) should you wish to make accurate wind observations, as the book covers wind measurements from the amateur perspective – including both the accuracy and durability of instruments exposed to 'the weather'.

[87] World Meteorological Organization, *Guide to Meteorological Instruments and Methods of Observation, WMO-No. 8* (World Meteorological Organization, 2008). Available online at www.wmo.int/pages/prog/gcos/documents/gruanmanuals/CIMO/CIMO_Guide-7th_Edition-2008.pdf

[88] The Australian Bureau of Meteorology has a useful page titled Solar Radiation Definitions at www.bom.gov.au/climate/austmaps/solar-radiation-glossary.shtml

[89] Burt, S., *The Davis Instruments Vantage Pro2 wireless AWS – an Independent Evaluation against UK-Standard Meteorological Instruments* (2009). Available online at http://measuringtheweather.com/wp-content/uploads/2012/06/Davis-Vantage-Pro2-AWS-review-2009-c-Stephen-Burt.pdf

[90] The Kipp & Zonen CMP3 sensor is described on the Kipp & Zonen website at www.kippzonen.com/Product/11/CMP-3-Pyranometer#.VLZm-SusU64

[91] Burt, S., *The Weather Observer's Handbook* (Cambridge University Press, 2012)

[92] World Meteorological Organization, *Manual on the Global Observing System; volume 1* (World Meteorological Organization, 2013). Available online at www.wmo.int/pages/prog/www/OSY/Manual/WMO544.pdf

[93] Burt, S., *Sunshine Recorders – an Overview* (2012). Available online at http://measuringtheweather.com/wp-content/uploads/2012/06/An-overview-of-sunshine-recorders-July-2012.pdf

[94] The University of Oregon Solar Radiation Monitoring Laboratory maintains a website that provides a program that can create a sun path chart for your locality: http://solardat.uoregon.edu/SunChartProgram.html

[95] The Blake-Larsen sunshine recorder is described at www.sunrecorder.net

[96] *Urban heat island introduction* is an interesting webpage produced by the Royal Meteorological Society at www.metlink.org/other-weather/urban-heat-islands/urban-heat-island-background illustrating the physics of the urban heat island, with numerous pointers to the results of local studies.

[97] Burt, S. and Brugge, R., *Climatological Averages for 1981–2010 and 2001–2010 for Stations Appearing in the Monthly Bulletin of the Climatological Observers Link* (Climatological Observers Link, 2011)

[98] *UK Climate – Historic Station Data*, published by the Met Office; available online at www.metoffice.gov.uk/public/weather/climate-historic/#?tab=climateHistoric

[99] *Monthly Weather Summary* and *Monthly Weather Bulletin*, published by Met Éireann, are available online at www.met.ie/climate/monthly-weather-reports.asp

[100] *Klimatologie; Maand- en jaarwaarden van de temperatuur, neerslag en luchtdruk*, published by KNMI; available online at www.knmi.nl/klimatologie/maandgegevens/index.html

[101] Land-based station data for sites worldwide can be found using this website, provided by the National Climate Data Center (USA): www.ncdc.noaa.gov/data-access/land-based-station-data

[102] The National Meteorological Library and Archive has a website at www.metoffice.gov.uk/learning/library

[103] A selection of digitized copies of the *Daily Weather Report*, made available by the Met Office, can be found at www.metoffice.gov.uk/learning/library/

archive-hidden-treasures/uk-daily-weather-report

[104] Recent issues of the *Daily Weather Summary*, provided by the Met Office, can be found online at www.metoffice.gov.uk/learning/library/publications/daily-weather-summary.

[105] Digitized volumes of *Symon's British Rainfall*, *British Rainfall* and *Monthly and Annual Totals of Rainfall*, provided by the Met Office, can be found at www.metoffice.gov.uk/learning/library/archive-hidden-treasures/british-rainfall

[106] The Met Office has the summary cover page for each issue of the *Monthly Weather Report* available online at www.metoffice.gov.uk/learning/library/archive-hidden-treasures/monthly-weather-report

[107] The Met Office webpages at www.metoffice.gov.uk/climate/uk/summaries are updated each month to include the latest month's weather in the UK. A brief description of the weather through the month is provided, along with maps, graphs and time-series of the regional variations in temperature, rain and sunshine.

[108] The Met Office digitized versions of *The Snow Survey of Great Britain* can be found at www.metoffice.gov.uk/learning/library/archive-hidden-treasures/snow-survey. In addition, summaries of Scottish snowbeds have appeared on an annual basis in the magazine *Weather*.

[109] The website of the Climatological Observers Link at www.colweather.org.uk contains information on accessing all their past monthly and annual bulletins back to May 1970.

[110] The National Hydrological Monitoring Programme produces the monthly *Hydrological Summary for the UK*. Issues of this report back to December 1988 can be downloaded from www.ceh.ac.uk/data/nrfa/nhmp/monthly_hs.html

[111] *The Monthly Climatic Data for the World* publication back to 1948 is provided by the National Climate Data Center at www.ncdc.noaa.gov/IPS/mcdw/mcdw.html. *See* also www1.ncdc.noaa.gov/pub/data/mcdw

[112] Met Office, *The Met Office Book of the British Weather* (David & Charles, 2010)

[113] The Met Office website containing climatological averages for the period 1981–2010 at about 300 weather stations can be found at www.metoffice.gov.uk/public/weather/climate

[114] The Met Éireann website at www.met.ie/climate-ireland/climate-of-ireland.asp provides details about the climate of the Republic of Ireland.

[115] Printed copies of worldwide climatological averages for the period 1961–1990 are available from the World Meteorological Organization at www.wmo.int/e-catalog/detail_en.php?PUB_ID=488&SORT=N&q=. They are also available on a CD from www.wmo.int/e-catalog/detail_en.php?PUB_ID=489&SORT=N&q=

[116] Details and back copies (from 1969 onwards) of the *Cumbria Weather Report* can be found at www.bramptonweather.co.uk/cumbriaweatherreport.html

[117] Details and archived copies of *Weather Front* can be found at www.rmets.org/weather-and-climate/weather/weather-front

[118] Burt, S., *The Weather Observer's Handbook* (Cambridge University Press, 2012)

[119] Details of national meteorological societies can be found at www.wmo.int/pages/partners/nat_met_soc_en.html

INDEX

absolute drought 110
absolute zero 120
accuracy, explanation of 124
aerosols 41
air frost 123
air mass 38, 57, 94
albedo 75
Alter shield 101
altocumulus 44, 47–49
   castellanus 49
   lenticularis 48
altostratus 44, 49–50, 56
analysis charts 92
anemometer 150
   hand-held 151
   siting 148
   vane-type 152
anthelion 71, 72
anti-condensation shield 136
anticyclone 86
arc, circumzenithal 71
   Hastings 72
   helic 72
   infralateral 72
   lower tangent 70–71
   Parry 72
   subhelic 72
   supralateral 72
   upper tangent 70–71
   Wegener 71–72
ash 83
ATDnet system 80
aurora 77
   australis 77
   borealis 77
automatic weather station (AWS) 13–15
   display console 14
   logger 14
   sensor 14
   wiring of sensors 15
AWS screens 116
AWS, pressure sensors 92
AWS, wind sensors 154

ball lightning 28
Ballot, Buys 93
barogram 89
barograph, open scale 88, 90
   siting 87
   small pattern 88
barometer, aneroid 84, 87–88
   checking 87
   Kew-pattern 90–91
   mercury 90
   precision aneroid 92
   siting 87
Beaufort
   letters 31–32
   wind scale 36
Beaufort, Admiral Sir Francis 31, 35
Bishop's ring 72
blogs 178
blood rain 83

blowing
   dust 28
   sand 28
   snow 24
blue jet 81
blue moon 75
blue sky 73
books, weather and climate 169–170
British Rainfall Organisation 17
British Summer Time (BST) 15

Campbell, John Francis 156
Celsius scale 119–120
Celsius, Anders 120
charts, surface pressure 92
circumzenithal arc 71
cirrocumulus 44, 47
cirrostratus 44, 47–48, 50, 69
cirrus 44–47
   anvil 55, 56
   spissatus 57
Citizen Weather Observer Program 176
climate zone indicator, urban 18
climate, definition 166
climatological averages 171
   creating 168
Climatological Observers Link 9, 11,
   17, 175
cloud 41
   amount 42
   formation 41
   genera 44
   luminance 43
   mother-of-pearl 73
   nacreous 73
   type 43
Cloud Appreciation Society 176
cloud base height, determining 56
   typical 44
clouds and depressions 57
CoCoRaHS 176
COL 9, 11, 17, 175
cold front 29, 58, 94
coloured rain 83
condensation trails 47
contrails 47
Coordinated Universal Time (UTC) 15
corona 72, 75
crepuscular rays 77
cumulonimbus 23, 26, 44, 49, 54–57, 78
cumulus 44, 49–50, 51–54
   development 52
   fair weather 54, 56
   fractus 54, 56
   pannus 49
cyclone 86–87

days with fog, definition 40
days with lying snow 65–66
Defoe, Daniel 35
depression 86
depressions, clouds and 57, 59
depressions, weather conditions 59

devils
   dust/fire/land/sand/snow/water/
     wind 27
dew 25, 63
dew point 121
   look-up table 132
diamond dust 23, 70
diffraction of light 75
drifting
   dust 28
   sand 28
   snow 24
drizzle 21
drought
   absolute 110
   meteorological 110
   partial 110
dust 83
   blowing 28
   drifting 28
dust devil 27
dust haze 28
dustpad 82
duststorms 28, 76

El Chichón 76
electrometeor 21, 28
evaporation 144
   annual cycle 145
   tank 144, 146
evaporimeter, Piche 144–146
evapotranspiration 144–145
Eyjafjallajökull, 83

Fahrenheit scale 119–120
Fahrenheit, Daniel Gabriel 120
fallstreaks 46
fen blow 28
fire devil 27
fog 24, 33, 172
   days with 40
   freezing 24
   ice 24
   shallow 24–25, 39
forecasting snow 64
forest fires 76
freezing fog 24
front
   cold 94
   occluded 94
   warm 94
frost, air 123
   ground 135
   hoar 25, 63
funnel clouds 26

gale 29, 32
glaze 25–26
glory 72
grading scheme, station 17
Greenwich Mean Time (GMT) 15
Griffith, Reverend Charles 98
Grímsvötn, 83

ground frost 135
ground ice 25–26
gust, definition 148

hail 23, 32, 56, 82–83
hailpad 22, 81
hailstones 82
halo
    22-degree 69–71
    phenomena 48, 69, 75
    simulations 71
Hastings arc 72
haze 28
haze, dust 28
haze, smoke 28
hectopascal 87
helic arc 72
hoar frost 25, 63
hook gauge 147
humidity 121
    calculators 131
    capacitor-based sensor 130
    variations 122
hurricane 27, 87
hydrometeor 21
hygrograph 128
hygrometer, Mason's 9, 14, 128

ice day 123
ice fog 24
ice pellets 23, 32, 81, 83
ice prisms 23–24
infralateral arc 72
installing equipment 16
instrument
    DIY 183
    exposure 16
    suppliers 180
inversion, temperature 51
ionosphere 80
iridescence 72–73
iridescent cloud 73, 75
Irish Meteorological Society 179
irization 73
isobar 86, 92

knot 34
Krakatoa 72, 76

lake breeze 167
land breeze 167
land devil 27
lapse rate of temperature 56
light, bending of 75
lightning 28, 78, 80
    air discharges 28
    ball 28
    cloud discharges 28
    detector 78
    ground discharges 28
    sheet 28
    streak 28
line squall 29
lithometeor 21, 27
lower tangent arc 70, 71
lying snow 33
    day with, definition 63

measurement
    accuracy 124
    precision 124
metadata
    instruments 20

photographs 20
    site 20
meteor 21
Meteorological Monitoring System
    (MMS) 130
millibar 85
mirage 75–76
mist 24
mock sun 70
moonbow 69
mother-of-pearl cloud 73
Mount Pinatubo 76
Mount St Helens 76
MSL pressure 87
    extremes 85
multilateration 80

nacreous cloud 73
nanometre 156
national meteorological societies 179
newsgroups 178
Newton, Isaac 67
nimbostratus 44, 49, 50, 56
northern lights 77

observation height 16
observation time 15
occluded front 94
okta 42
optical phenomena 67
    viewing angles 69
organizations, weather 175

parhelic circle 70–71
parhelion, 120-degree 72
parhelion, 22-degree 70
Parry arc 72
partial drought 110
Penman-Monteith method 145
photometeor 21, 29, 67
pollen 83
precipitation 29, 97
    continuous 29
    intensity 30–31
    intermittent 29
    rate of fall 30
precision, explanation of 124
present weather codes 31
press, local 173
pressure
    atmospheric 84
    change 96
    characteristic 96
    col 87
    correcting to MSL 94–95
    high 86
    low 86
    mean sea level (MSL) 87
    ridge 86
    semi-diurnal variation 95
    trough 86, 94
publications, weather-related 170–171
pyranometer 157

radiation
    diffuse 157
    direct 157
    global 157
    infra-red 156
    ultra-violet 156
        UV-A 156
        UV-B 156
        UV-C 156

radiosonde 174
rain 21
rain day, definition 108
rain, blood 83
rain, coloured 83
rainbow 67–68, 75
    double 68
    lunar 69
rainfall
    duration 107
    extremes 100
    intensity 107
    measurement, inverted funnel
        method 103
    measurement, warm water
        method 103
    observation time 97, 102
    throwing back the 102
    trace 106
raingauge
    CoCoRaHS 103, 104
    Davis Instrument 111
    entry-level 111
    exposure 97
    hail/ice/snow in 102
    heaters 108
    heavy snowfall 103
    height 97, 100
    Hellmann 104, 106
    manual 15, 97
    recording 97
    Snowdon 98–99
    storage 97
    tilting siphon 104–105
    tipping bucket 108
    types 97
Rayleigh scattering 74
record keeping 18
records
    future-proofing 19
    making a backup copy 20
red sky 75
red sunset 74
reflection of light 75
refraction of light 75
regional weather summaries 178
register
    cloud entries 58
    evaporation entries 147
    hail entries 83
    humidity entries 133
    pressure entries 96
    rainfall entries 111
    recording optical phenomena 77
    soil temperature entries 143
    state of the ground entries 64
    sunshine entries 165
    surface temperature entries 143
    temperature entries 133
    thunder entries 83
    visibility entries 40
    weather entries 32
    wind entries 38, 155
register of weather observations 18
relative humidity 121
    look-up table 132
rime 24–25
Ring europäischer
    Hobbymeteorologen 176
Royal Meteorological Society 179

Saharan dust 82
sand devil 27

sand
    blowing 28
    drifting 28
    falling 83
sandstorm 28
scattering, Rayleigh 74
scintillation 76
screen
    aspirated 118
    AWS 116
    DIY-type 114
    large 114
    location 112
    north-facing wall-mounted 115
    simple 114
    Stevenson 112–113
sea breeze 167
sensor, modern grass minimum 137
sferic 80
shallow fog 24–25, 39
sheet lightning 28
shimmer 76
showers 29, 56
site exposure 16
site security 16
Six, James 8
sky obscured 42
sleet 21, 23, 32
small hail 23
smoke haze 28
snow 21, 23, 32
    blowing 24
    depth measurements 64, 103
    devil 27
    drifting 24
    forecasting 64
    grains 22–23
    pellets 22–23
snowboard 103
snowflakes 21
software, suppliers 180
soil temperatures, measurement
        depths 134
solar radiation 156
soot 83
southern lights 77
space weather forecasting 77
Spanish plume 82–83
spouts 26
sprite 81
squall 29
squall, line 29
St Elmo's fire 80
state of the grass
    grass plot 60
    numerical codes 63
state of the ground
    bare soil plot 60
    numerical codes 61–62
    open ground 60
Stevenson screen 112, 113
Stevenson, Thomas 112
Stokes, George Gabriel 162
stratocumulus 44, 46, 50, 51, 53
stratus 44, 53
    fractus 50
streak lightning 28
subhelic arc 72
summaries, past weather 170
sun dog 70–71
sunshine 156, 158
    estimates from cloud cover 160

sunshine recorder, Blake-Larsen 159,
    165
    Campbell-Stokes 158–163
    Instromet 159, 163
    Jordan 159, 164
    Kipp & Zonen 158–159, 164–165
sunshine, site requirements 159–160
supralateral arc 72
surface pressure charts 92
surface temperatures 134
surface temperatures, terminal
    hours 134
Symons, George 140

tangent arc
    lower 70, 71
    upper 70, 71
TCO 10
Temperature
    annual cycle of soil 138
    AWS sensors 130–131
    dew point 121
    diurnal variation of soil 138
    dry bulb 119
    extremes 119–120
    grass minimum 136
    instruments 124
    maximum, throwing back 124
    measurement of 8–9
    probe for measuring soil 142
    scales 119–120
    surface and falls of snow 137
    wet bulb 119, 121
    what is? 119
    wind chill 127
thermograph 128
thermohygrograph 128, 129
thermometer
    bare soil minimum 137
    concrete minimum 137
    dry bulb 120, 126
    exposure 121
    grass minimum 136
    maximum 8, 120, 126
    mini temperature logger 125, 126
    minimum 8, 120, 126
    north-facing wall-mounted 116
    platinum resistance 130
    red spirit soil 141
    right-angled soil 139
    Six's 8, 14, 127
    stand-alone digital 125
    steel tube 140
    Symons-pattern 140
    wet and dry bulb 9
    wet bulb 120, 126
thermometer response times 128
thermometer screen 16
thunder 28–29, 32, 78, 83
thundersnow 29
thunderstorm 27–29, 54, 56, 78, 82
    climatology, UK 79
    distance from observer 78
    movement of storm 10
Thunderstorm Census Organisation 10
tornado 26, 27, 82
Tornado and Storm Research
    Organisation 10, 26, 176
Torricelli, Evangelista 85
TORRO 26
trace of rainfall 106
tropical cyclone 87

trough lines 94
twinkling of stars 76
typhoon 87

upper tangent arc 70–71
urban climate zone indicator 18
urban heat island 123, 167

vapour pressure 121
vector average of wind, explanation 148
Vereniging voor Weerkunde en
    Klimatologie 176
very wet day, definition 108
virga 57–58
visibility 24–25, 28, 34, 38
    at night 39
    codes 40
    definition 39
    descriptions 40
    measurement of 39
    over sea 39
volcanic ash 83
volcanic dust 83
volcanic eruptions 76

warm front 58, 94
water devil 27
waterspout 26–27
weather
    continuous 29, 32
    definition 166
    during past hour 29
    historical 170
    intermittent 29, 32
    local 166
    recent 29
    showers 29, 56
    types 21
    within sight 29, 32
Weather Observations Website 176
weather station observation summary
    sheet 19
weather station
    characteristics 17
    climatological 16
    grading scheme 17
    setting up 12
    synoptic 15
websites, software for weather 172–173
Wegener arc 71–72
wet day, definition 108
wet hours, definition 107
whirlwind 26–27
wind 34
wind chill 127
wind codes for register 38
wind devil 27
wind direction 35–36
    and cloud motion 37
wind speed 35
    conversion factors 34
    diurnal variation 149
    units 34
wind tower 152–153
wind vane 151
wind
    AWS sensors 154
    effective height 148
    instrumental observations 148
    non-instrumental observations 34
    run of the 152
    starting speeds of anemometer 149